LATEST ANGLICAN LITURGIES
1976–1984

ALCUIN CLUB COLLECTIONS No. 66

The Alcuin Club exists to promote the study of Christian liturgy in general, and in particular the liturgies of the Anglican Communion. Since its foundation in 1897 it has published over 130 books and pamphlets. Members of the Club receive publications of the current year *gratis*.

Information concerning the annual subscription, applications for membership and lists of publications is obtainable from the Treasurer, 5 St Andrew Street, London EC4A 3AB (telephone 01-583 7394).

LATEST ANGLICAN LITURGIES

1976–1984

EDITED BY

COLIN O. BUCHANAN

ALCUIN CLUB/SPCK

First published in 1985 in Great Britain by
SPCK
Holy Trinity Church
Marylebone Road
London NW1 4DU

in association with
Grove Books
Bramcote
Nottingham NG9 3DS

British Library Cataloguing in Publication Data

Latest Anglican Liturgies 1976–1984
1. Lord's Supper (Liturgy)
1. Buchanan, Colin, *1934–*
264'.035   BX5149.C5

ISBN 0–281–04139–3
ISBN 0–281–04140–7 Pbk

COPYRIGHT OF LITURGICAL TEXTS REPUBLISHED IN THIS VOLUME

Permission for publication has been obtained from the copyright holders shown below. The texts in respect of which copyright has been granted are shown by the code used in the volume, and the code is explained on pages viii–x below.

The Central Board of Finance of the Church of England (**EngA, EngB (Engl-2B)**); The Primus of the Scottish Episcopal Church on behalf of the College of Bishops (**Scot1, Scot2**); The Governing Body of the Church in Wales (**Wal1, Wal2**); The Standing Committee of the General Synod of the Church of Ireland (**Ire2**); The General Synod of the Anglican Church of Canada (**Can1A, Can4 (Can3)**) (the second eucharistic prayer in **Can4** and **Can3** is based on part on the ICEL text of Hippolytus, and was altered and adapted by permission of ICEL); The Chairman of the Provincial Liturgical Committee of the Church of the Province of the West Indies (**WIndR**); The Archbishop of Nigeria (**Nig**); The Chairman of the Synod of the Church of the Province of Tanzania (**TanR**); The General Secretary of the Church of North India (**CNIR**); The Standing Committee of the Anglican Church of Australia (**Aus1B, Aus5**); The Provincial Secretary of the Anglican Province of Papua New Guinea (**PNG**); The Provincial Secretary of the Church of the Province of New Zealand (**NZ1, NZ2, NZ3**); The Secretary of the Commission on Liturgy and Worship in the Province of Melanesia (**MelR**); The International Committee on English in the Liturgy (ICEL texts of Hippolytus and of the Roman Catholic second eucharistic prayer – see also under Canada above).

Formal permission for use of copyright does not apply to certain cases, but the goodwill of the following is also acknowledged:

The Custodian of the Text of the Book of Common Prayer of the Episcopal Church in the United States of America (**Amer1–1, 2–2, 3–3**); the Archbishop of West Africa (**WAfr**); The International Consultation on English Texts (ICET texts from *Prayers we have in Common*).

(Other acknowledgements are at the foot of page x below)

Printed in Great Britain by the University Press, Cambridge

CONTENTS

(Where a text is mentioned in brackets with an abbreviation in bold, its title can be found in the list of abbreviations on pages vi–viii below. Not all texts are shown in full in the chapters.)

FOLDERS IN DOCUMENT POCKET IN INSIDE BACK COVER
Texts introduced in Appendices C, D and E.

ABBREVIATIONS AND
TYPOGRAPHICAL RULES

LITURGICAL texts are represented throughout the book by a code in bold type as shown in the list below. The actual texts are to be found printed out in one of the four volumes, *The Liturgy in English* (**LiE**), *Modern Anglican Liturgies 1958–1968* (**MAL**), *Further Anglican Liturgies 1968–1975* (**FAL**), and this present volume *Latest Anglican Liturgies 1976–1984* (**LAL**). In each case the volume in which the text is so to be found is shown in the right-hand column. Where a text is only shown by description or *apparatus* to another text an asterisk is added to the volume code in the right-hand column. **LiE** also contained '1549', '1662 and Related Rites', and 'The Proposed English Revision of 1928', for which no alphabetical codes have been allocated. An attempt has been made to get the code to relate to the official title (e.g. 'Rite A' = '**EngA**'), but this has often not been possible.

Afr	The South African Liturgy (1929)	LiE
Amer	The American Liturgy (1928)	LiE
AmerR	The American Experimental Liturgy (1967)	MAL
Amer1	The American Experimental Liturgy (1970/3) 'The First Service'	FAL
Amer1–1	Rite One from the American Book of Common Prayer (1977)	LAL
Amer2	The American Experimental Liturgy (1970/3) 'The Second Service'	FAL
Amer2–2	Rite Two from the American Book of Common Prayer (1977)	LAL
Amer3	The American Experimental Liturgy (1970/3) 'The Order of Celebration'	FAL
Amer3–3	'The Order of Celebration' from the American Book of Common Prayer (1977)	LAL
Amer1–3	Liturgical Material common to **Amer1, Amer2,** and **Amer3,** and appended to them all (1970/3)	FAL
Aus1	The Australian 1662 Recension (1966)	MAL
Aus1A	The Australian 1662 Recension modernized (1972)	FAL
Aus1B	The 1662 Recension in *An Australian Prayer Book* (1978)	LAL
Aus2	The Australian 'A Modern Liturgy' (1966)	MAL
Aus3	The Australian Experimental Liturgy (1969)	FAL
Aus4	The Australian Experimental Liturgy (1973)	FAL
Aus5	The Second Order in *An Australian Prayer Book* (1978)	LAL
Bom	The Bombay Liturgy (1923)	*LiE
BomR	The Revised Form of the Bombay Liturgy (1948)	LiE
Braz	The Brazil Experimental Liturgy (1967)	MAL
BrazR	The Brazil Experimental Liturgy (1972)	FAL
Can	The Canadian 1662 Recension (1918)	*LiE
CanR	The Canadian Liturgy (1959)	LiE
Can1	The Canadian Alternative Liturgy (1974)	FAL
Can1A	The Traditional Language Rite in the Canadian *Book of Alternative Services* (1985)	LAL
Can2	[This number is left unused, but would have been a better numbering of **Can1** above]	
Can3	The 'Third Canadian Order' (1981)	*LAL
Can4	The Modern Language Rite in the Canadian *Book of Alternative Services* (1985)	LAL
Cey	The Ceylon Liturgy (1938)	LiE
Chil	The (South) Chilean Experimental Liturgy (1967)	MAL

ChilR	The Chilean Liturgy (1972)	FAL
CNI	The North India Liturgy (1973/4)	FAL
CNIR	The North India Liturgy (5th edition 1983)	LAL
CSI	The South India Liturgy (2nd edition 1954)	LiE
	(*also* Proper Prefaces, 3rd edition 1973)	MAL
CSIR	The Modern English South India Liturgy (1972)	FAL
EAUL	The United Liturgy of East Africa (1966)	MAL
Eng1	The English *Series 1* Liturgy (1966)	MAL
Eng1–2A	The English '*Series 1 and Series 2 Revised*' draft Liturgy (1975)	FAL
Eng1–2B	The Church of England '*Series 1 and 2 Revised*' Liturgy (1976)	*LAL
Eng2	The English *Series 2* Liturgy (1967)	MAL
Eng3	The English *Series 3* Liturgy (1973)	FAL
EngA	The Church of England Rite A Liturgy (1980)	LAL
EngB	The Church of England Rite B Liturgy (1980)	LAL
HK1	The Hong Kong and Macao Liturgy (1957)	MAL
HK2	The Hong Kong and Macao Experimental Bilingual Liturgy (1965)	MAL
Ind¹	The Indian 1662 Recension (1960)	*LiE
IndR	The Indian Liturgy (1960)	LiE
IndS	Propers contained in the Supplement to the C.I.P.B.C. Prayer Book (1966)	MAL
Iran	The Iran Experimental Liturgy (1967)	MAL
IranR	The Iran Experimental Liturgy (1971)	FAL
Ire	The Irish Liturgy (1926)	*LiE
IreR	The Irish Experimental Liturgy (1967)	MAL
Ire1	The Irish Experimental Liturgy (1972)	FAL
Ire2	The Liturgy from the Church of Ireland *Alternative Prayer Book* (1984)	LAL
Jap	The Japanese Liturgy (1959)	LiE
Kor	The Korean Liturgy (1939)	LiE
Kor1	The Korean Experimental Liturgy (1973)	FAL
Kor1A	The Korean Experimental Liturgy Revised (1980)	*LAL
Kuch	The Kuching Experimental Liturgy (1973)	FAL
LfA	A *Liturgy for Africa* (1964)	MAL
Mad	The Madagascar Liturgy (1945)	MAL
Mel	The Melanesian Liturgy (1972)	FAL
MLT	The modernization of **Eng2** in *Modern Liturgical Texts* (1968)	—
NG	The Papua New Guinea Liturgy (1970)	FAL
Nig	The Nigerian Liturgy (1983)	LAL
NUL	The United Liturgy for Nigeria (1965)	MAL
Nyas²	The Nyasaland Liturgy (?1929)	*LiE
NZ	The New Zealand Experimental Liturgy (1966)	MAL
NZR	The New Zealand Liturgy (1970)	FAL
NZ1	The New Zealand Alternative Liturgy (1984)	LAL
NZ2	The New Zealand Alternative Liturgy for Special Occasions (1984)	LAL

¹ The Code '**IndE**' was used in the writing of **MAL**, inconsistently with the coding set out in this section in both **LiE** and **MAL**, to indicate the Indian 1662 Recension, i.e. **Ind**. This is listed as under corrigenda to **MAL** in Appendix G to **FAL** (p. 421).

² These titles ('**Nyas**' and '**Rhod**', which is overleaf) are retained here for the sake of uniformity with **LiE**, in which the texts appear, and for no other reason. The countries and dioceses concerned have changed their names, and both the texts lapsed from use soon after (see chapter 12 in **FAL**). The countries are now called Malawi and Zambia respectively. It should also be noted that the dates here ascribed to the texts are guesswork based on bare inference. No dates appeared for them in **LiE**.

NZ3	The New Zealand 'Order of Celebration' (1984)	LAL
PNG	The Papua New Guinea rite (revised from **NG**) (1978)	*LAL
Rhod[3]	The Northern Rhodesia Liturgy (?1925)	LiE
SAfr1	The South African Experimental Liturgy (1969)	FAL
SAfr2	The South African '*Liturgy 1975*' (1975)	FAL
Scot	The Scottish Liturgy (1929)	LiE
ScotE	The Scottish 1662 Recension (1929)	*LiE
ScotR	The Scottish Experimental Liturgy (1966)	MAL
ScotRR	The 1970 form of **ScotR**	*FAL
ScotS	Propers authorized to supplement those in **Scot** and **ScotE** (1966)	MAL
Scot1	The Episcopal Church of Scotland Experimental Liturgy (1977)	LAL
Scot2	The Episcopal Church of Scotland 'Scottish Liturgy 1982'	LAL
Tan	The Tanzanian Liturgy (1973/4)	FAL
TanR	The Tanzanian Liturgy Revised (1977)	*LAL
WAfr	The Experimental Liturgy of the Church of the Province of West Africa (1980)	LAL
Wal	The Welsh Experimental Liturgy (1966)	MAL
WalR	The Welsh Modern English Study Liturgy (1972)	FAL
Wal1	The Rite from the Book of Common Prayer of the Church in Wales (1984)	LAL
Wal2	The Church in Wales Modern Language Liturgy (1984)	LAL
Wind	The West Indies Liturgy (1959)	LiE
Wind1	The Liturgy from the West Indies *Revised Services* (1980)	LAL
Zan	The Swahili Mass (Zanzibar Diocese) (1919)	LiE

[3] See note 2 above.

The liturgical texts have been laid out to conform as nearly as possible to their originals, subject to the need for standard type-sizes, and some uniformity of appearance. Disciplinary rubrics have usually been omitted, and notes standing before or after services have sometimes been reported in brief or presented in a smaller typeface. Numbers have been inserted in the margins to give easy reference to particular sections of text, and editorial footnotes below a section refer to the whole section thus demarcated by the numbering. In many cases the numbering is reprinted from the original, and this is indicated at the beginning of the text as set out here.

'ICET' ('International Consultation on English Texts') and 'CF' ('Common Forms') denote the two categories of 'Common Forms' set out once and for all in Appendix A. Very occasionally the code '**MAL** CF' is used to refer to forms in Appendix A to **MAL**. Variants from the Common Forms (ICET or CF) are printed as an *apparatus* wherever they occur. Occasionally other material is used similarly.

Italic type is used for rubrics. Roman type is used for the text of liturgies where the minister alone is directed to say or sing it. **Bold type** is used for the text of liturgies where it is either to be said or sung by the minister and people together, or by the people alone, or by the individual recipient at the administration. This type is often used where doubts exist, whether the doubt arises from an ambiguous rubric, or from the laying out in lines, or both. Rubrical directions from the original (e.g. *People :. .*) are retained even where a distinctive type as used here makes the original rubric appear redundant.

Asterisks * and square brackets [ ] are used as in the originals, and in fact almost always indicate optional items. Double square brackets ⟦ ⟧ enclose editorial comment, whether in the text or in footnotes (other footnotes are reprinted from the original). SMALL CAPITAL TYPE also denotes editorial comment, usually only of one word. OM means that a particular word or phrase is omitted, OMIT usually that a whole section is omitted.

All other punctuation and presentation reflects what is found in the originals. Where, through different printings, there are uncertainties as to what the original form is, every attempt has been made to recover the form authorized.

PREFACE

THIS volume stands fourth in a line of liturgical reference works. It follows Bernard J. Wigan (ed.), *The Liturgy in English* (Oxford University Press, 1962, 1964), Colin O. Buchanan (ed.), *Modern Anglican Liturgies 1958–1968* (Oxford University Press, 1968) and Colin O. Buchanan (ed.), *Further Anglican Liturgies 1968–1975* (Grove Books, Bramcote, 1975). Between them they provide a full set of Anglican eucharistic liturgies from the Reformation until Autumn 1984, along with considerable background information and supplementary material.[1]

I would not have been able to produce my own third volume for 1984 had it not been that the Alcuin Club found itself at a late stage with a gap in its annual series. This gave both the opportunity for this volume and the incentive to work fast on the texts. On the other hand, Alcuin Club volumes are limited in size by funds available, and the opportunity for this fourth volume has been balanced by restrictions on size to which the previous ones were not subject.

At the same time, the length of eucharistic rites has generally increased – sometimes through lengthy notes, more often through having a wide range of choice of forms of intercessions and of eucharistic prayers. This has meant trimming the introductions to the texts and omitting introductory chapters, and sometimes the judicious use of a small typeface for appendix material. Nevertheless, within these limitations it has been possible to provide a large amount of liturgical material, all of it recently authorized, almost all currently in use, and none of it otherwise readily available from all parts of the earth as it is here.[2] 1984 also proves (though this could hardly have been foreseen a few months ago) to be the great year when new texts are launched

---

[1] The two Oxford volumes, coded and known here as '**LiE**' and '**MAL**' respectively, are both out of print in 1984. The third volume, '**FAL**', is in print in both hardback and paperback editions.

[2] One omission I have had to accept is the text of the liturgies of the Spanish and Portuguese Reformed Episcopal Churches. These do not relate to the decade covered by the volume, but the dioceses concerned were joined to the Anglican Communion in 1979, and thus become part of the agenda here. I am editing the eucharistic liturgies in Grove Liturgical Study no. 43, *Liturgies of the Spanish and Portuguese Reformed Episcopal Churches* in June 1985. There are also texts from Brazil, Central Africa, Japan, South East Asia and Melanesia which are either not yet published or are still only at draft stage, or were not to hand in time for this volume, and these become the material in waiting for the next volume.

simultaneously in different parts of the world, and are thus caught red-hot in this volume.[3]

Some 'thou' form rites have reappeared, and in their case there is reference to forms in **LiE** and **MAL**, not least to the 'Common Forms' in **MAL**. There are also rites which are little changed from **FAL**, and are shown simply by an *apparatus* detailing those changes. In general the volume will be most useful if **FAL** is readily to hand also. I have made a very thorough effort to ensure the accuracy of what is printed, and I would be grateful if errors could be notified to me.

In the absence of introductory chapters about pan-Anglican trends or principles, I have simultaneously prepared Grove Liturgical Study no. 41, *Anglican Eucharistic Liturgy 1975–1985* (Grove Books, Bramcote, March 1985), and this Study, whilst it can stand on its own, relates to the texts here and serves as a general introduction.

Finally, my grateful thanks are due to the Society for the Promotion of Christian Knowledge for picking up both the need of the Alcuin Club and the desire of the editor to meet it. My thanks go also to those listed below who have taken endless pains (and in some cases given hospitality) to get the texts and presentation accurate. My College Council kindly gave me a sabbatical in Summer 1984, and I was able to travel. Thus the editorial task mirrors the contents of the volume – the work of editing has been done in England, Wales, Uganda, Australia, New Zealand, and the United States – and on aircraft. And my secretary, Pat Morris, has again been indispensable.

May this volume be useful under God in assisting those who study, use, or prepare liturgical texts.

COLIN BUCHANAN

[3] Thus, as with the two previous volumes, it is likely that this is being published at exactly the 'right' time to catch a rush of rites before a new lull begins. Several rites were still at proof stage in their own countries when the process of putting this volume into the press began.

ACKNOWLEDGEMENTS

Apart from those thanked on page iv for their permission to use copyright material, and those mentioned in the Preface above, many others have helped me, and I especially thank the following:

The Archbishop of Sydney; the Bishops of Bangor, Leicester, Mabula, Mount Kenya East, St Andrews; the Bishop in Peru; Bishop Christopher Robinson; the Deans of Lismore and of Waterford; the Archdeacon of Sabah

The Rev. Canons L. F. Bartlett, C. M. Guilbert, R. Hagesi, D. Holeton, S. S. Hox, M. H. K. Mbwana, J. P. Neves, A. Odukayo, B. Ullyett; the Rev. Professor E. Fasholé-Luke

The Revs. Joyce Bennett, J. R. Bowen, B. R. Carrell, P. Gibson, B. Hill, M. C. Kennedy, R. McCullough, H. C. Miller, Z. Nyilinkwaya, R. M. E. Paterson, P. Santram, D. Williams

Messrs. R. J. Brookes, J. Denton, L. Emery, J. Martin

CHAPTER 1

THE CHURCH OF ENGLAND

IN July 1975 'Series 1 and 2 Revised' (**Eng1-2A**[1]) began its course through Synod, gaining 'General Consideration'.[2] It went to its Revision Committee, and thus to its 'Revision Stage' in February 1976. At the same session of Synod, a policy was adopted of working towards an 'Alternative Service Book' by 1980. This was to include modern language services, for which a full revision of **Eng3** would provide the model, but also an adapted form of **Eng1-2A**. On 14 July 1976, the final form of **Eng1-2A** (called here **Eng1-2B**) was authorized from 1 November 1976 to 31 December 1979, by: Bishops 29–0; Clergy 105–52; Laity 115–35. The rite was published as a booklet and is shown below in *apparatus* form.

The Liturgical Commission put out questionnaires about **Eng3** in Winter 1976–77, and then redrafted it, incorporating the 1974 ICET texts (except the Lord's Prayer). It was published as a report (GS 364) on 18 May 1978, and went to General Synod. 'General Consideration' came on 11 July 1978, and the Revision Committee handled around 1200 suggested amendments, and produced their own new draft text (GS 364A), published on 8 February 1979. The most notable change was the bringing of eucharistic prayers derived from **Eng2** and **Eng1** into the main text, and the adding to them of a new prayer (printed third) based on Hippolytus.[3] Synod in February and July 1979 took nineteen hours to handle around 300 amendments, and the Revision Stage was completed with 'Provisional Approval' (only one against) on 6 July 1979. The text then went to the House of Bishops and, after some very minor drafting by the Bishops, returned to Synod to gain 'Final Approval' as **EngA** on 7 November 1979. Voting was: Bishops 33–4; Clergy 207–10; Laity 150–23. Authorization was initially from 1 May 1980 to 'the publication of the ASB' and was then extended to 31 December 1990.[4] The rite was published as a booklet (ASB 20) on 1 May 1980 then in the ASB, on 10 November 1980.

Eng1-2B was 'adapted' in General Synod in July and November 1979 for inclusion in the ASB also. In its unadapted form its authorization was extended in July 1979 to 'the date of publication of the ASB'. A

---

[1] Printed in **FAL** in its draft form (as it had then just been published).
[2] The procedures differ from those described in **FAL**. See *The Alternative Service Book 1980: A Commentary by the Liturgical Commission* (CIO, London, 1980), p. 16.
[3] See Appendix E for further details of the first and third Eucharistic Prayers.
[4] Final Approval for all the contents of the ASB on 9 November 1979 was given by: Bishops 13–0; Clergy 107–1; Laity 105–2.

special motion on 4 July 1979 to omit the adapted form 'Rite B' (here called **EngB**) from the ASB was defeated by 162 votes to 127. Then it was authorized on 9 November 1979 for use 'From the date of publication of the ASB' to 31 December 1990. **EngB** stands in the ASB as the only service not in modern language. **Eng1** was allowed to lapse in July 1980. **Eng2** and **Eng3** (unrevised) were extended in 1979 to the date of publication of the ASB, and in July 1980 to 31 December 1985, but Synod in 1984 and 1985 refused further extension.

THE ENGLISH RITE A LITURGY 1980 (EngA)

⟦The text of this liturgy was first published as a booklet, with the 'General Notes' from the ASB shown in the cover. The rubrics were mostly in blue, as were marginal numbers which referred to optional sections. In the ASB itself certain errors were corrected in the type-setting. A 1984 edition had further corrections. The numbering is original.⟧

THE ORDER FOR HOLY COMMUNION
also called THE EUCHARIST and THE LORD'S SUPPER

RITE A
NOTES

1 *PREPARATION   Careful devotional preparation before the service is recommended for every communicant.*

2 *THE PRESIDENT   The president (who, in accordance with the provisions of Canon B12 'Of the ministry of the Holy Communion', must have been episcopally ordained priest) presides over the whole service. He says the opening Greeting, the Collect, the Absolution, the Peace, and the Blessing; he himself must take the bread and the cup before replacing them on the holy table, say the Eucharistic Prayer, break the consecrated bread, and receive the sacrament on every occasion. The remaining parts of the service he may delegate to others. When necessity dictates, a deacon or lay person may preside over the Ministry of the Word.*

When the Bishop is present, it is appropriate that he should act as president. He may also delegate sections 32–49 to a priest.

3 *POSTURE   When a certain posture is particularly appropriate, it is indicated in the margin. For the rest of the service local custom may be established and followed. The Eucharistic Prayer (sections 38, 39, 40, and 41) is a single prayer, the unity of which may be obscured by changes of posture in the course of it.*

4 *SEASONAL MATERIAL   The seasonal sentences and blessings are optional. Any other appropriate scriptural sentences may be read at sections 1 and 50 at the discretion of the president and 'Alleluia' may be added to any sentence from Easter Day until Pentecost.*

5 *GREETINGS (section 2 etc.)   In addition to the points where greetings are provided, at other suitable points (e.g. before the Gospel and before the Blessing and Dismissal) the minister may say* 'The Lord be with you' *and the congregation reply* **'and also with you'.**

6 *PRAYERS OF PENITENCE   These are used either after section 4 or section 23 (but see Note 22 below for occasions when the Order following the pattern of the Book of Common Prayer is used).*

7 *KYRIE ELEISON (section 9)   This may be used in English or Greek. Alternative versions are set out in section 79.*

8   *GLORIA IN EXCELSIS (sections 10 and 73)*   *This canticle may be appropriately omitted during Advent and Lent, and on weekdays which are not Principal or Greater Holy Days. It may also be used at sections 1 and 16.*

9   *THE COLLECT (section 11)*   *The Collect may be introduced by the words* 'Let us pray' *and a brief bidding, after which silence may be kept.*

10   *READINGS*   *Where one of the three readings is to be omitted, provision for this is found in Table 3 of the Alternative Calendar and Lectionary according to the season of the year.*

11   *THE GOSPEL IN HOLY WEEK (section 17)*   *From Palm Sunday to the Wednesday in Holy Week, and on Good Friday, the Passion Gospel may be introduced:* 'The Passion of our Lord Jesus Christ according to *N* ', *and concluded:* 'This is the Passion of the Lord'. *No responses are used.*

12   *THE SERMON (section 18)*   *The sermon is an integral part of the Ministry of the Word. A sermon should normally be preached at all celebrations on Sundays and other Holy Days.*

13   *PROPER PREFACES*   *The Proper Prefaces are set out in section 76. They are obligatory when this is indicated in the seasonal propers but may be used on other suitable occasions. The Sunday Prefaces (31), (32), and (33) are for use with the Fourth Eucharistic Prayer and the Order following the pattern of the Book of Common Prayer.*

14   *SECOND EUCHARISTIC PRAYER (section 39)*   *The three paragraphs beginning* 'For he is your living Word' *and ending* 'a people for your own possession' *may be omitted if a Proper Preface is used.*

15   *ACCLAMATIONS*   *These are optional. They may be introduced by the president with the words* 'Let us proclaim the mystery of faith' *or with other suitable words or they may be used without introduction.*

16   *MANUAL ACTS*   *In addition to the taking of the bread and the cup at section 36 the president may use traditional manual acts during the Eucharistic Prayers.*

17   *WORDS OF INVITATION (section 45)*   *The words provided are to be used at least on Sundays and other Holy Days, and those in section 85 may be added. On other days those in section 85 may be substituted.*

18   *THE BLESSING (section 54)*   *In addition to the blessings provided here and in section 77 the president may at his discretion use others.*

19   *NOTICES*   *Banns of marriage and other notices may be published after section 2, section 19, or section 53.*

20   *HYMNS, CANTICLES, THE PEACE, THE COLLECTION AND PRESENTATION OF THE OFFERINGS OF THE PEOPLE, AND THE PREPARATION OF THE GIFTS OF BREAD AND WINE*   *Points are indicated for these, but if occasion requires they may occur elsewhere.*

21   *SILENCE*   *After sections 6, 13, 15, 17, 18, 26, before sections 42 and 51, and after the biddings in section 21, silence may be kept.*

22   *THE ORDER FOLLOWING THE PATTERN OF THE BOOK OF COMMON PRAYER (sections 22 and 57–75)*   *When this Order is being followed the Prayers of Penitence should not be used at section 4, as they are requisite at section 59. The Order provided should then be followed in its entirety.*

23   *MINISTRY TO THE SICK*   *When Holy Communion is ministered to the sick, the Laying on of Hands or Anointing may follow the Absolution (section 28); the alternative Eucharistic Prayer for use with the sick (section 84) may be used; and the service may be shortened if the needs of the patient require it.*

24   *A SERVICE WITHOUT COMMUNION*   *When there is no communion, the minister reads the service as far as the Absolution (section 28), and then adds the Lord's Prayer, the General Thanksgiving, and/or other prayers (see section 86) at his discretion, ending with the Grace. When such a service is led by a deacon or lay person,* 'us' *is said instead of* 'you' *in the Absolution.*

THE ORDER FOR HOLY COMMUNION RITE A

THE PREPARATION

1 *At the entry of the ministers AN APPROPRIATE SENTENCE may be used; and A HYMN, A CANTICLE, or A PSALM may be sung.*

2 *The president welcomes the people using these or other appropriate words.*

The Lord be with you *or*	The Lord is here.
All **and also with you.**	**His Spirit is with us.**

or Easter Day to Pentecost

Alleluia! Christ is risen.

All   **He is risen indeed. Alleluia!**

3 *This prayer may be said.*

All   **Almighty God...⟦CF 1⟧...our Lord. Amen.**

        hid] hidden

PRAYERS OF PENITENCE

4 *THE PRAYERS OF PENITENCE (sections 5–8) may be said here, or after section 23; if they are said here, sections 6–8 are always used. Alternative confessions may be used (see section 80).*

5 *THE COMMANDMENTS (section 78) or the following SUMMARY OF THE LAW may be said.*

Minister   Our Lord Jesus Christ said: The first commandment is this: 'Hear, O Israel, the Lord... ⟦CF 3⟧...than these.

All   **Amen. Lord, have mercy.**

        This is the first commandment] OM

6 *The minister invites the congregation to confess their sins in these or other suitable words (see section 25).*

God so loved the world that he gave his only Son Jesus Christ to save us from our sins, to be our advocate in heaven, and to bring us to eternal life.

Let us confess our sins, in penitence and faith, firmly resolved to keep God's commandments and to live in love and peace with all men.

7 *All*   **Almighty God, our heavenly Father,**
        we have sinned against you and against our fellow
            men,
        in thought and word and deed,
        through negligence, through weakness,
        through our own deliberate fault.

We are truly sorry,
and repent of all our sins.
For the sake of your Son Jesus Christ, who died for us,
forgive us all that is past;
and grant thát we may serve you in newness of life
to the glory of your name. Amen.

8 *President* Almighty God...⟦CF 5⟧...our Lord. **Amen.**

you...your] *you...your* THROUGHOUT

---

9 *KYRIE ELEISON may be said (see also section 79).*

Lord, have mercy.
Lord, have mercy.

Christ, have mercy.
Christ, have mercy.

Lord, have mercy.
Lord, have mercy.

10 *GLORIA IN EXCELSIS may be said.*
All **Glory to God...⟦ICET 4⟧...the Father. Amen.**

11 *The president says THE COLLECT.*

THE MINISTRY OF THE WORD

12 *Either two or three readings from scripture follow, the last of which is always the Gospel.*

13 *Sit*
OLD TESTAMENT READING

At the end the reader may say

This is the word of the Lord.
All **Thanks be to God.**

14 *A PSALM may be used.*

15 *Sit*
NEW TESTAMENT READING (EPISTLE)

At the end the reader may say

This is the word of the Lord.
All **Thanks be to God.**

16 *A CANTICLE, A HYMN, or A PSALM may be used.*

17 *Stand*
THE GOSPEL. When it is announced

All **Glory to Christ our Saviour.**

At the end the reader says

This is the Gospel of Christ.

All **Praise to Christ our Lord.**

18 *Sit*

THE SERMON

19 *Stand*

THE NICENE CREED *is said on Sundays and other Holy Days, and may be said on other days.*

All **We believe**...⟦ICET 3⟧...**to come. Amen.**

**incarnate from] incarnate of
[and the Son]]** OMIT BRACKETS

THE INTERCESSION

20 *INTERCESSIONS AND THANKSGIVINGS are led by the president, or by others. The form below, or one of those in section 81, or other suitable words, may be used.*

21 *This form may be used*
(a) with the insertion of specific subjects between the paragraphs;
(b) as a continuous whole with or without brief biddings.

Not all paragraphs need be used on every occasion.
Individual names may be added at the places indicated.
This response may be used before or after each paragraph.

Minister Lord, in your mercy
All **hear our prayer.**

Let us pray for the Church and for the world, and let us thank God for his goodness.

Almighty God, our heavenly Father, you promised through your Son Jesus Christ to hear us when we pray in faith.

Strengthen *N* our bishop and all your Church in the service of Christ; that those who confess your name may be united in your truth, live together in your love, and reveal your glory in the world.

Bless and guide Elizabeth our Queen; give wisdom to all in authority; and direct this and every nation in the ways of justice and of peace; that men may honour one another, and seek the common good.

Give grace to us, our families and friends, and to all our neighbours; that we may serve Christ in one another, and love as he loves us.

Comfort and heal all those who suffer in body, mind, or spirit...; give them courage and hope in their troubles; and bring them the joy of your salvation.

Hear us as we remember those who have died in the faith of Christ...; according to your promises, grant us with them a share in your eternal kingdom.

Rejoicing in the fellowship of (*N* and of) all your saints, we commend ourselves and all Christian people to your unfailing love.

Merciful Father,

All   **accept these prayers**
for the sake of your Son,
our Saviour Jesus Christ. Amen.

22 *The Order following the pattern of the Book of Common Prayer continues at section 57.*

PRAYERS OF PENITENCE

23 *THE PRAYERS OF PENITENCE (sections 24–28) are said here, if they have not been said after section 4; if they are said here, sections 26–28 are always used.*
Alternative confessions may be used (see section 80).

24 *THE COMMANDMENTS (section 78) or the following SUMMARY OF THE LAW may be said.*

Minister   Our Lord Jesus...⟦CF 3, as at no. 5⟧...than these.

All   **Amen. Lord, have mercy.**

25 *The minister may say*

God so loved the world that he gave his only Son Jesus Christ to save us from our sins, to be our advocate in heaven, and to bring us to eternal life.

or one or more of these SENTENCES.

Hear...⟦CF 4⟧...propitiation for our sins. (1 *John* 2. 1)
does sin] sins

26 *Minister*   Let us confess our sins, in penitence and faith, firmly resolved to keep God's commandments and to live in love and peace with all men.

27 *All*   **Almighty God**...⟦as at no. 7⟧...**your name. Amen.**

28 *President*   Almighty God...⟦CF 5⟧...our Lord. **Amen.**
you...your] *you...your* THROUGHOUT

29 *All may say*

We do not presume...⟦CF 6⟧...**he in us. Amen.**

The alternative prayer at section 82 may be used.

THE MINISTRY OF THE SACRAMENT
THE PEACE

30 *Stand*

The president says either of the following or other suitable words (see section 83).

Christ is our peace.
He has reconciled us to God in one body by the cross.
We meet in his name and share his peace.

or   We are the Body of Christ.
In the one Spirit we were all baptized into one body.
Let us then pursue all that makes for peace
and builds up our common life.

He then says

The peace of the Lord be always with you
All   **and also with you.**

31 *The president may say*

Let us offer one another a sign of peace.

and all may exchange a sign of peace.

THE PREPARATION OF THE GIFTS

32 *The bread and wine are placed on the holy table.*

33 *The president may praise God for his gifts in appropriate words to which all respond*

Blessèd be God for ever.

34 *The offerings of the people may be collected and presented. These words may be used.*

**Yours, Lord, is the greatness, the power,
the glory, the splendour, and the majesty;
for everything in heaven and on earth is yours.
All things come from you,
and of your own do we give you.**

35 *At the preparation of the gifts A HYMN may be sung.*

THE EUCHARISTIC PRAYER
THE TAKING OF THE BREAD AND CUP AND THE GIVING OF THANKS

36 *The president takes the bread and cup into his hands and replaces them on the holy table.*

37 *The president uses one of the four EUCHARISTIC PRAYERS which follow.*

38 FIRST EUCHARISTIC PRAYER

President	The Lord be with you *or* The Lord is here.
All	**and also with you.** **His Spirit is with us.**
President	Lift up your hearts.
All	**We lift them to the Lord.**
President	Let us give thanks to the Lord our God.
All	**It is right to give him thanks and praise.**

President   It is indeed right,
it is our duty and our joy,
at all times and in all places
to give you thanks and praise,
holy Father, heavenly King,
almighty and eternal God,
through Jesus Christ your only Son our Lord.

For he is your living Word;
through him you have created all things from the
    beginning,
and formed us in your own image.

Through him you have freed us from the slavery of sin,
giving him to be born as man and to die upon the cross;
you raised him from the dead
and exalted him to your right hand on high.
Through him you have sent upon us
your holy and life-giving Spirit,
and made us a people for your own possession.

PROPER PREFACE, when appropriate (section 76)

Therefore with angels and archangels,
and with all the company of heaven,
we proclaim your great and glorious name,
for ever praising you and saying:

All   **Holy, holy, holy Lord,**
God of power and might,
heaven and earth are full of your glory.
Hosanna in the highest.

This ANTHEM may also be used.

Blessed is he who comes in the name of the Lord.
Hosanna in the highest.

President   Accept our praises, heavenly Father,
through your Son our Saviour Jesus Christ;
and as we follow his example and obey his command,
grant that by the power of your Holy Spirit
these gifts of bread and wine
may be to us his body and his blood;

Who in the same night that he was betrayed,
took bread and gave you thanks;
he broke it and gave it to his disciples, saying,
Take, eat; this is my body which is given for you;
do this in remembrance of me.
In the same way, after supper
he took the cup and gave you thanks;
he gave it to them, saying,
Drink this, all of you;
this is my blood of the new covenant,
which is shed for you and for many for the forgiveness
   of sins.
Do this, as often as you drink it,
in remembrance of me.

All   **Christ has died:**
Christ is risen:
Christ will come again.

President   Therefore, heavenly Father,
we remember his offering of himself
made once for all upon the cross,
and proclaim his mighty resurrection and glorious
   ascension.
As we look for his coming in glory,
we celebrate with this bread and this cup
his one perfect sacrifice.

Accept through him, our great high priest,
this our sacrifice of thanks and praise;
and as we eat and drink these holy gifts
in the presence of your divine majesty,
renew us by your Spirit,
inspire us with your love,
and unite us in the body of your Son,
Jesus Christ our Lord.

Through him, and with him, and in him,
by the power of the Holy Spirit,
with all who stand before you in earth and heaven,
we worship you, Father almighty,
in songs of everlasting praise:

All   **Blessing and honour and glory and power
be yours for ever and ever. Amen.**

Silence may be kept.

The service continues with THE LORD'S PRAYER at section 42 on p. . . . .

39 SECOND EUCHARISTIC PRAYER

President	The Lord be with you *or*	The Lord is here.
All	**and also with you.**	**His Spirit is with us.**

President   Lift up your hearts.
All   **We lift them to the Lord.**

President   Let us give thanks to the Lord our God.
All   **It is right to give him thanks and praise.**

President   It is indeed right,
it is our duty and our joy,
at all times and in all places
to give you thanks and praise,
holy Father, heavenly King,
almighty and eternal God,
through Jesus Christ your only Son our Lord.

The following may be omitted if a Proper Preface is used.

For he is your living Word;
through him you have created all things from the
beginning,
and formed us in your own image.

Through him you have freed us from the slavery of sin,
giving him to be born as man and to die upon the cross;
you raised him from the dead
and exalted him to your right hand on high.

Through him you have sent upon us
your holy and life-giving Spirit,
and made us a people for your own possession.

PROPER PREFACE, when appropriate (section 76)

Therefore with angels and archangels,
and with all the company of heaven,

we proclaim your great and glorious name,
for ever praising you and saying:

All　**Holy, holy, holy Lord,
God of power and might,
heaven and earth are full of your glory.
Hosanna in the highest.**

This ANTHEM may also be used.

**Blessed is he who comes in the name of the Lord.
Hosanna in the highest.**

President　Hear us, heavenly Father,
through Jesus Christ your Son our Lord,
through him accept our sacrifice of praise;
and grant that by the power of your Holy Spirit
these gifts of bread and wine
may be to us his body and his blood;

Who in the same night that he was betrayed,
took bread and gave you thanks;
he broke it and gave it to his disciples, saying,
Take, eat; this is my body which is given for you;
do this in remembrance of me.
In the same way, after supper
he took the cup and gave you thanks;
he gave it to them, saying,
Drink this, all of you;
this is my blood of the new covenant,
which is shed for you and for many for the forgiveness
of sins.
Do this, as often as you drink it,
in remembrance of me.

All　**Christ has died:
Christ is risen:
Christ will come again.**

President　Therefore, Lord and heavenly Father,
having in remembrance his death once for all upon the
cross,
his resurrection from the dead,
and his ascension into heaven,
and looking for the coming of his kingdom,
we make with this bread and this cup
the memorial of Christ your Son our Lord.

Accept through him this offering of our duty and service;
and as we eat and drink these holy gifts
in the presence of your divine majesty,
fill us with your grace and heavenly blessing;
nourish us with the body and blood of your Son,
that we may grow into his likeness
and, made one by your Spirit,
become a living temple to your glory.

Through Jesus Christ our Lord,
by whom, and with whom, and in whom,
in the unity of the Holy Spirit,
all honour and glory be yours, almighty Father,
from all who stand before you in earth and heaven.
now and for ever. **Amen.**

Silence may be kept.

The service continues with THE LORD'S PRAYER at section 42 on p. . . . .

40 THIRD EUCHARISTIC PRAYER

President	The Lord be with you *or*	The Lord is here.
All	**and also with you.**	**His Spirit is with us.**

President   Lift up your hearts.
All   **We lift them to the Lord.**

President   Let us give thanks to the Lord our God.
All   **It is right to give him thanks and praise.**

President   Father, we give you thanks and praise
through your beloved Son Jesus Christ,
your living Word through whom you have created all
    things;

Who was sent by you, in your great goodness, to be our
    Saviour;
by the power of the Holy Spirit he took flesh
and, as your Son, born of the blessed Virgin,
was seen on earth
and went about among us;

He opened wide his arms for us on the cross;
he put an end to death by dying for us
and revealed the resurrection by rising to new life;
so he fulfilled your will and won for you a holy people.

PROPER PREFACE, when appropriate (section 76)

Therefore with angels and archangels,
and with all the company of heaven,
we proclaim your great and glorious name,
for ever praising you and saying:

All   **Holy, holy, holy Lord,**
God of power and might,
heaven and earth are full of your glory.
Hosanna in the highest.

This ANTHEM may also be used.
Blessed is he who comes in the name of the Lord.
Hosanna in the highest.

President   Lord, you are holy indeed, the source of all holiness;
grant that, by the power of your Holy Spirit,
and according to your holy will,
these your gifts of bread and wine
may be to us the body and blood of our Lord Jesus
    Christ;

Who in the same night that he was betrayed,
took bread and gave you thanks;
he broke it and gave it to his disciples, saying,
Take, eat; this is my body which is given for you;
do this in remembrance of me.
In the same way, after supper
he took the cup and gave you thanks;
he gave it to them, saying,
Drink this, all of you;
this is my blood of the new covenant,
which is shed for you and for many for the forgiveness
    of sins.
Do this, as often as you drink it,
in remembrance of me.

All   **Christ has died:**
Christ is risen:
Christ will come again.

President   And so, Father, calling to mind his death on the cross,
his perfect sacrifice made once for the sins of all men,
rejoicing at his mighty resurrection and glorious
    ascension,
and looking for his coming in glory,
we celebrate this memorial of our redemption;

We thank you for counting us worthy
to stand in your presence and serve you;
we bring before you this bread and this cup;

We pray you to accept this our duty and service,
a spiritual sacrifice of praise and thanksgiving;

Send the Holy Spirit on your people
and gather into one in your kingdom
all who share this one bread and one cup,
so that we, in the company of all the saints,
may praise and glorify you for ever,
through him from whom all good things come,
Jesus Christ our Lord;

By whom, and with whom, and in whom,
in the unity of the Holy Spirit,
all honour and glory be yours, almighty Father,
for ever and ever. **Amen.**

Silence may be kept.

*The service continues with THE LORD'S PRAYER at section 42 on
p. . . . .*

41 FOURTH EUCHARISTIC PRAYER

President	The Lord be with you	*or*	The Lord is here.
All	**and also with you.**		**His Spirit is with us.**

President Lift up your hearts.
All **We lift them to the Lord.**

President Let us give thanks to the Lord our God.
All **It is right to give him thanks and praise.**

President It is indeed right,
it is our duty and our joy,
at all times and in all places
to give you thanks and praise,
holy Father, heavenly King,
almighty and eternal God,
creator of heaven and earth,
through Jesus Christ our Lord:

PROPER PREFACE, when appropriate (section 76)

The following is used when no Proper Preface is provided.

For he is the true high priest,
who has loosed us from our sins

and has made us to be a royal priesthood to you,
our God and Father.
Therefore with angels and archangels,
and with all the company of heaven,
we proclaim your great and glorious name,
for ever praising you and saying:

All **Holy, holy, holy Lord,**
God of power and might,
heaven and earth are full of your glory.
Hosanna in the highest.

This ANTHEM may also be used.

Blessed is he who comes in the name of the Lord.
Hosanna in the highest.

President All glory to you, our heavenly Father:
in your tender mercy
you gave your only Son Jesus Christ
to suffer death upon the cross for our redemption;
he made there
a full atonement for the sins of the whole world,
offering once for all his one sacrifice of himself;
he instituted,
and in his holy gospel commanded us to continue,
a perpetual memory of his precious death
until he comes again.

Hear us, merciful Father, we humbly pray,
and grant that by the power of your Holy Spirit
we who receive these gifts of your creation,
this bread and this wine,
according to your Son our Saviour Jesus Christ's holy
    institution,
in remembrance of the death that he suffered,
may be partakers of his most blessed body and blood;

Who in the same night that he was betrayed,
took bread and gave you thanks;
he broke it and gave it to his disciples, saying,
Take, eat; this is my body which is given for you;
do this in remembrance of me.
In the same way, after supper
he took the cup and gave you thanks;
he gave it to them, saying,
Drink this, all of you;

this is my blood of the new covenant,
which is shed for you and for many for the forgiveness
of sins.
Do this, as often as you drink it,
in remembrance of me.

All   **Christ has died:**
Christ is risen:
Christ will come again.

President   Therefore, Lord and heavenly Father,
in remembrance of the precious death and passion,
the mighty resurrection and glorious ascension
of your dear Son Jesus Christ,
we offer you through him this sacrifice of praise and
thanksgiving.

Grant that by his merits and death,
and through faith in his blood,
we and all your Church may receive forgiveness of our
sins
and all other benefits of his passion.
Although we are unworthy, through our many sins,
to offer you any sacrifice,
yet we pray that you will accept this,
the duty and service that we owe;
do not weigh our merits, but pardon our offences,
and fill us all who share in this holy communion
with your grace and heavenly blessing.

Through Jesus Christ our Lord,
by whom, and with whom, and in whom,
in the unity of the Holy Spirit,
all honour and glory be yours, almighty Father,
now and forever. **Amen.**

Silence may be kept.

THE COMMUNION
THE BREAKING OF THE BREAD AND
THE GIVING OF THE BREAD AND CUP

42   *THE LORD'S PRAYER is said either as follows or in its traditional*
form.
President   As our Saviour taught us, so we pray.

All   **Our Father**... ⟦ICET 1⟧... **for ever. Amen.**
Save us from the time of trial and] Lead us not into temptation but

43 *The president breaks the consecrated bread, saying*

We break this bread
to share in the body of Christ.

All **Though we are many, we are one body,
because we all share in one bread.**

44 *Either here or during the distribution one of the following anthems may be said.*

Lamb of God...⟦ICET 8(b)⟧...**us peace.**

or **Jesus, Lamb of God**...⟦ICET 8(a)⟧...**your peace.**

45 *Before the distribution the president says*

Draw near with faith. Receive the body of our Lord Jesus Christ which he gave for you, and his blood which he shed for you.

Eat and drink in remembrance that he died for you, and feed on him in your hearts by faith with thanksgiving.

Additional words of invitation may be used (see section 85).

46 *The president and people receive the communion. At the distribution the minister says to each communicant*

The body of Christ keep you in eternal life.
The blood of Christ keep you in eternal life.

or The body of Christ.
The blood of Christ.

The communicant replies each time **Amen**, *and then receives.*

Alternative words of distribution may be found in section 66.

47 *During the distribution hymns and anthems may be sung.*

48 *If either or both of the consecrated elements be likely to prove insufficient, the president himself returns to the holy table and adds more, saying these words.*

Father, giving thanks over the bread and the cup according to the institution of your Son Jesus Christ, who said, Take, eat; this is my body (and/or Drink this; this is my blood), we pray that this bread/wine also may be to us his body/blood, to be received in remembrance of him.

49 *Any consecrated bread and wine which is not required for purposes of communion is consumed at the end of the distribution or after the service.*

AFTER COMMUNION

50 *AN APPROPRIATE SENTENCE may be said and A HYMN may be sung.*

51 *Either or both of the following prayers or other suitable prayers are said* *(see section 86).*

52 *President* Father of all...⟦CF 8⟧...our Lord. **Amen.**

in this hope that we have grasped] firm in the hope you have set before us

or

53 *All* **Almighty God...⟦CF 9⟧...praise and glory. Amen.**

THE DISMISSAL

54 *The president may say this or an alternative BLESSING (section 77).*

The peace of God...⟦CF 10⟧...you always. **Amen.**

55 *President* Go in peace to love and serve the Lord.
   All **In the name of Christ. Amen.**

or

   President Go in the peace of Christ.
   All **Thanks be to God.**

From Easter Day to Pentecost 'Alleluia! Alleluia!' *may be added after both the versicle and the response.*

56 *The ministers and people depart.*

THE ORDER FOLLOWING THE PATTERN OF THE BOOK OF COMMON PRAYER

(continued from section 22)

57 *The priest prepares the bread and wine on the holy table, the offerings of the people may be presented, and A HYMN may be sung.*

58 *THE COMMANDMENTS (section 78) or the following SUMMARY OF THE LAW may be said.*

   Minister Our Lord...⟦CF 3, as at no. 5⟧ ...than these.

   All **Amen. Lord, have mercy.**

59 *The priest invites the congregation to confess their sins in these or other suitable words (see section 25). Alternative confessions may be used (see section 80).*

Let us confess our sins, in penitence and faith, firmly resolved to keep God's commandments and to live in love and peace with all men.

60 *All* **Almighty God... ⟦as at no. 7⟧...your name. Amen.**

61 *Priest* Almighty God...⟦CF 5⟧...our Lord. **Amen.**
   you...your] *you...your* THROUGHOUT

62 *The priest says these SENTENCES*

  Hear...⟦CF 4⟧...propitiation for our sins. (1 *John* 2.1)
  does sin] sins

63 **Priest** Lift up your hearts.
  All **We lift them to the Lord.**

  Priest Let us give thanks to the Lord our God.
  All **It is right to give him thanks and praise.**

  Priest It is indeed right,
   it is our duty and our joy,
   at all times and in all places
   to give you thanks and praise,
   holy Father, heavenly King,
   almighty and eternal God,
   through Jesus Christ our Lord.

PROPER PREFACE, when appropriate (section 76)

   Therefore with angels and archangels,
   and with all the company of heaven,
   we proclaim your great and glorious name,
   for ever praising you and saying:
  All **Holy, holy, holy Lord,**
   God of power and might,
   heaven and earth are full of your glory.
   Hosanna in the highest.

64 *All* **We do not presume**...⟦CF 6⟧...**he in us. Amen.**

65 *Priest* Almighty God, our heavenly Father,
   in your tender mercy
   you gave your only Son Jesus Christ
   to suffer death upon the cross for our redemption;
   he made there
   a full atonement for the sins of the whole world,
   offering once for all his one sacrifice of himself;
   he instituted,
   and in his holy gospel commanded us to continue,
   a perpetual memory of his precious death
   until he comes again.

   Hear us, merciful Father,
   we humbly pray,
   and grant that we who receive these gifts of your
    creation,
   this bread and this wine,
   according to your Son our Saviour Jesus Christ's holy
    institution,

in remembrance of the death that he suffered,
may be partakers of his most blessed body and blood;

Who in the same night that he was betrayed,
Here the priest takes the paten.
took bread and gave you thanks;
he broke it, *Here he breaks the bread.*
and gave it to his disciples, saying,
Take, eat;
Here he lays his hand on all the bread.
this is my body which is given for you;
do this in remembrance of me.
In the same way, after supper
Here he takes the cup.
he took the cup and gave you thanks;
he gave it to them, saying,
Drink this, all of you;
Here he lays his hand on all the vessels of wine to be consecrated.
this is my blood of the new covenant,
which is shed for you and for many for the forgiveness
of sins.
Do this, as often as you drink it,
in remembrance of me. **Amen.**

66 *The priest and people receive the communion. At the distribution the minister says to the communicants the following words, or those in sections 45 and 46.*

The body... ⟦CF 7(a)⟧...with thanksgiving.
The blood... ⟦CF 7(b)⟧...be thankful.
everlasting] eternal   TWICE

67 *If either or both of the consecrated elements be likely to prove insufficient, the priest himself returns to the holy table and adds more, and consecrates according to the form in section 65, beginning, 'Our Saviour Christ in the same night...', for the bread, and at 'In the same way, after supper our Saviour...', for the cup.*

68 *Any consecrated bread and wine which is not required for purposes of communion is consumed at the end of the distribution or after the service.*

69 *THE LORD'S PRAYER is said either as follows or in its traditional form.*

Priest   As our Saviour taught us, so we pray.
Our Father... ⟦ICET 1, as at no. 42⟧...**for ever. Amen.**

70 *One or other of the following prayers or one of those at sections 52 and 53 is used.*

71   Lord and heavenly Father, we your servants entirely desire your fatherly goodness mercifully to accept this our sacrifice of praise and thanksgiving, and to grant that, by the merits and death of your Son Jesus Christ, and through faith in his blood, we and all your Church may receive forgiveness of our sins and all other benefits of his passion.

And here we offer and present to you, O Lord, ourselves, our souls and bodies, to be a reasonable, holy, and living sacrifice, humbly beseeching you that all we who are partakers of this holy communion may be fulfilled with your grace and heavenly benediction.

And although we are unworthy, through our many sins, to offer you any sacrifice, yet we pray that you will accept this, the duty and service that we owe, not weighing our merits but pardoning our offences, through Jesus Christ our Lord; by whom and with whom, in the unity of the Holy Spirit, all honour and glory are yours, Father almighty, now and for ever. **Amen.**

or

72   Almighty and everliving God, we heartily thank you that you graciously feed us, who have duly received these holy mysteries, with the spiritual food of the most precious body and blood of your Son our Saviour Jesus Christ, and assure us thereby of your favour and goodness towards us and that we are true members of the mystical body of your Son, the blessed company of all faithful people, and are also heirs, through hope, of your eternal kingdom, by the merits of the most precious death and passion of your dear Son. And we humbly beseech you, heavenly Father, so to assist us with your grace, that we may continue in that holy fellowship, and do all such good works as you have prepared for us to walk in; through Jesus Christ our Lord, to whom, with you and the Holy Spirit, be all honour and glory, now and for ever. **Amen.**

73 *GLORIA IN EXCELSIS or A HYMN may be sung.*

All   **Glory to God**... ⟦ICET 4⟧... **God the Father. Amen.**

74 *Priest*   The peace of God... ⟦CF 10⟧... always. **Amen.**

75 *The ministers and people depart.*

APPENDICES

76 *PROPER PREFACES*

Suitable for use with all Eucharistic Prayers (sections 38, 39, 40, and 41) and the Order following the pattern of the Book of Common Prayer (section 63).

[The Proper Prefaces which follow here are to be found in Appendix C.]

77 *ALTERNATIVE BLESSINGS*

[The Seasonal and other Blessings which follow here are to be found in Appendix D.]

78 *THE COMMANDMENTS*

Either A :

Minister	Our Lord Jesus Christ said, If you love me, keep my commandments; happy are those who hear the word of God and keep it. Hear then these commandments which God has given to his people, and take them to heart.
	I am the Lord your God: you shall have no other gods but me. You shall love the Lord your God with all your heart, with all your soul, with all your mind and with all your strength.
All	**Amen. Lord, have mercy.**
Minister	You shall not make for yourself any idol. God is spirit, and those who worship him must worship in spirit and in truth.
All	**Amen. Lord, have mercy.**
Minister	You shall not dishonour the name of the Lord your God. You shall worship him with awe and reverence.
All	**Amen. Lord, have mercy.**
Minister	Remember the Lord's day and keep it holy. Christ is risen from the dead: set your minds on things that are above, not on things that are on the earth.
All	**Amen. Lord, have mercy.**
Minister	Honour your father and mother. Live as servants of God; honour all men; love the brotherhood.
All	**Amen. Lord, have mercy.**
Minister	You shall not commit murder. Be reconciled to your brother; overcome evil with good.
All	**Amen. Lord, have mercy.**
Minister	You shall not commit adultery. Know that your body is a temple of the Holy Spirit.
All	**Amen. Lord, have mercy.**
Minister	You shall not steal. Be honest in all that you do and care for those in need.
All	**Amen. Lord, have mercy.**
Minister	You shall not be a false witness. Let everyone speak the truth.
All	**Amen. Lord, have mercy.**

Minister	You shall not covet anything which belongs to your neighbour. Remember the words of the Lord Jesus: It is more blessed to give than to receive. Love your neighbour as yourself, for love is the fulfilling of the law.
All	**Amen. Lord, have mercy.**
or B :	
Minister	God spoke all these words, saying, I am the Lord ... ⟦CF 2, including bracketed parts, with response **'Amen. Lord, have mercy'** as above to first nine commandments⟧ ... You shall not covet (your neighbour's house, you shall not covet your neighbour's wife, or his manservant, or his maidservant, or his ox, or his ass, or) anything that is your neighbour's.
All	**Lord, have mercy on us, and write all these your laws in our hearts.**

God; you shall have] God (who brought you out of the land of Egypt, out of the house of bondage). You shall have
but me] before me
any graven] a graven
nor the likeness] or any likeness
or in the ... or in the] or that is in the ... or that is in the
under the earth]] OMIT BRACKET
nor worship them] or serve them: for I the Lord your God am a jealous God, visiting the iniquity of the fathers upon the children to the third and the fourth generation of those who hate me, but showing steadfast love to thousands of those who love me, and keep my commandments).
in vain.] in vain (for the Lord will not hold him guiltless who takes his name in vain).
to keep holy the sabbath day] the sabbath day, to keep it holy.
that you have to do] your work.
the sabbath of] a sabbath to
God] God; in it you shall not do any work, you, or your son, or your daughter, your manservant, or your maidservant, or your cattle, or the sojourner who is within your gates; for in six days the Lord made heaven and earth, the sea, and all that is in them, and rested the seventh day; therefore the Lord blessed the sabbath day and hallowed it.)
mother.] mother (that your days may be long in the land which the Lord your God gives you).
commit murder] kill
[against your neighbour]] OMIT BRACKETS

79 *KYRIE ELEISON*

Section 9 may be said in one of the following forms.

Lord, have mercy (upon us.)   Kyrie eleison.
Lord, have mercy (upon us.)   Kyrie eleison.
Lord, have mercy (upon us.)   Kyrie eleison.

Christ, have mercy (upon us.) Christe eleison.
Christ, have mercy (upon us.)   Christe eleison.
Christ, have mercy (upon us.) Christe eleison.

Lord, have mercy (upon us.)   Kyrie eleison.
Lord, have mercy (upon us.)   Kyrie eleison.
Lord, have mercy (upon us.)   Kyrie eleison.

80 *ALTERNATIVE CONFESSIONS*

Either A :

All	**Almighty God, our heavenly Father,**
	we have sinned against you and against our fellow men,

in thought and word and deed,
in the evil we have done
and in the good we have not done,
through ignorance, through weakness,
through our own deliberate fault.
We are truly sorry,
and repent of all our sins.
For the sake of your Son Jesus Christ, who died for
   us,
forgive us all that is past;
and grant that we may serve you in newness of life
to the glory of your name. Amen.

or B :

All   Almighty God, our heavenly Father,
we have sinned against you,
through our own fault,
in thought and word and deed,
and in what we have left undone.
For your Son our Lord Jesus Christ's sake,
forgive us all that is past;
and grant that we may serve you in newness of life
to the glory of your name. Amen.

or C :

All   Father eternal, giver of light and grace,
we have sinned against you and against our fellow
   men,
in what we have thought,
in what we have said and done,
through ignorance, through weakness,
through our own deliberate fault.
We have wounded your love,
and marred your image in us.
We are sorry and ashamed,
and repent of all our sins.
For the sake of your Son Jesus Christ, who died for
   us,
forgive us all that is past;
and lead us out from darkness
to walk as children of light. Amen.

81 *ALTERNATIVE FORMS OF INTERCESSION*

Either A:

Minister	Let us pray for the whole Church of God in Christ Jesus, and for all men according to their needs.
	O God, the creator and preserver of all mankind, we pray for men of every race, and in every kind of need: make your ways known on earth, your saving power among all nations. (Especially we pray for...) Lord, in your mercy
All	**hear our prayer.**
Minister	We pray for your Church throughout the world: guide and govern us by your Holy Spirit, that all who profess and call themselves Christians may be led into the way of truth, and hold the faith in unity of spirit, in the bond of peace, and in righteousness of life. (Especially we pray for...) Lord, in your mercy
All	**hear our prayer.**
Minister	We commend to your fatherly goodness all who are anxious or distressed in mind or body; comfort and relieve them in their need; give them patience in their sufferings, and bring good out of their troubles. (Especially we pray for...) Merciful Father,
All	**accept these prayers for the sake of your Son, our Saviour Jesus Christ. Amen.**

or B:

Minister	In the power of the Spirit and in union with Christ, let us pray to the Father.
	Hear our prayers, O Lord our God.
All	**Hear us, good Lord.**
Minister	Govern and direct your holy Church; fill it with love and truth; and grant it that unity which is your will.
All	**Hear us, good Lord.**
Minister	Give us boldness to preach the gospel in all the world, and to make disciples of all the nations.
All	**Hear us, good Lord.**
Minister	Enlighten your ministers with knowledge and understand-

ing, that by their teaching and their lives they may proclaim your word.

All **Hear us, good Lord.**

Minister Give your people grace to hear and receive your word, and to bring forth the fruit of the Spirit.

All **Hear us, good Lord.**

Minister Bring into the way of truth all who have erred and are deceived.

All **Hear us, good Lord.**

Minister Strengthen those who stand; comfort and help the faint-hearted; raise up the fallen; and finally beat down Satan under our feet.

All **Hear us, good Lord.**

Minister Guide the leaders of the nations into the ways of peace and justice.

All **Hear us, good Lord.**

Minister Guard and strengthen your servant Elizabeth our Queen, that she may put her trust in you, and seek your honour and glory.

All **Hear us, good Lord.**

Minister Endue the High Court of Parliament and all the Ministers of the Crown with wisdom and understanding.

All **Hear us, good Lord.**

Minister Bless those who administer the law, that they may uphold justice, honesty, and truth.

All **Hear us, good Lord.**

Minister Teach us to use the fruits of the earth to your glory, and for the good of all mankind.

All **Hear us, good Lord.**

Minister Bless and keep all your people.

All **Hear us, good Lord.**

Minister Help and comfort the lonely, the bereaved, and the oppressed.

All **Lord, have mercy.**

Minister Keep in safety those who travel, and all who are in danger.

All **Lord, have mercy.**

Minister Heal the sick in body and mind, and provide for the homeless, the hungry, and the destitute.

All **Lord, have mercy.**

Minister	Show your pity on prisoners and refugees, and all who are in trouble.
All	**Lord, have mercy.**
Minister	Forgive our enemies, persecutors, and slanderers, and turn their hearts.
All	**Lord, have mercy.**
Minister	Hear us as we remember those who have died in the peace of Christ, both those who have confessed the faith and those whose faith is known to you alone, and grant us with them a share in your eternal kingdom.
All	**Lord, have mercy.**
Minister	Father, you hear those who pray in the name of your Son: grant that what we have asked in faith we may obtain according to your will; through Jesus Christ our Lord. **Amen.**

82 *ALTERNATIVE PRAYER OF HUMBLE ACCESS* (*section 29*)

Most merciful Lord,
your love compels us to come in.
Our hands were unclean,
our hearts were unprepared;
we were not fit
even to eat the crumbs from under your table.
But you, Lord, are the God of our salvation,
and share your bread with sinners.
So cleanse and feed us
with the precious body and blood of your Son,
that he may live in us and we in him;
and that we, with the whole company of Christ,
may sit and eat in your kingdom. Amen.

83 *A SELECTION OF OTHER INTRODUCTORY WORDS TO THE PEACE* (*section 30*)

[The Seasonal Introductory Words which follow here are to be found in Appendix D.]

84 *A EUCHARISTIC PRAYER FOR USE WITH THE SICK*

President	The Lord be with you	*or*	The Lord is here.
All	**and also with you.**		**His Spirit is with us.**
President	Lift up your hearts.		
All	**We lift them to the Lord.**		
President	Let us give thanks to the Lord our God.		
All	**It is right to give him thanks and praise.**		

President   It is indeed right,
it is our duty and our joy,
to give you thanks, holy Father,
through Jesus Christ our Lord.

Through him you have created us in your image;
through him you have freed us from sin and death;
through him you have made us your own people by the
    gift of the Holy Spirit.

Hear us, Father,
through Christ your Son our Lord,
and grant that by the power of your Holy Spirit
these gifts of bread and wine
may be to us his body and his blood;

Who in the same night that he was betrayed,
took bread and gave you thanks;
he broke it and gave it to his disciples, saying,
Take, eat; this is my body which is given for you;
do this in remembrance of me.
In the same way, after supper
he took the cup and gave you thanks;
he gave it to them, saying,
Drink this, all of you;
this is my blood of the new covenant,
which is shed for you and for many for the forgiveness of
    sins.
Do this, as often as you drink it,
in remembrance of me.

Therefore, Father,
proclaiming his saving death and resurrection
and looking for his coming in glory,
we celebrate with his bread and this cup
his one perfect sacrifice.

Accept through him, our great high priest,
this our sacrifice of thanks and praise,
and grant that we who eat this bread and drink this cup
may be renewed by your Spirit and grow into his likeness;

Through Jesus Christ our Lord,
by whom, and with whom, and in whom,
all honour and glory be yours, Father,
now and for ever. **Amen.**

85 *ADDITIONAL WORDS OF INVITATION TO COMMUNION*
which may be used after section 45

Either A :

President	Jesus is the Lamb of God who takes away the sins of the world. Happy are those who are called to his supper.
All	**Lord, I am not worthy to receive you,** **but only say the word, and I shall be healed.**

or B :

President	The gifts of God for the people of God.
All	**Jesus Christ is holy,** **Jesus Christ is Lord,** **to the glory of God the Father.**

or C : Easter Day to Pentecost

President :	Alleluia! Christ our Passover is sacrificed for us.
All	**Alleluia! Let us keep the feast.**

86 *ALTERNATIVE FINAL PRAYER*
Especially suitable for a service without Communion

All	**Almighty God,** **we offer you our souls and bodies,** **to be a living sacrifice,** **through Jesus Christ our Lord.** **Send us out into the world...⟦Cf 9⟧...glory. Amen.**

THE ENGLISH RITE B LITURGY 1980 (EngB)

⟦This Rite is derived from **Eng1–2B**, itself the amended and authorized form of **Eng1–2A**, published in **FAL**. The text was then 'adapted' to become **EngB**, and the presentation was conformed (for incorporation in the ASB) to the presentation of **EngA**. **Eng1–2B** is shown here by an *apparatus*. The numbering is original.⟧

THE ORDER FOR HOLY COMMUNION RITE B
NOTES

⟦**Eng1–2B** has first two Notes on '*POSTURE*' and on '*SAYING AND SINGING*' as in **Eng1–2A**. In **EngB** these are excluded, as they come in the 'General Notes' at beginning of the ASB. Note 1 below is thus numbered '*3*' in **Eng1–2B**, and so on. **Eng1–2B** omits the word '*section*' when it occurs in a bracket following the title of a Note.⟧

1   *SEASONAL MATERIAL*   The seasonal sentences (sections 1, 43) and blessings (section 54) are optional. Any other appropriate scriptural sentences may be read at sections 1 and 43 at the discretion of the priest and 'Alleluia' may be added to any sentence from Easter Day until Pentecost (Whit Sunday).

Eng1–2b: *SEASONAL MATERIAL   The proper prefaces in Thanksgiving A and those for Christmas, Passiontide, Easter, and Ascension in Thanksgiving B (28) are obligatory; but the seasonal sentences (1, 39) and the seasonal blessings (48) are optional. The use of one portion of the optional material does not necessitate the use of the other portions. On any occasion for which no suitable sentence is provided, the priest may use a sentence of his own choice.*

2   *1662 MATERIAL   It is permitted to use the 1662 text of the Gloria (sections 5, 48), the Creed (section 14), the Intercession (sections 17, 18), the Confession (section 21), the Absolution (section 22), and the Lord's Prayer (sections 33, 36, 44) instead of the texts printed here.*

Eng1–2B: *5, 48*] *6, 44   17, 18*] *17   21*] *20   22*] *21   33, 36, 44*] *29, 32, 40*
[**Eng1–2B** has Note 5 on '*SERIES 2 MATERIAL*' as in **Eng1–2A**, save that for '*34*' read '*30*', for '*46*' '*43*', for '*49*' '*46*', and for '*those*' '*the texts*'. Note 3 below is then '*6*', and so on.]

3   *GLORIA IN EXCELSIS (section 5)   This canticle is also appropriate at sections 1, 11, and 48.*

Eng1–2B (no. 6): *GLORIA*] *The GLORIA 5*] *6   1, 11, and 48*] *2 and 4*

4   *COLLECTS AND READINGS   The collects and readings are either those set out in this book or those in the Book of Common Prayer, together with any others approved by the General Synod.*

[**Eng1–2B** has '*7 THE COLLECTS*' and '*8 THE LESSONS*' as nos. 8 and 9 in **Eng1–2A**.]

5   *THE SERMON   The sermon (section 13) is an integral part of the Ministry of the Word. A sermon should normally be preached at all celebrations on Sundays and other Holy Days.*

Eng1–2B (no. 9): *The sermon . . . Word*] OM   *at all celebrations*] OM
                           A sermon should normally] *Normally a sermon should*   *other*] OM

6   *THE PEACE   The priest may accompany the words of the Peace (sections 24, 25) with a handclasp or similar action; and both the words and the action may be passed through the congregation.*

[**Eng1–2B** (no. 10) has the section number ('*25*') after the title.]

7   *THE PRAYERS OF INTERCESSION AND THE THANKSGIVING (sections 17, 18, and 30, 31)   The use of the first Intercession does not presume the use of the first Thanksgiving. Either Prayer of Intercession may be used with either Thanksgiving.*

Eng1–2B (no. 11): *INTERCESSION*] ADDS '(*17*)'   *the first Intercession*] *Intercession A*
                           17, 18, and 30, 31] *28*   *the first Thanksgiving*] *Thanksgiving A*

8   *PROPER PREFACES   The Proper Prefaces set out for use in the first Thanksgiving and those for Christmas, Passiontide, Easter and Ascension in the second Thanksgiving are obligatory.*

Eng1–2B: OMIT (SEE VARIANT AT NOTE 1 ABOVE)

9   *THE FIRST THANKSGIVING (section 30)   The Prayer of Humble Access may, if desired, be said after the Sanctus; and the Thanksgiving may end after the words,* 'Do this, as oft as ye shall drink it, in remembrance of me'; *in which case the people then say* **Amen.**

Eng1–2B (no. 12): *FIRST THANKSGIVING*] *THANKSGIVING A   30*] *28*

10   *THE BLESSING (section 49)   In addition to the blessings provided here and at section 54 the priest may at his discretion use others.*

Eng1–2B: OMIT

11   *NOTICES   Banns of marriage and other notices may be published after section 1, section 12, or section 42, if they are not published at section 15.*

Eng1–2B: OMIT (SEE VARIANT RE NOTE 12 BELOW)

12   *HYMNS, CANTICLES, THE PEACE, THE COLLECTION AND PRESENTATION OF THE OFFERINGS OF THE PEOPLE, AND THE PREPARATION OF THE GIFTS OF BREAD AND WINE   Points are indicated for these, but if occasion requires they may occur elsewhere.*

Eng1–2B: 14   *HYMNS, CANTICLES, NOTICES, OFFERINGS OF THE PEOPLE, AND THE PLACING OF THE BREAD AND WINE   Points are indicated for the singing of hymns and canticles, the publication of banns of marriage and other notices, the collection and presentation of the offerings of the people, and the placing of the bread and wine upon the holy table: but if occasion requires, there are other points at which they may occur. In particular, hymns may be sung after the Communion.*

13   *SILENCE   After sections 8, 10, 12, 13, 20, 43 and after the biddings in sections 17, 18 silence may be kept.*

Engl–2B: OMIT

14   *A SERVICE WITHOUT COMMUNION   When there is no communion the minister reads the service as far as the Absolution (section 22) and then adds the Lord's Prayer (section 36), the General Thanksgiving, and/or other prayers at his discretion, ending with the Grace. When such a service is led by a deacon or lay person, 'us' is said instead of 'you' in the Absolution.*

Engl–2B (no. 13): *there is*] *there is to be*   22] 21   36] 32   *and/or*] *and*   ADDS AT END '(21)'

THE ORDER FOR HOLY COMMUNION RITE B

[In **Engl–2B** Seasonal Sentences follow here as section 1, and the sections below are numbered '2' and so on. In **EngB** itself the Seasonal Sentences are part of the ASB proper provision for each Sunday and Holy day, and are not printed as part of the rite, and are thus not printed here.]

THE WORD AND THE PRAYERS
THE PREPARATION

1   *At the entry of the ministers A SENTENCE may be used ; and A HYMN, A CANTICLE, or A PSALM may be sung.*

Engl–2B (no. 2): *SENTENCE*] *sentence* (pp. 4–5)

2   *The minister may say*

The Lord be with you

All   **and with thy spirit.**

3   *This prayer may be said.*

All   **Almighty God...[MAL CF 2]...our Lord. Amen.**

Engl–2B (no. 4): *This*] *The following*

4   *One of the following may be used.*

Either THE COMMANDMENTS (section 55) ;
or THE SUMMARY OF THE LAW (section 56) ;
or KYRIE ELEISON in English or Greek (section 57),
each petition being said once, twice, or three times.

[**Engl–2B** (no. 5) has page numbers in place of section numbers]

5   *GLORIA IN EXCELSIS may be said.*

All   **Glory to God...[MAL CF 5]...the Father. Amen.**
              Thou that takest...upon us]   OM [see FAL, page 62, footnote]
              most high] the Most High

Engl–2B (no. 6): *GLORIA*] *The canticle Gloria*

6   *THE COLLECT*

Engl–2B (no. 7): *THE COLLECT*] *The collect of the day*

THE MINISTRY OF THE WORD

7   *Either two or three readings from scripture follow, the last of which is always the Gospel.*

Engl–2B: OMIT

8 *Sit*

OLD TESTAMENT READING

At the end the reader may say

> This is the word of the Lord.

All **Thanks be to God.**

Eng1–2B: *OLD TESTAMENT READING]* *A lesson from the Old Testament may be*
read
the reader may say] there may be said
Reader

ADDS AT END *Silence may be kept.* [And similarly after sections 10 and 12]

9 *A PSALM may be used.*

Eng1–2B: *used] said*

10 *Sit*

NEW TESTAMENT READING (EPISTLE)

At the end the reader may say

> This is the word of the Lord.

All **Thanks be to God.**

Eng1–2B: *Sit]* OM
NEW TESTAMENT READING (EPISTLE)] *A Lesson from the Old or*
New Testament shall be read
the reader may say] there may be said
Reader

11 *A CANTICLE, A HYMN, or A PSALM may be used.*

Eng1–2B: *used] sung*

12 *Stand*

THE GOSPEL. *When it is announced*

All **Glory be to thee, O Lord.**

At the end the reader says

> This is the Gospel of Christ.

All **Praise be to thee, O Christ.**

Eng1–2B: *The Gospel]* *A lesson from the Gospels shall be read.*
the reader says] of the Gospel.
This...Christ] OM

13 *Sit*

THE SERMON

Eng1–2B: ADDS AT END *At the end silence may be kept.*

14 *Stand*

THE NICENE CREED *is said on Sundays and other Holy Days, and*
may be said on other days.

Eng1–2B: *is said] is said, at least*   *other] greater*   *and...days]* OM

All **I believe...** [**MAL CF 6**] **...world to come. Amen.**

PRAYERS OF INTERCESSION

15 *Banns of marriage and other notices may be published ; the offerings of the
people may be collected and presented ; a hymn may be sung ; and verses
of scripture may be read.*

16 *INTERCESSIONS are led by the priest, or by others. These may be
introduced by biddings.*

*It is not necessary to include specific subjects in any section of the following
prayers.*

*The set passages may follow one another as a continuous whole, or this
versicle and response may be used after each paragraph.*

Minister	Lord, in thy mercy
All	**hear our prayer.**

Eng1–2B: *led...others] offered...other persons
        or this versicle...***our prayer]*** without the versicles and responses*

Either section 17 or section 18 is used.

Eng1–2B: *section 17 or section 18 is] Intercession A or Intercession B shall be*

[In **Eng1–2B** the two Intercessions (17) are lettered A and B and are printed in parallel
columns. The versicle and response are printed out after each paragraph of spoken text
in both Intercessions. The rubrics '*Minister*' and '*All*' are omitted.]

17 *FIRST INTERCESSION*

Minister	Let us pray for the whole Church of God in Christ Jesus, and for all men according to their needs.
	Almighty and...[**MAL** CF 8]...world without end. **Amen.**

to grant them everlasting light] according to thy promises, to grant them
        refreshment, light

[Indented rubric in **MAL** CF is footnote to page, indicated by asterisk:
*If the offerings of the people have not been presented these words in brackets are omitted.
Eng1–2B: *In brackets]* OM

Fifth paragraph of prayer omitted in error in **MAL** CF 8, but present in **MAL** CF 7
(cf. **FAL** page 422), is included.]

The service continues at either section 19 or section 20.
Eng1–2B: OM

---

18 *SECOND INTERCESSION*

Minister	Let us pray for the whole Church of God in Christ Jesus, and for all men according to their needs.
	Almighty God, who hast promised to hear the prayers of those who ask in faith :
	Here he may pray for the Church throughout the world, especially for the diocese and its bishop ; and for any particular needs of the Church.

Grant that we and all who confess thy name may be united in thy truth, live together in thy love, and show forth thy glory in the world.

Here he may pray for the nations of the world, for this kingdom, and for all men in their various callings.

Give wisdom to all in authority, bless Elizabeth our Queen, and direct this nation and all nations in the ways of justice and of peace; that men may honour one another, and seek the common good.

Here he may pray for the local community; for families, friends, and particular persons.

Give grace to us, our families and friends, and to all our neighbours in Christ, that we may serve him in one another, and love as he loves us.

Here he may pray for the sick, the poor, and those in trouble, and for the needs of particular persons.

Save and comfort those who suffer, that they may hold to thee through good and ill, and trust in thy unfailing love.

Here he may commemorate the departed; he may commend them by name.

Hear us as we remember those who have died in faith, and grant us with them a share in thy eternal kingdom.

Merciful Father,

All **accept these prayers,**
for the sake of thy Son,
our Saviour Jesus Christ. Amen.

Eng1–2B (no. 17B): hast] has [possibly misprint in **Eng1–2A**, authorized in **Eng1–2B**]
bishop; *and*] *bishop*;
AT END OF EACH RUBRIC ADD *Silence may be kept*
of peace] peace
Merciful Father] Lord, in thy mercy

PRAYERS OF PENITENCE

19 *The minister may say one or more of THE COMFORTABLE WORDS.*

Eng1–2B (no. 18): *The minister may say*] OM
ADD AT END *may be said by the minister*

Hear what comfortable... [**MAL** CF 12]... propitiation for our sins. (1 *John* 2.1)

saith] says THROUGHOUT
also] OM TWICE
Jesus Christ came] Christ Jesus came [see **FAL**, page 422, footnote]

[**Eng1–2B** OMITS SCRIPTURE REFERENCES.]

20 *Minister*   *(Ye that do ...⟦**MAL** CF 9⟧... holy ways;) draw near with faith, and take this holy sacrament to your comfort; and make your humble confession to almighty God (meekly kneeling upon your knees).

or   Seeing we have a great high priest who has passed into the heavens, Jesus the Son of God, let us draw near with a true heart, in full assurance of faith, and make our confession to our heavenly Father.

⟦**Eng1–2B** (no. 19) has rubric '*The minister says*' then '*either*' and '*or*' at the head of two parallel columns.⟧

21 *Kneel*

⟦**Eng1–2B** (no. 20) has rubric '*The minister and people make the following confession.*'⟧

All   **Almighty God, our heavenly Father,**
we have sinned against thee,
through our own fault,
in thought, and word, and deed,
and in what we have left undone.
We are heartily sorry,
and repent of all our sins,
For thy Son our Lord Jesus Christ's sake,
forgive us all that is past;
and grant that we may serve thee in newness of life,
to the glory of thy name. Amen.

⟦**Eng1–2B** (no. 21) has rubric '*The priest says the absolution*' and omits '*priest*' below⟧

22 *Priest*   Almighty God...⟦CF 5⟧...our Lord. **Amen.**
you...your] *you...your*   THROUGHOUT ⟦not in **Eng1–2B**⟧
Eng1–2B: Amen] *All* **Amen.**

⟦**Eng1–2B** has rubric (no. 22): '*One or more of the Comfortable Words may be said here, if they have not already been said at section 18.*'⟧

23 *All may say*

Eng1–2B: *All may say*]   *The following prayer may be said :*
All

We do not presume...⟦MAL CF 13⟧...he in us. Amen.
property] nature
that our sinful...precious blood, and] *(that...and)

THE MINISTRY OF THE SACRAMENT
⟦**Eng1–2B** has 'THE COMMUNION'⟧

THE PEACE

24 *Stand*
Priest   We are the Body of Christ.
By one Spirit we were all baptized into one body.

---

* *The words in brackets may be omitted.*

Endeavour to keep the unity of the Spirit
in the bond of peace.

He then says

The peace of the Lord be always with you

All **and with thy spirit.**

Eng1–2B:*Priest] The priest says*
He then says] 25 *The priest gives the Peace to the congregation, saying:*

25 *All may exchange a sign of peace.*

Eng1–2B: OMITS

THE PREPARATION OF THE BREAD AND WINE

26 *The priest begins THE OFFERTORY.*

The bread and the wine are placed on the holy table.

Eng1–2B: *THE OFFERTORY] the offertory. A hymn may be sung, verses of scripture*
may be read, and the offerings of the people may be collected and presented if this
has not already been done.
The bread...table] OM

27 *The offerings of the people may be collected and presented if this has not*
already been done.

These words may be used.

Thine, O Lord, is the greatness and the power
and the glory and the victory and the majesty.
All that is in heaven and earth is thine.
All things come of thee, O Lord,
and of thine own do we give thee.

Eng1–2B: *The offerings...may be used] The bread and wine are brought to the holy table,*
and this sentence may be said.

28 *At the preparation of the gifts A HYMN may be sung.*

Eng1–2B: OMITS

THE THANKSGIVING

29 *The priest says THE PRAYER OF CONSECRATION using either*
section 30 or section 31.

Eng1–2B (no. 28): *using...31] Either Prayer A or Prayer B shall be said*
⟦In **Eng1–2B** the two Thanksgivings are printed in parallel columns, headed 'A' and
'B' and with an opening rubric '*The priest says*' printed under the 'A' or 'B', then
no marginal rubrics.⟧

30 *FIRST THANKSGIVING*

Priest The Lord be with you
All **and with thy spirit.**

Priest Lift up your hearts.
All **We lift them up unto the Lord.**

Priest	Let us give thanks unto the Lord our God.
All	**It is meet and right so to do.**
Priest	It is very meet, right, and our bounden duty,

that we should at all times and in all places give thanks unto
    thee,
O Lord, holy Father,
almighty, everlasting God,
Creator of heaven and earth,

PROPER PREFACE, when appropriate (section 52)

[The Proper Prefaces, which are printed after the service, are to be found here in Appendix C. In **Eng1–2B** the rubric reads '*Here follows the Proper Preface*.' and the Proper Prefaces are printed at this point.]

The following is used when no Proper Preface is provided.

[**Eng1–2B** (at the end of the Proper Prefaces):

The following is used] *Sundays when...provided*] (*when no other Proper Preface is appointed*)]

through Jesus Christ our Lord; for he is the true High
Priest, who has washed us from our sins, and has made us
to be a kingdom and priests unto thee, our God and Father.

Therefore with angels and archangels,
and with all the company of heaven,
we laud and magnify thy glorious name,
evermore praising thee and saying:

Holy, holy, holy, Lord God of Hosts,
heaven and earth are full of thy glory.
Glory be to thee, O Lord most high. (Amen.)

(Blessed is he that cometh in the name of the Lord.
Hosanna in the highest.)

All glory be to thee,
almighty God, our heavenly Father,
who of thy tender mercy
didst give thine only Son Jesus Christ
to suffer death upon the cross for our redemption;
who made there,
by his one oblation of himself once offered,
a full, perfect, and sufficient sacrifice, oblation, and
    satisfaction
for the sins of the whole world;
and did institute,
and in his holy gospel command us to continue,
a perpetual memory of that his precious death,
until his coming again.

Hear us, O merciful Father,
we most humbly beseech thee;
and grant that by the power of thy Holy Spirit,
we receiving these thy creatures of bread and wine,
according to thy Son our Saviour Jesus Christ's holy
    institution,
in remembrance of his death and passion,
may be partakers of his most blessed body and blood.
Who, in the same night that he was betrayed,
took bread;
Here the priest is to take the paten into his hands.
and when he had given thanks,
he brake it, *Here he may break the bread.*
and gave it to his disciples, saying, Take, eat;
Here he is to lay his hand upon the bread.
this is my body which is given for you:
do this in remembrance of me.
Likewise after supper he took the cup;
Here he is to take the cup into his hand.
and when he had given thanks,
he gave it to them, saying, Drink ye all of this;
Here to lay his hand upon the cup.
for this is my blood of the New Testament,
which is shed for you and for many
for the remission of sins:
do this, as oft as ye shall drink it,
in remembrance of me.

Wherefore, O Lord and heavenly Father,
we thy humble servants,
having in remembrance
the precious death and passion of thy dear Son,
his mighty resurrection and glorious ascension,
entirely desire thy fatherly goodness
mercifully to accept this our sacrifice of praise and
    thanksgiving;
most humbly beseeching thee to grant that
by the merits and death of thy Son Jesus Christ,
and through faith in his blood,
we and all thy whole Church
may obtain remission of our sins,
and all other benefits of his passion.
And although we be unworthy through our manifold
    sins

to offer unto thee any sacrifice,

yet we beseech thee to accept this our bounden duty and
service,

not weighing our merits but pardoning our offences.

We pray that all we who are partakers of this holy
communion

may be fulfilled with thy grace and heavenly benediction,

Through Jesus Christ our Lord,

by whom, and with whom, and in whom,

in the unity of the Holy Spirit,

all honour and glory be unto thee,

O Father almighty,

world without end. **Amen.**

Silence may be kept.

The service continues at either section 32 or section 33 or section 34.

⟦**Eng1–2B** (28A) provides for 'manual acts' by symbols referring to footnotes, where
rubrics like the ones in the text above are printed (but with an '*and*' added before the
third and the fifth). The rubrics and rule at the end of the Thanksgiving are omitted.⟧

---

31 *SECOND THANKSGIVING*

Priest	The Lord be with you
All	**and with thy spirit.**
Priest	Lift up your hearts.
All	**We lift them up unto the Lord.**
Priest	Let us give thanks unto the Lord our God.
All	**It is meet and right so to do.**
Priest	It is very meet, right, and our bounden duty,

that we should at all times and in all places give thanks
unto thee,

O Lord, holy Father,

almighty, everlasting God,

through Jesus Christ

thine only Son our Lord:

Because through him thou hast created all things from
the beginning,

and fashioned us men in thine own image;

through him thou didst redeem us from the slavery of
sin,

giving him to be born as man, to die upon the cross,

and to rise again for us:

through him thou hast made us a people for thine own
possession,
exalting him to thy right hand on high,
and sending forth through him thy holy and life-giving
Spirit.

PROPER PREFACE, when appropriate (section 53)

[The Proper Prefaces, which are printed after the service, are to be found here in
Appendix C. In **Eng1–2B** the rubric reads '*Here follows the Proper Preface*', and the
Proper Prefaces are printed at this point.]

Therefore with angels and archangels,
and with all the company of heaven,
we laud and magnify thy glorious name,
evermore praising thee and saying,

Holy, holy, holy, Lord God of hosts,
heaven and earth are full of thy glory.
Glory be to thee, O Lord most high.

(Blessed is he that cometh in the name of the Lord.
Hosanna in the highest.)

Hear us, O Father,
through Christ thy Son our Lord;
through him accept our sacrifice of praise;
and grant that by the power of thy Holy Spirit
these gifts of bread and wine
may be unto us his body and blood.

Who, in the same night that he was betrayed,
took bread;
Here the priest is to take the bread into his hands.
and when he had given thanks to thee,
he broke it,
and gave it to his disciples, saying, Take, eat;
this is my body which is given for you:
do this in remembrance of me.

Likewise after supper he took the cup;
Here he is to take the cup into his hands.
and when he had given thanks to thee,
he gave it to them saying, Drink ye all of this;
for this is my blood of the new covenant,
which is shed for you and for many
for the remission of sins:
do this, as oft as ye shall drink it, in remembrance of me.

Wherefore, O Lord and heavenly Father,
with this bread and this cup
we make the memorial of his saving passion,
his resurrection from the dead,
and his glorious ascension into heaven,
and we look for the coming of his kingdom.

We pray thee to accept this our duty and service,
and grant that we may so eat and drink these holy things
in the presence of thy divine majesty,
that we may be filled with thy grace and heavenly
   blessing.

Through Jesus Christ our Lord,
by whom, and with whom, and in whom,
in the unity of the Holy Spirit,
all honour and glory be unto thee,
O Father almighty,
world without end. **Amen.**

Silence may be kept.

Eng1–2B: O Father Almighty] O Father Almighty, from the whole company of earth
and heaven, throughout all ages.

⟦**Eng1–2B** (no. 28B) provides for the 'manual acts' by symbols referring to footnotes,
where the two rubrics are printed. The rubric and the rule at the end of the
Thanksgiving are omitted.⟧

---

32 *THE BENEDICTUS may follow, if it has not already been said.*

> **Blessed is he that cometh in the name of the Lord.
> Hosanna in the highest.**

33 *The priest and people together say THE LORD'S PRAYER either here
or at section 36, or at section 44. (The text is printed at section 36.)*

Eng1–2B (no. 29): *say] may say*   36] 32   TWICE   44] 40

THE COMMUNION

*THE BREAKING OF THE BREAD AND
THE GIVING OF THE BREAD AND CUP*
⟦**Eng1–2B** has only ' *THE BREAKING OF THE BREAD*'⟧

34 *The priest breaks the consecrated bread, if he has not already done so, saying*

Eng1–2B (no. 30): *breaks] shall break*

> We break...⟦as **Eng A**, no. 43⟧... **in one bread.**

35 *Either here or during the distribution this anthem may be said.*

> **O Lamb...⟦MAL CF 14⟧...thy peace.**

Eng1–2B (no. 31): *Either...distribution]*   OM
                ADDS   '*All*'   BEFORE TEXT

[[**Eng1–2B** has heading here '*THE GIVING OF THE BREAD AND CUP*']]

36 *The priest and people may say* THE LORD'S PRAYER, *if it has not already been said.*

Priest   As our Saviour has taught us, so we pray.

Our Father, who...[[MAL CF 1]]...and ever. Amen.

in earth] on earth
them that] those who

37 *The priest and people receive the communion.*

Eng1–2B (no. 33): *people] the other communicants*

The communion may be administered in one of the following ways :

38 *The minister says to each communicant*

The Body...[[CF 7(a)]]...with thanksgiving.
The Blood...[[CF 7(b)]]...be thankful.
to] unto   TWICE

Eng1–2B (no. 34): ABOVE THE RUBRIC ADDS '*either* (*a*)'
The minister says] One of the ministers delivers the bread
ADDS AT END '*saying*'
AFTER WORDS FOR BREAD EXTRA RUBRIC:
'*and one of the ministers delivers the cup to each communicant, saying :*'

39 *or*

The priest first says to all the communicants

Draw near and receive the body of our Lord Jesus Christ, which was given for you, and his blood, which was shed for you. Take this in remembrance that Christ died for you, and feed on him in your hearts by faith with thanksgiving.

One of the ministers then delivers the bread to each communicant, saying

The body of Christ.

or   The body of Christ preserve your body and soul unto everlasting life.

or   The body of our Lord Jesus Christ, which was given for you, preserve your body and soul unto everlasting life.

One of the ministers then delivers the cup to each communicant, saying

The blood of Christ.

or   The blood of Christ preserve your body and soul unto everlasting life.

or   The blood of our Lord Jesus Christ, which was shed for you, preserve your body and soul unto everlasting life.

The communicant may reply each time **Amen,** *and then receives.*

Eng1–2B (no. 35): BEGINS *or* (*b*)

40 *During the distribution HYMNS and ANTHEMS may be sung.*

Eng 1–2B (no. 36): *distribution]* administration

41 *If either or both of the consecrated elements are likely to prove insufficient, the priest returns to the holy table and adds more, with these words.*

> Having given thanks to thee, O Father, over the bread and the cup according to the institution of thy Son Jesus Christ, who said, Take, eat; this is my body (*and/or* Drink this; this is my blood) we pray that this bread/wine also may be to us his body/blood, and be received in remembrance of him.

42 *Any consecrated bread and wine which is not required for purposes of communion is consumed at the end of the distribution, or after the service.*

Eng1–2B (no. 38): *distribution]* administration
after] immediately after

AFTER COMMUNION

Eng 1–2B: AFTER COMMUNION] AFTER THE COMMUNION

43 *AN APPROPRIATE SENTENCE may be said (pp. . . .) and A HYMN may be sung.*

Eng1–2B (no. 39): *AN. . .sung]* A seasonal sentence may be said

[The seasonal sentences are printed on pp. 42 and 43 of the ASB (i.e. before all the services) and are covered here in Appendix D. In **Eng1–2B** they are printed at this point, and are followed by a rubric '*Silence may be kept.*']

44 *The priest and people say THE LORD'S PRAYER, if it has not already been said. (The text is printed at section 36.)*

Eng1–2B (no. 40): *say]* shall say   36] 32

45 *Either or both of the following PRAYERS or either of those in the Appendices (section 58) are said.*

Eng1–2B (no. 41): *either of]* OM
Appendices (section 58 are)] Appendix shall be

46 *Priest*   Almighty and. . . ⟦**MAL** CF 18⟧. . . without end. **Amen.**
       Ghost] Spirit

Eng1-2B (no. 42): **Amen]** *All* **Amen**

47 *All*   **Almighty God**. . . ⟦CF 9⟧. . . **praise and glory. Amen.**
       you. . .your] thee. . .thy THROUGHOUT

48 *GLORIA IN EXCELSIS may be used, if it has not been used already (the text is printed at section 5); or some other suitable canticle or hymn may be sung.*

Eng1–2B (no. 44): *GLORIA]* The canticle Gloria
(the text. . .section 5)] OM

THE DISMISSAL

Eng1–2B: OM

49 *The priest may say this or an alternative BLESSING (section 54).*

Eng1–2B (no. 45): *an alternative Blessing (section 54)*] *the appropriate seasonal blessing*

The peace...⟦CF 10⟧...always. **Amen.**

Eng1–2B: ADDS RUBRIC *'All'* BEFORE **'Amen'**.

50 *Priest*   Go in peace and serve the Lord.
    All   **In the name of Christ. Amen.**

    or

    Priest   Go in the peace of Christ.
    All   **Thanks be to God.**

Eng1–2B (no. 46): BEGINS *The priest dismisses the people, saying: either* Go...Christ] Go in peace to love and serve the Lord.

51 *The ministers and people depart.*

APPENDICES ⟦Eng1-2B: APPENDIX⟧

52 *PROPER PREFACES FOR THE FIRST THANKSGIVING*

⟦The Proper Prefaces which follow here are those for **Engl** to be found in **MAL** Appendix C. There are some tiny changes recorded in Appendix C here. In **Eng1–2B** the Prefaces are printed in Thanksgiving A.⟧

53 *PROPER PREFACES FOR THE SECOND THANKSGIVING*

⟦The Proper Prefaces which follow here are those originally compiled for **Eng3**, and then adapted into 'thou' form for **Eng1-2A** (see **FAL**, page 67 and Appendix C). These are to be found in Appendix C here. In **Eng1-2B** the Prefaces are printed in Thanksgiving B.⟧

54 *ALTERNATIVE BLESSINGS*

⟦The Seasonal and other Blessings which follow here are to be found in Appendix D. In **Eng1-2B** the Blessings are printed after no. 51 (47 in **Eng1-2B**) as no. 48.⟧

55 *THE COMMANDMENTS* ⟦**Eng1-2B**: *THE TEN COMMANDMENTS*⟧

    Minister   God spake these words...⟦**MAL** CF 3 without the bracketed portions⟧...**in our hearts, we beseech thee.**

56 *THE SUMMARY OF THE LAW* ⟦**Eng1-2B**: *OUR LORD'S SUMMARY OF THE LAW*⟧

    Minister   Our Lord Jesus Christ said: Hear O Israel...⟦**MAL** CF 4(b)⟧...and the prophets.

    All   **Lord, have mercy upon us,**
            and write all these thy laws in our hearts,
            we beseech thee.

57 *KYRIE ELEISON* ⟦**Eng1-2B**: *THE KYRIES*⟧

Lord, have mercy...⟦as at **EngA**, no. 79⟧...Kyrie eleison.

58 *ALTERNATIVE PRAYERS*

Either of the following prayers may be used instead of those in sections 46 and 47.

Eng1-2B: *Either...prayers] These*　　46] *42*　　47] *43*

Priest	O Lord and heavenly Father, we thy humble servants entirely desire thy fatherly goodness mercifully to accept this our sacrifice of praise and thanksgiving; most humbly beseeching thee to grant that by the merits and death of thy Son Jesus Christ, and through faith in his blood, we and all thy whole Church may obtain remission of our sins, and all other benefits of his passion. And here we offer and present unto thee, O Lord, ourselves, our souls and bodies, to be a reasonable, holy, and lively sacrifice unto thee; humbly beseeching thee, that all we, who are partakers of this Holy Communion, may be fulfilled with thy grace and heavenly benediction. And although we be unworthy, through our manifold sins, to offer unto thee any sacrifice, yet we beseech thee to accept this our bounden duty and service, not weighing our merits, but pardoning our offences; through Jesus Christ our Lord, by whom, and with whom, in the unity of the Holy Ghost, all honour and glory be unto thee, O Father almighty, world without end. **Amen.**
All	**Almighty Lord, and everlasting God,** **we offer and present unto thee ourselves, our souls and bodies,** **to be a reasonable, holy, and living sacrifice unto thee:** **humbly beseeching thee,** **that all we, who are partakers of this Holy Communion,** **may be fulfilled with thy grace and heavenly benediction.** **And although we be unworthy, through our manifold sins,** **to offer unto thee any sacrifice,** **yet we beseech thee to accept this our bounden duty and service,** **not weighing our merits, but pardoning our offences;** **through Jesus Christ our Lord,** **to whom, with thee and the Holy Ghost,** **be all honour and glory, world without end.** **Amen.**

CHAPTER 2

THE SCOTTISH EPISCOPAL CHURCH

SINCE 1975 the Liturgy Committee of the Scottish Episcopal Church has produced two new eucharistic liturgies, to be used in succession to each other alongside existing Scottish (and English[1]) uses. In 1977 the first *Experimental Liturgy 1977* (**Scot1**), was recommended by the Provincial Synod for authorization by the College of Bishops, which was done in November 1977. It was published as an 'orange bookie' and was the first Scottish Episcopal text to address God as 'you'. It was superseded in 1982 by the more definitive *Scottish Liturgy 1982* (**Scot2**), a 'blue bookie' authorized by the College of Bishops in March 1982. This altered the text of **Scot1** at most points of the rite.

THE EPISCOPAL CHURCH IN SCOTLAND EXPERIMENTAL LITURGY 1977 (Scot1)

〖The numbering of this rite is original. The bold type is editorial.〗

EXPERIMENTAL LITURGY 1977

〖On the inside front cover are the following notes:

NOTES

1. *Sections introduced by a rubric in italics may be omitted.*
   〖For this edition, where italic is used for all rubrics, an obelisk (†), is used as in **Scot2**.〗
2. *In the Introductory Rites, the local congregation is expected to make its own selection, suitable to the occasion, from Sections 1–7.*〗

INTRODUCTORY RITES

1 *An Entrance Hymn.*†

2 *An Introductory Sentence.*† *This may also be used as a versicle and response.*
   Priest: Blessed be the Lord our God
   All: **Blessed be the Father, Son and Holy Spirit**

   〖There follow seasonal sentences, which are printed here in Appendix D〗

3 *The Priest greets the congregation:* Grace and peace to you from God our Father and the Lord Jesus Christ.
   All: **Amen.**

4 *The Priest prepares the congregation explaining the theme of the service.*†

5 *The collect for Purity :*†
   Almighty God, to you... 〖CF 1〗 **...our Lord. Amen.**
   whom]you

---

[1] See chapter 1 above for English uses during this period.

6 *The Kyries:*†

Priest:	Lord, have mercy.
All:	**Lord, have mercy.**
Priest:	Christ, have mercy.
All:	**Christ, have mercy.**
Priest:	Lord, have mercy.
All:	**Lord, have mercy.**

⟦An unnumbered rubric follows '*The Confession and Absolution may form part of the Introductory Rites.*' It is followed by the text of no. 13 below, rubric and text enclosed within a ruled box. '*Silence*' has no brackets.⟧

7 *The Gloria in excelsis:*†

Glory to God . . . ⟦ICET 4⟧ . . . **the Father. Amen.**
AFTER THE FOURTH LINE INSERT (**with God the Son, Jesus Christ, and God the Holy Spirit.**)

8 *The Collect of the Day.*

LITURGY OF THE WORD

Either two or three readings from Scripture follow, the last reading being from a Gospel.

9 *Before the Old Testament reading and/or the Epistle:*
Reader: The book of (epistle to) . . . ch . . . , v . . . .
After these readings:
Reader: Thanks be to God.
Before the Gospel:
Reader: The Gospel according to . . . ch . . . , v . . . .
After the Gospel:
Reader: This is the Gospel of Christ.
People: **Praise be to you, Lord Jesus Christ.**
A Psalm may follow the Old Testament Reading.†
A Psalm, Canticle or Hymn may precede the Gospel.†

10 *A sermon, or other exposition of the Word.*†

11 *The Nicene Creed (This may be omitted on week days).*
We believe . . . ⟦ICET 3⟧ . . . **world to come. Amen.**

THE INTERCESSIONS

12 *Prayer shall be offered for the universal Church, its members and its mission*
the nation and all in authority
the world and the concerns of the local community
those who suffer and those in need
the departed (on lesser Saints' Days, the commemoration of a Saint may be made here.)
Either of the forms provided may be used.†

Adaptations and insertions may be made to both forms.†
Any similar form may be used.†

FORM A

(*This prayer may also be used in a continuous form omitting the matter
printed in italics*).

Leader : Let us pray for the Church and for the world... ⟦as **Eng3**,
in **FAL** pages 52–54, save that the biddings 'We give
thanks for/we pray for', and the versicles and responses are
printed here in italic (to indicate that they may be omitted),
and the single word '(*Silence*)' occurs⟧...**Accept these
prayers for the sake of your Son, our Saviour, Jesus
Christ. Amen.**

FORM B

Leader : In the power of the Spirit and in union with Christ, let us
pray to the Father.

All : **We pray, O Lord.** ⟦and similarly after each petition
below⟧

Leader : For peace on earth, for the well-being of the Church and
for the unity of all peoples

Leader : For all your people and especially *N.* our bishop

Leader : For Elizabeth our Queen, for all in government and
authority and for the leaders of nations.

Leader : For all who serve the life of this city (town, village,...) and
the life of every community

Leader : For the aged and infirm, for the lonely and the unloved,
the sick and the suffering and for those who serve them

Leader : For the poor and the oppressed, for the unemployed and
the destitute and for all who care for them

Leader : For refugees and prisoners and for those who suffer for
their faith

Leader : For...*Intercessions appropriate to the occasion may be
added.*†

Leader : For all who have died in the hope of resurrection and for
all the departed

*Silence may be kept during which people may add their own petitions,
privately or aloud.*†

Leader : In communion with (...and) all the Saints, we commend
ourselves and one another to you, O Lord.

All : **Accept these prayers for the sake of your Son, our
Saviour, Jesus Christ. Amen.**

THE CONFESSION AND ABSOLUTION

13 Priest : God is love, and we are his children. There is no room for
fear in love: we love because he loved us first.
Let us confess our sins in penitence and faith.

All :	**We confess to God almighty, the Father, the Son and the Holy Spirit, and to all our fellow members in the Body of Christ, that we have sinned in thought, word and deed, and in what we have left undone.**

(Silence)†

Most loving Father, where sin has divided and scattered, may your love make one again; where sin has brought weakness, may your power heal and strengthen; where sin has brought death, may your Spirit raise to new life.

Priest : God who is both power and love, set you free from your sins, help you to new ways of living and give you the power and healing of his Holy Spirit.

All : **Amen.**

Priest : The Lord has freed us from our sin.

All : **Thanks be to God.**

THE PEACE

14 *All Stand*

Priest : We meet in Christ's name: let us share his peace.

All : **Peace be with you.**

The congregation greet one another according to local custom.†

LITURGY OF THE SACRAMENT
THE TAKING OF THE BREAD AND THE WINE

15 *The bread and wine are placed on the altar and the alms of the people may be presented.*

A Hymn†

16 *Prayers of Offering*†[1]

Priest : Blessed are you, Lord, God of all creation;
through your goodness we have this bread to offer,
which earth has given and human hands have made:
may it become for us the bread of life.

All : **Blessed be God for ever.**

Priest : Blessed are you, Lord, God of all creation;
through your goodness we have this wine to offer,
fruit of the vine and work of human hands;
may it become the cup of our salvation.

All : **Blessed be God for ever.**

---

[1] 〚This rubric is printed as though mandatory, but is corrected by a note at the end of the reprinted copy.〛

THE GREAT THANKSGIVING

17 *All stand*

*DIALOGUE:
an invitation to
praise and
thanksgiving 'to
suppress all
worldly thoughts'
(St Cyprian)*

Priest :	The Lord be with you.
All :	**And also with you.**
Priest :	Lift up your hearts.
All :	**We lift them to the Lord.**
Priest :	Let us give thanks to the Lord our God.
All :	**It is right to give him thanks and praise.**

Priest :   Worship and praise belong to you,
Father, in every place and at all times.
All power is yours.
You are without beginning and without end.
You called into being all that is;
you created the heavens and established the earth,
giving life to all.
Through your Son Jesus Christ
our life and yours are brought together
in a wonderful exchange:
divinity is bound to human nature
and manhood taken up to God.
Through your Holy Spirit,
you call all human kind to new birth
in a creation restored by love.
As children of your redeeming purpose
we offer you our praise.
Therefore with Angels and Archangels
and with the whole company of heaven,
we sing the hymn of your unending glory:

All :   **Holy, Holy, Holy Lord,**

*SANCTUS: an
anthem to God's
glory.*

God of power and might.
Heaven and earth are full of your glory.

BENEDICTUS: **Hosanna in the highest.**

*the greeting of him
who came in the
flesh, comes in the
sacrament and is
still to come*

Blessed is he who comes in the name of the Lord.
Hosanna in the highest.

Priest :   Glory and thanksgiving be to you, most loving Father,

*CHRISTO-
LOGICAL
PRAYER:
thanksgiving to
God for all that
was accomplished
in the life, death
and resurrection
of Jesus.*

for the gift of your Son born in human flesh.
He is the Word existing beyond time,
both source and final purpose,
bringing to wholeness all that is made.
We thank you
that through him you have freed us from our sin,

giving him to die upon the cross,
and to rise again for us.

The appropriate Seasonal Prayer is added here

⟦The 'Seasonal Prayers' take the same form as 'Proper Prefaces' in other rites, though
they are in a different place in the Eucharistic Prayer. They are printed on a facing page
in the booklet, and are to be found here in Appendix C.⟧

Priest : On the night before he died,

NARRATIVE
OF THE
INSTITU- he took bread and gave you thanks.
He broke the bread,
TION : an gave it to his disciples and said:
account of the 'Take, eat.
Last Supper. This is my Body: it is broken for you.'
After supper he took the cup;
he offered you thanks,
he gave it to them and said:
'Drink this, all of you.
This is my Blood of the new covenant:
it is poured out for you and for all men,
that sins may be forgiven.
Do this in remembrance of me.'

Priest : **We now obey your Son's command.**

and People :† **We recall his blessed passion and death,**

ANAMNESIS
AND OBLA- **his glorious resurrection and ascension;**
TION : the **and we look for the coming of his kingdom.**
work of Christ is **United with him, we offer you these gifts**
recalled and **and ourselves with them;**
linked with our
offering. **one, holy, and living sacrifice.**

Priest : Hear us, most merciful Father,

EPICLESIS : and send your Holy Spirit upon us
we ask for the and upon this bread and this wine,
descent of the
Holy Spirit as that overshadowed by his life-giving power
the divine they may be the Body and Blood of your Son,
response to our and we may be kindled with the fire of your love
obedience. and renewed for the service of your kingdom.

Priest : **Help us who are bound into the fellowship of your**

and People :† **whole Church**

PRAYER OF **to live and work to your praise and glory.**
PETITION : as **May we grow together in unity and love**
members of the
Church we pray **until at last, in a renewed creation,**
for her whole life **we share the life of the Saints,**
and mission. **in the company of the Virgin Mary, the Apostles and**
Prophets,
and of all our brothers and sisters
living and departed.

Priest :   Accept our offering through Jesus Christ our Lord, through
DOXOLOGY: whom, with whom and in whom, all honour and glory be
a concluding act   to you, Lord of all Ages, world without end.
of praise.

18 *The Lord's Prayer*
  Priest :   As our Saviour has taught us, so we pray:
  All :   **Our Father...⟦ICET 1⟧...for ever. Amen.**

      Save us from...and] Do not bring us to...but
      (Silence)†

   ## THE BREAKING OF THE BREAD

19 *Priest :*   We break this bread,
        Seal of communion in Christ's Body once broken,
        Pledge that his Church may be the wheat
        which bears its fruit in dying.
  All :   **Lord, unite us in this sign.**

20 *The Agnus Dei.*†
        Lamb of God...⟦ICET 8(b)⟧...us peace.

   ## THE GIVING OF THE BREAD AND CUP

21 *Priest :*   Happy are those who are invited to the marriage supper of
        the Lamb. Come. All is now ready.

  Either[1]†
  All :   **Lord, I am not worthy to receive you, but only say the
        word, and I shall be healed.**
  or [1]†   **We do not presume...⟦CF 6⟧...he in us. Amen.**
        this your table] your table

22 *At the administration.*
   The Body of Christ given for you.
   The Blood of Christ shed for you.
   The communicant replies : **Amen.**

23 *During the administration, a Communion Hymn may be sung.*†

   ## THE POST-COMMUNION PRAYER

24 *The texts before the following prayers may be used either as sentences or
   as versicles and responses.*†
   Give thanks to the Lord, for he is gracious.
   For his mercy endures for ever.
   We have broken the Bread which is Christ's Body, we have tasted the
   Wine of Life; we thank you for these gifts by which we are made one
   in Jesus and drawn into the new creation which is your will for all
   mankind; through him who died for us and rose again, your Son, Christ
   our Lord. Amen.

   ⟦There follow ten seasonal texts and prayers on the same pattern. See Appendix D.⟧

   [1] ⟦A reprinted edition notes that it is not required that one of these be used.⟧

The Gloria in Excelsis (if not used at 7 above)†
Glory to God...〖ICET 4 as at §7〗...**the Father. Amen.**

CONCLUDING RITES

25 *The Blessing :*†
The peace of God...〖CF 10〗...always. **Amen.**

26 *Priest :*   Go in peace to love and serve the Lord.
   All :   **In the name of Christ. Amen.**

27 *A final hymn*†

THE EPISCOPAL CHURCH IN SCOTLAND
'SCOTTISH LITURGY 1982' (Scot 2)
〖The numbering is original, save for nos. 27–30 which are editorial.〗
SCOTTISH LITURGY 1982
〖On the inside front cover, facing the first page of text, the following notes appear:
*The Liturgy is printed with a minimum of instructions out of a conviction that worship in
a contemporary idiom must be adapted to suit particular times and places.
The words printed in **bold type** are intended for use by the people as well as the celebrant.
All those sections marked* † *may be included or omitted according to the season or the
circumstances.
Indications are also given where alternatives are provided.*〗

PREPARATION

1 *Welcome*

Grace and peace to you from God our Father and the Lord
Jesus Christ.
Amen.

2 *Peace (or at 16)*

We meet in Christ's name.
Let us share his peace.

3 *Collect for Purity*†

Almighty God...〖CF 1〗...our Lord. Amen.
hid] hidden

4 *Summary of the Law*†

Our Lord Jesus Christ said: The first commandment is
this: 'Hear, O Israel, the Lord our God is the
only...〖CF 3〗...than these.
Amen. Lord, have mercy.

This is the first commandment] OM

5 *Confession and Absolution (or at 15)*

God is love and we are his children.
There is no room for fear in love.
We love because he loved us first.

Let us confess our sins in penitence and faith.

Silence

**God our Father, we confess to you
and to our fellow members in the Body of Christ
that we have sinned in thought, word and deed,
and in what we have failed to do.
We are truly sorry.
Forgive us our sins,
and deliver us from the power of evil,
for the sake of your Son who died for us,
Jesus Christ, our Lord.**

God, who is both power and love,
forgive *us* and free *us* from *our* sins,
heal and strengthen *us* by his Spirit,
and raise *us* to new life in Christ our Lord.

Amen.

6 *Kyrie†*

Lord, have mercy.
Lord, have mercy.
Christ, have mercy.
Christ, have mercy.
Lord, have mercy.
Lord, have mercy.

7 *Gloria†*

Glory to God...⟦ICET 4⟧...the Father, Amen.

AFTER THE FOURTH LINE INSERT **(with God the Son, Jesus Christ, and God the Holy Spirit)**

3, 4, 6 *and* 7 *are selected according to the season or the occasion*

8 *Collect of the day*

THE LITURGY OF THE WORD

9 *Old Testament Reading†*

10 *Epistle*

11 *Gospel*

When it is announced:
Glory to Christ our Saviour.

At end:
Give thanks to the Lord for his glorious Gospel.
Praise to Christ our Lord.

12 *Sermon†* or other exposition of the Word.

13 *Nicene Creed†*

We believe…〚ICET 3〛…**world to come. Amen.**

incarnate from] incarnate of
(and the Son)] OM BRACKETS

14 *Intercessions*

Prayer is offered
for the world and its people,
for those who suffer and those in need,
for the Church and its members.

15 *Confession and Absolution if not used at 5*

God is love…〚as at no. 5 above〛…in Christ our Lord.
Amen.

16 *Peace if not used at 2*

We meet in Christ's name.
Let us share his peace.

THE LITURGY OF THE SACRAMENT
THE TAKING OF THE BREAD AND THE WINE

17 *Offering*

Silence
or

Let us present our offerings to the Lord.

Yours, Lord, is the greatness, the power, the glory, the
splendour, and the majesty; for everything in heaven
and on earth is yours.

All things come from you, and of your own we give you.

See Appendix for alternative use.

THE GREAT THANKSGIVING

18 *Eucharistic Prayer*

The Lord be with you.
And also with you.
Lift up your hearts.
We lift them to the Lord.
Let us give thanks to the Lord our God.
It is right to give him thanks and praise.

Worship and praise belong to you, Father,
in every place and at all times.

All power is yours.
You created the heavens and established the earth;
you sustain in being all that is.

In Christ your Son our life and yours
are brought together in a wonderful exchange.
He made his home among us
that we might for ever dwell in you.

Through your Holy Spirit
you call us to new birth
in a creation restored by love.

As children of your redeeming purpose
we offer you our praise,
with angels and archangels
and the whole company of heaven,
singing the hymn of your unending glory:

Holy, Holy, Holy Lord,
God of power and might.
Heaven and earth are full of your glory.
Hosanna in the highest.

Blessed is he who comes in the name of the Lord.
Hosanna in the highest.

Glory and thanksgiving be to you,
most loving Father,
for the gift of your Son born in human flesh.

He is the Word existing beyond time,
both source and final purpose,
bringing to wholeness all that is made.
Obedient to your will he died upon the Cross.
By your power you raised him from the dead.
He broke the bonds of evil
and set your people free
to be his Body in the world.
On the night when he was given up to death,
knowing that his hour had come,
having loved his own,
he loved them to the end.
At supper with his disciples
he took bread and offered you thanks.
He broke the bread,
and gave it to them, saying:

'Take, eat.
This is my Body: it is broken for you.'
After supper, he took the cup,
he offered you thanks,

and gave it to them saying:
'Drink this, all of you.
This is my Blood of the new covenant;
it is poured out for you, and for all,
that sins may be forgiven.
Do this in remembrance of me.'

ANAMNESIS AND OBLATION: the work of Christ is recalled and linked with our offering.

We now obey your Son's command.
We recall his blessed passion and death,
his glorious resurrection and ascension:
and we look for the coming of his Kingdom.
Made one with him, we offer you these gifts
and with them ourselves,
a single, holy, living sacrifice.

EPICLESIS: we ask for the descent of the Holy Spirit as the divine response to our obedience.

Hear us, most merciful Father,
and send your Holy Spirit upon us
and upon this bread and this wine,
that, overshadowed by his life-giving power,
they may be the Body and Blood of your Son,
and we may be kindled with the fire of your love
and renewed for the service of your Kingdom.
Help us, who are baptised into the fellowship of
  Christ's Body
to live and work to your praise and glory;

PRAYER OF PETITION: as members of the Church we pray for her whole life and mission.

may we grow together in unity and love
until at last, in your new creation,
we enter into our heritage
in the company of the Virgin Mary,
the apostles and prophets,*
and of all our brothers and sisters
living and departed.

DOXOLOGY: a concluding act of praise.

Through Jesus Christ our Lord,
with whom, and in whom,
in the unity of the Holy Spirit,
all honour and glory be to you,
Lord of all ages,
world without end. **Amen.**

THE SHARING OF THE BREAD AND THE WINE

19 *Breaking of the Bread*

Silence

or

The living bread is broken for the life of the world.
Lord, unite us in this sign.

* Appropriate commemoration of a particular Saint may be made here.

20 *Lord's Prayer*

As our Saviour has taught
us, so we pray:

**Our Father in heaven
...⟦ICET 1⟧...for ever.
Amen.**
**Save us from] Do not bring
us to**
and deliver] but deliver

As our Saviour Christ has
commanded and taught
us, we are bold to say:

**Our Father, who art
...⟦MAL CF 1⟧...ever
and ever. Amen.**
in earth] on earth
them that] those who

21 *Communion*

At the giving of the bread:
The Body of Christ given for you.

At the giving of the cup:
The Blood of Christ shed for you.

The Communicant replies **Amen.**

22 *Communion Song†*

Lamb of God...⟦ICET 8(b)⟧...us peace.

or **Jesus, Lamb of God...⟦ICET 8(a)⟧...your peace.**

THANKSGIVING AND SENDING OUT

23 *Sentence*

An appropriate seasonal sentence may be used

⟦None are printed here or elsewhere.⟧

Give thanks to the Lord, for he is gracious.
And his mercy endures for ever.

24 *Prayers*

One of the following is said

(a) Father, we have broken the bread which is Christ's body,
we have tasted the wine of his new life. We thank you for
these gifts by which we are made one in him and drawn
into that new creation which is your will for all mankind;
through him who died for us and rose again, your Son, our
Saviour Jesus Christ. **Amen.**

(b) Father of all...⟦CF 8⟧...our Lord. **Amen.**

in this hope that we have grasped] firm in the hope you have set before us

(c) Father, your steadfast purpose is the completion of all
things in your Son. May we who have received the pledges
of the kingdom, live by faith, walk in hope and be renewed
in love, until the world reflects your glory and you are all
in all; through Jesus Christ our Lord. **Amen.**

25 *Blessing†*

The peace of God...[CF 10]...always. Amen.
A seasonal variant may be used

26 *Dismissal*

Go in peace to love and serve the Lord.
In the name of Christ. Amen.

APPENDIX
FORMS OF INTERCESSION

27 *Form 1*

Through Jesus, whom we confess as Lord,
we give thanks and praise to the Father,
calling on him who is judge of all:
Father, your kingdom come.

Father, your kingdom come.

For all the peoples of the world;
that they may know you as the God of peace,
we pray to you, O Lord:

Father, your kingdom come.
[This response follows each paragraph]

For nations, for leaders and governments;
that integrity may mark all their dealings,
we pray to you O Lord:

For all who labour for righteousness;
that your presence and help may give them courage,
we pray to you, O Lord:

For communities torn by dissension and strife;
that your forgiveness may bring them healing,
we pray to you, O Lord:

For the anxious, the lonely, the bereaved;
that consolation and peace may be theirs,
we pray to you, O Lord:

For the Church, your household and family;
that she may be firm in the confession of her hope,
we pray to you, O Lord:

For... our Bishop, and for all who bear Christ's name;
that their lives may proclaim your glory,
we pray to you, O Lord:

For those who are separated from us by death;
that theirs may be the kingdom which is unshakeable,
we pray to you, O Lord:

O God of peace,
who brought again from the dead our Lord Jesus,
that great Shepherd of the sheep:
make us perfect in all goodness to do your will
and to be what you would have us be;
through him to whom be glory for ever,
Jesus Christ our Lord. **Amen.**

28 *Form 2*   O God the Father of our Lord Jesus Christ,
in whom you chose us, before the foundation of the world,
and destined us in love to be your own:
help us to pray for all your children.

For the life of the world;
that your peace may be known and may prevail:

For...
Lord, hear us.
Lord, graciously hear us.

⟦The same pattern then follows after each section of prayer⟧
For all who suffer injury, death or loss;
that they may know the hope to which you call us:

For all who exercise rule and authority;
that they may acknowledge your power:

For the Church which is Christ's body;
that it may live for the praise of your glory:

O God, you exerted your strength and power
when you raised Christ from the dead,
putting everything in subjection beneath his feet:
accept the prayers which we offer in his name
for the world you have created and redeemed;
through him in whom you have set forth
the mystery of your will,
to unite all things in heaven and on earth,
your Son, our Lord Jesus Christ. **Amen.**

29 *Form 3*   To him who alone is God
let us make our requests with thanksgiving,
through the one mediator, the man Christ Jesus.

I ask your prayers for peace in the life of the world...
Pray for God's peace.

Silence

I ask your prayers for all who suffer injury, sickness and
    loss...
Pray for all who are afflicted.

Silence

I ask your prayers for all who wield authority and influence...
Pray for all who exercise power.

Silence

I ask your prayers for our bishop(s)...and for all whom
Christ has appointed to his service...
Pray for God's people.

Silence

I ask your prayers for...

Silence

Give thanks to God for all in whom Christ has been
    honoured,
(especially...)

Silence

O God, whose will it is that all should find salvation
and come to know the truth:
receive the prayers and petitions
which we offer in faith and love;
through him who gave proof of your purpose,
and who sacrificed himself
to win freedom for all mankind,
Jesus Christ our Lord. **Amen.**

ALTERNATIVE USE AT OFFERTORY

30 *Prayers of Offering*

Blessed are you, Lord God of all creation;
through your goodness we have this bread to offer,
which earth has given and human hands have made;
it will become for us the bread of life.
Blessed be God for ever.
Blessed are you, Lord God of all creation;
through your goodness we have this wine to offer,
fruit of the vine and work of human hands;
it will become the cup of our salvation.
Blessed be God for ever.

CHAPTER 3

THE CHURCH IN WALES

Wal was originally authorized for ten years' use in 1966, but its period was extended as the proposed definitive replacement for it was not ready.[1] When the Liturgical Commission brought a revised rite to the Governing Body, it failed, on its third reading in April 1979, to gain the necesary two-thirds majority in each House, largely because **Wal** itself was so well entrenched.[2] A more cautious adaptation of **Wal** was then undertaken, and its three readings went through without difficulty in April 1980, September 1980, and September 1981.[3] The rite remained in 'thou' form of address to God, with minor changes of language (such as 'Spirit' for 'Ghost' in the Creed) being admitted alongside that.

The rite as accepted in 1981 needed slight further harmonization in order to conform to the presentation of the whole set of liturgical material which would be in the projected *Book of Common Prayer*. The decision of the Governing Body in September 1983 to provide this definitive Book led into a last stage of adaptation. The revised rite (published below as **Wal1**) is contained within Volume 1 of the Book with its propers, and a bilingual English and Welsh Book is also published. In general the services in the definitive Book replace all previous authorized services, but a bare permission to continue the use of 1662 communion was contained in the Bill providing for the revision of the communion service. The Book was published in August 1984, and authorized from 30 September 1984. Wales is unique in the Anglican Communion in having an 'ancient language' modern Prayer Book.

Whilst the Province has been very cautious about modern language, there has been provided a modern language eucharist to be used alongside the definitive one.[4] This was presented to the Governing Body for authorization in April 1984 in a paperback book containing a modern Welsh text in parallel with it, and a full set of propers, and this was then authorized for 'experimental use'. The intention is that it should form part of a Volume III to the Book of Common Prayer in due course. The text is printed below as **Wal2**, and its independence of **Wal1** is clearly visible. It is now available in hardback.

[1] The text of **Wal** is printed in **MAL**, pp. 163–172.
[2] The voting was: Bishops 6–0; Clergy 65–38; Laity 70–68.
[3] The voting was: Bishops 6–0; Clergy 82–4; Laity 101–14.
[4] There was a 'study rite' in 1972, published as **WalR** in **FAL**, pp. 82–88, but interest in it appears to have been slight.

THE RITE FROM *THE BOOK OF COMMON PRAYER FOR USE IN THE CHURCH IN WALES* 1984 (Wal1)

[The text is in Volume 1 of the Prayer Book, and is printed on the right-hand side of the page in the bilingual Book, facing the Welsh text opposite. The numbering below is editorial.]

THE ORDER FOR THE CELEBRATION OF THE HOLY EUCHARIST

GENERAL RUBRICS

1. *The Holy Eucharist is the principal act of Christian worship. Every confirmed person should communicate regularly and frequently after careful preparation, which should include self-examination leading to repentance and reconciliation. It is the responsibility of the Priest to teach and help his people in these matters. He should instruct them in the use of private confession, which is available for all who cannot otherwise find the assurance of God's forgiveness. (See Appendix IV).*

2. *It is the duty of a Christian to contribute gladly and liberally to the maintenance of the worship of God and the proclamation of the Gospel.*

3. *The Eucharist is the Sacrament of our fellowship in the Body of Christ. The Priest shall therefore warn any communicants who by their public conduct bring the Church into disrepute that they ought not to receive the Holy Mysteries until they amend their way of life. If they do not heed the warning, the Priest shall report the matter to the Bishop and proceed as he directs.*

THE PREPARATION

1 *A hymn, psalm or anthem may be sung.*

Kneel

2 In the Name of the Father, and of the Son, and of the Holy Spirit. **Amen.**

3 Almighty God, unto whom...[CF 1]...our Lord. **Amen.**
your...you] thy...thee

4 Lord, have mercy.   *or*   Kyrie, eleison.
Lord, have mercy.   **Kyrie, eleison.**
Lord, have mercy.   Kyrie, eleison.

Christ, have mercy.   **Christe, eleison.**
Christ, have mercy.   Christe, eleison.
Christ, have mercy.   **Christe, eleison.**

Lord, have mercy.   Kyrie, eleison.
Lord, have mercy.   **Kyrie, eleison.**
Lord, have mercy.   Kyrie, eleison.

or

Lord, have mercy upon us.
Christ, have mercy upon us.
Lord, have mercy upon us.

5   *or THE TEN COMMANDMENTS*

After each of the first nine commandments shall be said or sung :
Lord, have mercy upon us, and incline our hearts to keep this law.

After the tenth commandment shall be said or sung :
Lord, have mercy upon us, and write all these thy laws in our hearts, we beseech thee.
God said:
1. I am the Lord...[CF 2, without brackets in nos. 2 and 9, and without the bracketed words in no. 4]...covet anything that is your neighbour's.

but me] before me
any graven] a graven
nor the] or any
or in the] or that is in the TWICE
nor worship] or serve
to keep holy the sabbath day] the sabbath day, to keep it holy
commit murder] kill

6 Let us humbly confess our sins to Almighty God.

Almighty God, our Heavenly Father,
we have sinned against thee,
in thought and word and deed,
and in what we have left undone.
We are truly sorry and repent of all our sins.
Have mercy upon us, most merciful Father;
forgive us all that is past;
and grant that we may ever hereafter
serve and please thee in newness of life,
to the honour and glory of thy Name;
through Jesus Christ our Lord. Amen.

7 *The Priest says :*
Almighty God have mercy...[CF 5]...our Lord. **Amen.**

keep...eternal] bring you to everlasting life

Stand

8 *Gloria in Excelsis* (*on Sundays and festivals*).
Glory be to God on high...[**MAL** CF 5]...**the Father. Amen.**

Thou that takest...upon us] OM [See **FAL**, page 62, footnote] .
Ghost] Spirit

THE MINISTRY OF THE WORD

9 The Lord be with you;
And with your spirit.

The Collect or Collects of the day.

Sit

10 *The Old Testament Lesson. The reader says:*
The reading from...

11 *The Epistle. The reader says:*
The reading from...

12 *The Psalm.*

Stand

13 *The Gospel. The readers says:*
Hear the Holy Gospel according to Saint...
Glory be to thee, O Lord.

After the Gospel:
Praise be to thee, O Christ.

Sit

14 *The Sermon follows the reading of the Gospel.*

Stand

15 *The Nicene Creed (on Sundays and festivals).*
I believe in one God...⟦MAL CF 6⟧...to come. Amen.
Ghost] Spirit TWICE
sitteth on] is seated at
proceedeth] proceeds
spake] spoke
believe one] believe in One

16 *Banns of Marriage and other notices.*

Kneel

THE INTERCESSION

Either

17 *The minister may ask the people to pray for the various needs of the universal Church and the world, the local Church and community, and for particular needs. After each bidding silence shall be kept. Then is said:*
Lord, in thy mercy,
Hear our prayer.

After the final bidding shall be said:
We bless thy holy Name for the grace and virtue declared [in...and] in all thy Saints: grant that we, rejoicing in their fellowship and following their good examples, may at thy Son's appearing be set with them on his right hand and be made partakers of thy heavenly kingdom.
Hear us, O heavenly Father, for the sake of Jesus Christ, our only Mediator and Advocate, to whom with thee and the Holy Spirit be all honour and glory, world without end. Amen.

Or

18 *Notice may first be given of special objects of prayer and thanksgiving.*
Let us pray for the whole Church of Christ and for all men according
to their needs.

Almighty and everlasting God, we humbly beseech thee to inspire
continually the universal Church with the spirit of truth, unity, and
concord, that all who confess thy holy Name may agree in the truth of
thy holy Word, and live in unity and godly love.

> Lord, in thy mercy,
> **Hear our prayer.**

Give grace, O heavenly Father, to all Bishops, Priests and Deacons, and
specially to thy servant N. our Bishop, that they may by their life and
doctrine proclaim thy true and living Word and rightly and duly
administer thy Holy Sacraments.

> Lord, in thy mercy,
> **Hear our prayer.**

To all thy people give thy heavenly grace, and specially to this
congregation here present; that they may serve thee in holiness and
righteousness all the days of their life.

> Lord, in thy mercy,
> **Hear our prayer.**

We beseech thee, O Lord, to direct with thy heavenly wisdom those who
rule over the nations of the world, that thy people may be faithfully and
justly governed; bless thy servant *Elizabeth our Queen* and all who
exercise authority under *her*.

> Lord, in thy mercy,
> **Hear our prayer.**

Of thy goodness, O Lord, help and comfort all those who are in trouble,
sorrow, need, sickness, or any other adversity,* granting them a happy
issue out of all their afflictions.

> Lord, in thy mercy,
> **Hear our prayer.**

We commend to thy gracious keeping, O Lord, all thy servants departed
this life in thy faith and fear,* beseeching thee to grant us with them
everlasting light and peace.

> Lord, in thy mercy,
> **Hear our prayer.**

Finally, we bless thy holy Name for the grace and virtue declared
[in...and] in all thy Saints. Grant that we, rejoicing in their fellowship

* *Here sick or departed persons may be mentioned by name.*

and following their good examples, may at thy Son's appearing be set with them on his right hand and be made partakers of thy heavenly kingdom.

Hear us, O heavenly Father, for the sake of Jesus Christ, our only Mediator and Advocate, to whom with thee and the Holy Spirit be all honour and glory, world without end. Amen.

THE MINISTRY OF THE SACRAMENT

Stand

19 The peace of the Lord be always with you;
And with your spirit.

THE OFFERTORY

20 *One of the sentences may be said.*

A hymn, psalm or anthem may be sung.

The offerings of the people are brought to the Priest and presented at the altar.

The priest sets the bread and wine on the altar.

⟦The Offertory Sentences which follow here are to be found in Appendix B⟧

Then may be said :

All things come of thee:
And of thine own do we give thee.

THE GREAT THANKSGIVING

21 The Lord be with you;
And with your spirit.

Lift up your hearts;
We lift them up unto the Lord.

Let us give thanks unto our Lord God;
It is meet and right so to do.

The Priest continues :

It is very meet, right and our bounden duty, that we should at all times, and in all places, give thanks unto thee, O Lord, Holy Father, Almighty, Everlasting God.

If appointed, the Proper Preface in Appendix I ; otherwise on Sundays :

Through Jesus Christ out Lord, who by his death has destroyed death, and by his rising to life again has restored to us everlasting life.

⟦The Proper Prefaces which are printed in Appendix I to the service are described here in Appendix C⟧

Therefore with Angels and Archangels, and with all the company of heaven, we laud and magnify thy glorious Name, evermore praising thee and saying:

Holy, Holy, Holy, Lord God of Hosts,
heaven and earth are full of thy glory.
Glory be to thee. O Lord most high.

Blessed is he who comes in the Name of the Lord.
Hosanna in the highest.

Kneel

All glory, praise and thanksgiving be unto thee Almighty God our heavenly Father, creator and sustainer of all things, maker of man in thine own image, who gavest thine only Son Jesus Christ to take our nature upon him and to suffer death upon the Cross for our redemption. There he made the one perfect and sufficient sacrifice for the sins of the whole world; and did institute, and in his Holy Gospel command us to continue, a perpetual memorial of that his precious death until his coming again.

Therefore we beseech thee, O merciful Father, to sanctify with thy Holy Spirit these thy gifts of Bread and Wine, that we, receiving them according to thy Son our Saviour Jesus Christ's holy institution, may be partakers of his most precious Body and Blood:

Who in the same night that he was betrayed, took Bread
    (*Here the Priest takes the Bread into his hands*)

and when he had given thanks, he broke it, and gave it to his disciples, saying, Take, eat, this is my Body which is given for you: Do this in remembrance of me.

Likewise after supper he took the Cup
    (*Here the Priest takes the Cup into his hands*)

and when he had given thanks, he gave it to them, saying, Drink ye all of this, for this is my Blood of the New Covenant, which is shed for you and for many for the remission of sins: Do this, as oft as ye shall drink it, in remembrance of me.

Wherefore, O Lord and heavenly Father, making the memorial of the blessed Passion, mighty Resurrection, and glorious Ascension, of thy dearly beloved Son as he hath commanded us, rejoicing in his gift of the Holy Spirit, and looking for his coming again with power and great glory, we thy servants, with all thy holy people, do set forth before thy Divine Majesty this Bread of eternal life and this Cup of everlasting salvation.

And we beseech thee to accept this our sacrifice of praise and thanks-giving, and to grant to us and thy whole Church remission of our sins and all other benefits of his Passion. And we pray that all we, who are partakers of this holy Communion, may be fulfilled with thy grace and heavenly benediction and be numbered in the glorious company of thy saints.

Through Jesus Christ our Lord, by whom, in whom, and with whom, in the unity of the Holy Spirit, all honour and glory be unto thee, O Father Almighty, throughout all ages, world without end.

All say: **Amen.**

22 *The Priest breaks the Bread, saying:*
The Bread which we break;
Is it not the communion of the Body of Christ?
We who are many are one Bread, one Body;
For we are all partakers of the one Bread.

23 *Then may be said:*
We do not presume ... ⟦CF 6⟧ ... **he in us. Amen.**
your] **thy** THROUGHOUT
merciful] **O merciful**
you are] **thou art**
nature] **property**

24 *Then may be said here or during the Communion.*
O Lamb of God ... ⟦**MAL** CF 14⟧ ... **thy peace.**

THE COMMUNION

25 As our Saviour Jesus Christ has taught us we are bold to say:
Our Father, who art ... ⟦**MAL** CF 1⟧ ... **and ever. Amen**
in earth] **on earth**
them that] **those who**

26 Draw near and receive the Body and Blood of our Lord Jesus Christ given for you, and feed on him in your hearts by faith with thanksgiving.

27 *The priest receives Holy Communion and the Sacrament is administered with these words:*
The Body of Christ keep you in eternal life. **Amen.**
The Blood of Christ keep you in eternal life. **Amen.**

28 *If additional consecration is required, the form in Appendix II shall be used.*

29 *The priest, with such other communicants as he may call to him, reverently consumes any part of the consecrated elements not required for purposes of Communion, and the vessels are cleansed.*

30 *A hymn may be sung while this is being done.*

THE POST-COMMUNION

31 *The priest may read the verse or verses from the proper psalm marked with the symbol* ‡.

O give thanks unto the Lord, for he is gracious;
For his mercy endureth for ever.

Either

32 Almighty and everlasting God, we thank thee for the spiritual food of the Body and Blood of thy Son, our Saviour Jesus Christ, which thou hast given us in these holy mysteries, assuring us thereby of thy favour and goodness towards us who are members of the mystical body of thy Son, and heirs through hope of thy eternal kingdom:
Wherefore, we offer and present unto thee, O Lord,
ourselves, our souls and bodies,
to be a reasonable, holy, and living sacrifice unto thee,
beseeching thee
to keep us, by thy grace, in this holy fellowship
and to enable us to do all those good works
which thou hast prepared for us to walk in;
through Jesus Christ our Lord,
to whom with thee and the Holy Spirit
be all honour and glory,
world without end. Amen.

Or

33 Almighty God, we thank thee for feeding us with the Body and Blood of thy Son Jesus Christ, through whom we offer to thee our souls and bodies to be a living sacrifice. Send us out in the power of thy Spirit to live and work to thy praise and glory. **Amen.**

THE DISMISSAL

34 The Lord be with you;
And with your spirit.

35 *The Priest may then say :*
[The peace of God... [CF 10]...always. **Amen.**
And the blessing] and] The blessing
among] amongst

36 Let us go forth in peace:
In the Name of Christ. Amen.

APPENDIX 1

37   *PROPER PREFACES*

[The Proper Prefaces which are printed here are those for **Wal** recorded in **MAL**, but with slight changes recorded here in Appendix C]

APPENDIX II

38 *FORM OF ADDITIONAL CONSECRATION*

If the consecrated bread proves insufficient, the Priest returns to the altar, takes bread, and says:

Father, almighty and everliving God, hear the prayer and thanksgiving which we offer through Jesus Christ our Lord; who in the same night that he was betrayed, took Bread and when he had given thanks, he broke it, and gave it to his disciples, saying, Take, eat, this is my Body which is given for you: Do this in remembrance of me.

If it is necessary to consecrate in both kinds, the Priest takes wine, and continues:

Likewise after supper he took the Cup and when he had given thanks, he gave it to them saying, Drink ye all of this, for this is my Blood of the New Covenant, which is shed for you and for many for the remission of sins: Do this, as oft as ye shall drink it, in remembrance of me.

For the blessing of the Cup only, the Priest says:

Father, almighty and everlasting God, hear the prayer and thanksgiving which we offer through Jesus Christ our Lord; who in the same night that he was betrayed, took the Cup and when he had given thanks, he gave it to his disciples, saying, Drink ye all of this, for this is my Blood of the New Covenant, which is shed for you and for many for the remission of sins: Do this, as oft as ye shall drink it, in remembrance of me.

APPENDIX III

39 *GENERAL DIRECTIONS*

1. *The Holy Table shall be covered with a clean white cloth.*

2. *The bread and wine are to be provided by the churchwardens at the expense of the parish. The bread shall be wheat bread, whether leavened or unleavened, and the wine pure grape wine to which a little water may be added.*

3. *It is the Bishop's right to be the celebrant of the Eucharist and to preach; if he is not the celebrant, he pronounces the Absolution and gives the Blessing.*

4. *As far as possible the celebrant should be seen to preside over the whole of the Eucharist in order to emphasise the unity of the service.*

5. *When a Deacon is present he should read the Gospel and assist in the administration of the Sacrament and may if necessary lead the Post-Communion. A Deacon may administer Holy Communion from the reserved Sacrament.*

6. *A Deacon or Reader may say such parts of the service to the end of the Intercession (omitting the Absolution) as may be required.*

7. *Subject to the regulations of the Church in Wales, a lay person may assist in the administration of the Holy Communion. At the discretion of the parish priest, lay persons may read the Old Testament Lesson and Epistle and lead the Intercession.*

8. *When the Ministry of the Sacrament is not to follow the Ministry of the Word the service shall end with the Lord's Prayer and the Grace.*

9. *On weekdays which are not Holy Days, the Psalm and either the Old Testament Lesson or the Epistle may be omitted.*

10. *The directions 'Stand', 'Kneel', 'Sit', indicate the postures which are appropriate for the people at various stages of the service.*

11. *Appropriate parts of the service may be either said or sung.*

12. *The use of silence is commended as a means of recollection, especially before the General Confession and immediately after the Communion of the People.*

40 〚There follows an 'APPENDIX IV' – '*A FORM OF CONFESSION AND ABSOLUTION*'. As this is a form for private use, it is not reproduced here.〛

THE CHURCH IN WALES MODERN LANGUAGE
LITURGY 1984 (Wal2)

〚This is also available in a bilingual edition. The numbering is editorial〛

THE HOLY EUCHARIST IN MODERN LANGUAGE

WE PREPARE FOR WORSHIP

Kneel

1 *A hymn, psalm or anthem may be sung.*

2 In the name of God, Father, Son and Holy Spirit. **Amen.**
   (*And in Eastertide :*
   Alleluia. Christ is risen!
   Alleluia. The Lord is risen indeed!)

3 Father, our hearts are open to you.
   No secrets are hidden from you.
   Cleanse us by your Holy Spirit,
   that we may perfectly love and worship you;
   through Jesus Christ our Lord. **Amen.**

4 Lord of all compassion;
   have mercy on us.

   Heavenly Father, we have sinned in thought, word and deed.
   We have failed to do what we ought to have done.
   We are sorry and truly repent.
   Have mercy on us and forgive us all our sins,
   that we may serve you in newness of life
   to the glory of your name;
   through Jesus Christ our Lord. Amen.

5 Almighty God have mercy on you,
   forgive you and set you free from sin,
   strengthen you in goodness,
   and keep you in eternal life;
   through Jesus Christ our Lord. **Amen.**

Stand

6 *Gloria in Excelsis* (*on Sundays and festivals*).
   Glory to God...〚ICET 4〛...**the Father. Amen.**

7 Let us pray.
   The Collect or Collects of the day.

WE PROCLAIM THE WORD OF GOD

Sit

8 *The Old Testament Reading. The reader says:*
   The reading from...

9 *The New Testament Reading. The reader says:*
The reading from...

10 *The Psalm.*

Stand

11 *The Gospel. The reader says:*

Listen to the Gospel of Christ according to Saint...
Glory to Christ our Saviour.

After the Gospel:
Praise to Christ our Lord.

Sit

12 *The Sermon follows the reading of the Gospel.*

Stand

13 *Nicene Creed (on Sundays and festivals).*
We believe... ⟦ICET 2⟧ ...to come. Amen.

[and the Son]] OMIT BRACKETS

14 *Banns of Marriage and other notices.*

WE PRAY WITH THE CHURCH

Kneel

Either

15 *The minister may ask the people to pray for the various needs of the universal Church and the world, the local Church and community, and for particular needs. After each bidding silence shall be kept. Then is said:*

Lord, in your mercy;

hear our prayer.

After the final bidding:

We give you thanks and praise for all your saints. Rejoicing in their fellowship and following their example, we ask you to grant us with them a share in your eternal kingdom.
Hear us, Father, for the sake of your Son, our Saviour Jesus Christ. To him, with you and the Holy Spirit, be all honour and glory, now and for ever. Amen.

or

16 Father, we pray for your holy catholic Church;
That we all may be one.

Grant that every member of Christ's Body may truly serve you;
That your name may be glorified by all people.

We pray for all bishops, priests, and deacons;
That they may be faithful ministers of your Word and Sacraments.

We pray for all who govern and hold authority among the nations of the world;
That there may be justice and peace on the earth.

Give us grace to do your will in all that we undertake;
That our works may be acceptable in your sight.

Have compassion on those who suffer from any grief or trouble;
That they may be set free from their distress.

To the departed give eternal rest;
Let light perpetual shine upon them.

We praise you for your saints who have entered into your joy;
May we also rejoice in your heavenly kingdom.

Let us pray for our own needs and those of others.

Silence

The People may add their own petitions.

Lord, hear the prayers of your people, for the sake of your Son our Saviour Jesus Christ. **Amen.**

or

17 Let us pray.

Almighty and everliving God, hear the prayers which we offer in faith:

For peace and for the salvation of all mankind,
Lord, hear us.

For the one holy catholic and apostolic Church, and for the unity of all Christian people,
Lord, hear us.

For bishops, priests and deacons, and especially for *N.* our bishop,
Lord, hear us.

For those who learn and those who teach the Christian faith,
Lord, hear us.

For all who live and work in this parish (place),
Lord, hear us.

For families and for those who live alone,
Lord, hear us.

For the sick and those in any kind of distress,
Lord, hear us.

For all in authority, and especially for *N.* our *Queen,*
Lord, hear us.

For those who work for peace, justice and righteousness throughout the
    world,
Lord, hear us.

For...
Lord, hear us.

We thank you, Lord, for all your saints, and for all your servants who
have died in your faith and fear. We commend ourselves, and one
another, and our whole life to you, Lord God, through Jesus Christ our
Saviour. **Amen.**

Stand

18 The peace of the Lord be always with you;
And also with you.

19 *A hymn, psalm or anthem may be sung.*

20 *The collection is brought to the priest.*

21 *The priest sets the bread and wine on the altar.*
   He may say:

Grant, Lord, that we who rejoice in the sacrament of your Son's death
and resurrection may greet him when he comes in glory, and may enter
into the everlasting joy of heaven; through the same Christ our Lord.
Amen.

THE GREAT THANKSGIVING

22 The Lord be with you;
And also with you.

Lift up your hearts;
We lift them to the Lord.

Let us give thanks to the Lord our God;
It is right to give him thanks and praise.

It is indeed right, it is our duty and our joy at all times and in all places
to give you thanks, holy Father, all-powerful and ever-living God:

If appointed, the Proper Preface in Appendix I; otherwise, on Sundays:
through Jesus Christ our Lord, who by his death has destroyed death,
and by his rising to life again has restored to us everlasting life.

[The other Prefaces, which are printed in the Rite in Appendix 1, are to be found here
in Appendix C]

And so with the hosts of angels and all the company of heaven, we
proclaim the glory of your name, and join in their unending hymn of
praise:

**Holy, holy, holy Lord, God of power and might,
heaven and earth are full of your glory.
Hosanna in the highest.**

**Blessed is he who comes in the name of the Lord.
Hosanna in the highest.**

We acclaim you, holy Father, glorious in power. You created all things
and formed us in your own image. We thank you that, because all have
fallen into sin, you gave your only Son, Jesus Christ, to be made man,
to die on the Cross and to rise again for our salvation.

On the night he was betrayed, he took bread,
   (*Here the priest takes the bread into his hands*)
and when he had given thanks, he broke it and gave it to his disciples,
saying, Take, eat, this is my Body which is given for you. Do this in
remembrance of me.

In the same way after supper he took the cup,
   (*Here the priest takes the cup into his hands*)
and when he had given thanks, he gave it to them, saying, Drink from
this, all of you, for this is my Blood of the New Covenant, which is shed
for you and for many for the forgiveness of sins. Do this, as often as
you drink it, in remembrance of me.
this, as often as you drink it, in remembrance of me.

Therefore, heavenly Father, as we now proclaim his death and resurrection, we offer to you these your gifts, this Bread and this Cup, and
we ask you to accept our sacrifice of thanks and praise. Send your Holy
Spirit on us and on these gifts, that we who share in this holy
Communion may be united in peace and love with all your faithful
people through Jesus Christ our Lord. Through him, with him, in him,
in the unity of the Holy Spirit, all honour and glory are yours, almighty
Father, now and for ever. **Amen.**

23 **Christ has died.
Christ is risen.
Christ will come again.**

24 *The priest breaks the Bread, saying :*
   We break this Bread to share in the Body of Christ.
   **Though we are many we are one Body, for we all share in one
      Bread.**

25 Because Jesus taught us, we boldly say:
   Our Father in heaven...⟦ICET 1⟧...**for ever. Amen.**

26 Come, let us receive the Body and Blood of our Lord Jesus Christ, given
   for us, and feed on him in our hearts by faith with thanksgiving.

27 *The priest receives Holy Communion, and administers the Sacrament with
these words :*
The Body of Christ. **Amen.**
The Blood of Christ. **Amen.**

28 *During the Communion, this anthem may be used :*
Jesus, Lamb of God...⟦ICET 8(a)⟧...**your peace.**

29 *If additional consecration is required, the form in Appendix II shall be used.
The priest reverently consumes any part of the consecrated elements
remaining. He may call other communicants to assist him. The vessels are
then cleansed.*

30 *A hymn may be sung.*

WE GO OUT IN GOD'S STRENGTH

31 Give thanks to the Lord, for he is good:
his love is everlasting.

We thank you, Father, for giving us the Body and Blood of your Son
　　in this holy Sacrament,
through which we are assured of the hope of eternal life.
We offer ourselves to you as a living sacrifice.
Keep us in the fellowship of his Body the Church,
and send us out in the power of your Spirit
to live and work to your praise and glory. **Amen.**

32 The Lord be with you;
And also with you.

Go out into the world in peace;
In the name of Christ. Amen.

(*Or in Eastertide :*
Go out in the power of the Risen Christ. Alleluia!
Thanks be to God. Alleluia!)

APPENDIX I
33 ### *PROPER PREFACES*
⟦The Proper Prefaces which are printed here are to be found in Appendix C⟧

APPENDIX II
34 ### *A FORM OF ADDITIONAL CONSECRATION*

*If the consecrated bread is insufficient, the priest returns to the altar, takes
bread, and says :*
Holy Father, hear the prayer and thanksgiving which we offer through
Jesus Christ our Lord; on the night he was betrayed, he took bread,

and when he had given thanks, he broke it and gave it to his disciples, saying, Take, eat, this is my Body which is given for you. Do this in remembrance of me.

If it is necessary to consecrate in both kinds, the priest takes wine, and continues:

In the same way after supper he took the cup and when he had given thanks, he gave it to them, saying, Drink from this, all of you, for this is my Blood of the New Covenant, which is shed for you and for many for the forgiveness of sins. Do this, as often as you drink it, in remembrance of me.

For the blessing of the cup only, the priest says:

Holy Father, hear the prayer and thanksgiving which we offer through Jesus Christ our Lord; on the night he was betrayed, he took the cup, and when he had given thanks, he gave it to his disciples, saying, Drink from this, all of you, for this is my Blood of the New Covenant, which is shed for you and for many for the forgiveness of sins. Do this, as often as you drink it, in remembrance of me.

APPENDIX III
GENERAL DIRECTIONS

35

1. *The Holy Table shall be covered with a clean white cloth.*

2. *The bread and wine are to be provided by the churchwardens at the expense of the parish. The bread shall be wheat bread, whether leavened or unleavened, and the wine pure grape wine to which a little water may be added.*

3. *It is the Bishop's right to be the celebrant of the Eucharist and to preach; if he is not the celebrant, he pronounces the Absolution and gives the Blessing.*

4. *As far as possible the celebrant should be seen to preside over the whole of the Eucharist in order to emphasise the unity of the service. He may give a Blessing at the end.*

5. *When a deacon is present he should read the Gospel and assist in the administration of the Sacrament.*

6. *A deacon or reader may say such parts of the service to the end of the prayers of the people (omitting the Absolution) as may be required.*

7. *Subject to the regulations of the Church in Wales, a lay person may assist in the administration of the Holy Communion. At the discretion of the parish priest, lay persons may read the Old Testament Lesson and Epistle and lead the prayers of the people.*

8. *The opening and closing prayers of the service may be said by the priest alone, or by the priest and people, as desired.*

9. *When there is no Communion, the prayers of the people shall be followed by the Lord's Prayer and the Grace.*

10. *On weekdays which are not Holy Days, the Psalm and either the Old Testament Lesson or the Epistle may be omitted.*

11. *Appropriate parts of the service may be either said or sung.*

12. *The use of silence is commended as a means of recollection, especially before the General Confession and immediately after the Communion of the people.*

CHAPTER 4

THE CHURCH OF IRELAND

The first revision of the 1972 rite (**Ire1**) was proposed by the Liturgical Advisory Committee to the 1980 General Synod. It was rejected in the House of Laity there, apparently because the balance of the draft was not thought to be wholly representative of the spectrum of the Church of Ireland. New members were added to the Committee, and new drafting led to an altered text coming before the 1981 Synod, and being confirmed by the 1982 Synod. The crucial features of the new rite (**Ire2**) were that the Eucharistic Prayer from **Ire1** was left with only tiny verbal changes, but the main Eucharistic Prayer from **Aus5** was added as an alternative use.

After 1982 the new '*Alternative Prayer Book 1984*' was in preparation, and the text of **Ire2** took its place in that. The rite itself became lawful on 1 July 1984, and the Book was published by Collins Liturgical Publications on 18 September 1984. An official 'inauguration' was held in Armagh cathedral on 18 October 1984, and the whole Book was in use from 28 October 1984.

THE LITURGY FROM THE CHURCH OF IRELAND *ALTERNATIVE PRAYER BOOK 1984* (Ire2)

〖The Alternative Prayer Book 1984 is published in two colours. References here to 'the Book' refer to it. The numbering is original, except nos. 34–37, which are editorial.〗

AN ORDER FOR THE CELEBRATION OF THE HOLY COMMUNION:
also called THE LORD'S SUPPER or THE EUCHARIST

Stand
1 *The appropriate greeting shall be used and a sentence of Scripture may be said.*

Priest
The Lord be with you.
And also with you.

or
Grace to you and peace from God our Father
and the Lord Jesus Christ. (*Phil.* 1.2)
Thanks be to God.

[There follow four Sentences of Scripture (with responses) for major seasons, which are to be found here in Appendix D.]

The Sentences of Scripture are on pp.... [i.e. others earlier in the Book]

2 *All say*

Almighty God... [CF 1] **...Christ our Lord. Amen.**

hid] **hidden**

3 *This canticle may be omitted in Advent and Lent and on weekdays which are not holy days.*

Glory to God... [ICET 4] **...God the Father. Amen.**

4 *The priest says THE COLLECT of the day.*

THE MINISTRY OF THE WORD

Sit

5 *THE OLD TESTAMENT READING*

The reader says

The Old Testament reading is from...chapter...beginning at verse....

At the end of the reading he may say

This is the word of the Lord.

Thanks be to God.

Silence may be kept.

6 *THE PSALM*

After the reading, one of the appointed Psalms, or a part of it, may be said or sung.

7 *THE EPISTLE*

The reader says

The Epistle is from...chapter...beginning at verse....

At the end of the reading he may say

This is the word of the Lord.

Thanks be to God.

8 *A canticle, psalm, hymn or anthem may be sung.*

Stand

9 *THE GOSPEL*

The minister who reads the Gospel says

The Holy Gospel is written in the Gospel according to... in the... chapter beginning at verse...

Glory to Christ our Saviour.

At the end of the reading the minister says
This is the Gospel of Christ.
Praise to Christ our Lord.

10 *THE SERMON may be preached here or after the Creed.*

11 *THE NICENE CREED is said at least on Sundays and the greater festivals.*

We believe... [ICET 3] ... **world to come. Amen.**
incarnate from] incarnate of
[and the Son]]   OMIT BRACKETS

12 *Banns of Marriage are read here.*
A hymn may be sung.

THE INTERCESSIONS

13 *The Intercessions and Thanksgivings are led by the priest or by others appointed by him, using either of the following forms :*

THE FIRST FORM

Let us pray.

Almighty and everliving God
hear the prayers which we offer in faith:

For peace, and for the salvation of all men,
  Lord, in your mercy
  hear our prayer.

For the one holy catholic and apostolic Church,
and for the unity of all Christian people,
  Lord, in your mercy
  hear our prayer.

For all who minister in the Church,
for bishops, priests and deacons,
  Lord, in your mercy
  hear our prayer.

For those who learn and those who teach the Christian faith,
  Lord, in your mercy
  hear our prayer.

For all who live and work in this parish,
  Lord, in your mercy
  hear our prayer.

For families, and for those who live alone,
  Lord, in your mercy
  hear our prayer.

For the sick and afflicted, and for those who care for them,
Lord, in your mercy
hear our prayer.

For all in authority, and especially for
(*N.I.*) Elizabeth our Queen,
(*R.I.*) our President,
Lord, in your mercy
hear our prayer.

For those who work for peace, justice and righteousness throughout the world,
Lord, in your mercy
hear our prayer.

For...
Lord, in your mercy
hear our prayer.

Rejoicing in the fellowship of your holy apostles and martyrs, and of all your servants departed this life in your faith and fear, we commend ourselves and one another and our whole life to you, Lord God; through Jesus Christ our Saviour. **Amen.**

THE SECOND FORM

Let us pray.

Almighty God, our heavenly Father,
you promised through your Son Jesus Christ
to hear the prayers of those who ask in faith:

We pray for your Church in all the world...
for this diocese and for...our bishop
for...

Grant that we, and all who confess your name,
may be united in your truth,
live together in your love,
and reveal your glory in the world.

Lord, in your mercy
hear our prayer.

We pray for the nations of the world...
for this country and for
(*N.I.*) Elizabeth our Queen,
(*R.I.*) our President,
for all in authority
and for the communities in which we live and work...

Guide the people of this land and of all the nations
in the ways of justice and of peace,
that we may honour one another
and serve the common good.

Lord, in your mercy
hear our prayer.

We pray for the sick...the poor...
and those in trouble...(and for...)

Save and comfort all who suffer,
that they may hold to you through good and ill,
and trust in your unfailing love.

Lord, in your mercy
hear our prayer.

We bless your holy name for all your servants
who have died in faith, (for...)

We rejoice in the faithful witness of your people
in every age, and pray that we may share with them
the joys of your eternal kingdom.

**Merciful Father,
accept these our prayers
for the sake of your Son
our Saviour Jesus Christ.   Amen.**

PENITENCE

14 *The priest says*

Hear what our Lord Jesus Christ says: You shall love...〚CF 3〛...
as yourself. On these two commandments depend all the law and the
prophets. (*Matt.* 22.37–39)

heart,...soul,] heart and...soul
and with all your strength] OM
first] first and great
The second is this] And the second is like it: You shall

**Lord, have mercy on us,
and write these your laws in our hearts.**

or

Hear these commandments which God has given to his people, and take
them to heart.

〚The Decalogue follows as in **EngA** no. 78A, but with the response above printed after
the fourth and tenth commandments (the first commandment includes 'and' before
'with all your mind' and the response to the tenth '**all these your laws**'). The first
half of each is printed in capitals, and references are added to the second half.〛

or

The Ten Commandments may be read in the shorter form as printed in capitals above, or in full (p.... [[i.e. no. 35]])

15 *The priest, or one of the ministers, says*

God so loved the world that he gave his only Son Jesus Christ to save us from our sins, to intercede for us in heaven, and to bring us to eternal life.

or

He may say one or more of the following sentences:

Jesus says, come to me... [[CF 4]]... propitiation for our sins. (1 *John* 2.1, 2)

who labour] that labour
give you rest] refresh you
whoever believes] all who believe
Hear...says] OM TWICE
saying...acceptance] is a true saying, and worthy by all men to be received
anyone does sin] any man sin

16 *Then he says*

Let us therefore confess our sins in penitence and faith, firmly resolved to keep God's commandments, and to live in love and peace with all men.

17 *After a short pause for self examination, all say*

Almighty God, our heavenly Father,
we have sinned in thought and word and deed,
and in what we have left undone.
We are truly sorry, and we humbly repent.
For the sake of your Son, Jesus Christ,
have mercy on us and forgive us,
that we may walk in newness of life
to the glory of your name. Amen.

18 *The priest, or the bishop if he is present, pronounces the absolution:*

Almighty God... [[CF 5]]... Christ our Lord. **Amen.**
upon] on
life eternal] eternal life

19 *All then say together*

We do not presume... [[CF 6]]... **he in us. Amen.**

drink his blood] ADD **that our sinful bodies may be made clean by his body,**
              and our souls washed through his most precious blood,
              and

THE PEACE

Stand

20 *The priest says*
Christ is our peace.
He has reconciled us to God
in one body by the cross.
We meet in his name and share his peace.

or

Jesus said, A new commandment I give to you,
that you love one another:
even as I have loved you,
that you also love one another. (*John* 13.34)

21 *He then says*
The peace of the Lord be always with you.
And also with you.
Those present may give one another a sign of peace.

THE OFFERTORY

22 *The priest may say one or more sentences of Scripture,* (p.... [i.e. no. 36]).
A hymn may be sung.

The alms of the people may be brought to the Lord's Table.

The bread and wine for communion are placed on the Lord's Table if this has not already been done.

All may say together

**Lord, yours is the greatness
and the power and the glory
and the victory and the majesty;
for all things come from you
and of your own we give you.** (1 *Chron.* 29.11, 14)

THE MINISTRY OF THE SACRAMENT
THE TAKING OF THE BREAD AND WINE AND THE GIVING OF THANKS
Stand

23 *The priest takes the bread and wine into his hands. He may say*
Christ our passover has been sacrificed for us;
therefore let us celebrate the feast. (1 *Cor.* 5.7, 8)

24 *The priest says*
The Lord be with you.   *or*   The Lord is here.
And also with you.   **His Spirit is with us.**

Lift up your hearts.
We lift them up to the Lord.

Let us give thanks to the Lord our God.
It is right to give him thanks and praise.

Father, almighty and everliving God,
at all times and in all places
it is right for us to give you thanks and praise:

When there is a proper preface it follows here (pp.... ff [i.e. at no. 34])

[The Proper Prefaces are to be found here in Appendix C.]

And so with all your people,
with angels and archangels,
and with all the company of heaven,
we proclaim your great and glorious name,
for ever praising you and saying:

Holy, holy, holy Lord,
God of power and might,
heaven and earth are full of your glory.
Hosanna in the highest.

The congregation may kneel
Blessed are you, Father,
the creator and sustainer of all things;
you made man in your own image,
and more wonderfully restored him
when you freed him from the slavery of sin;
for in your love and mercy
you gave your only Son Jesus Christ to become man
and suffer death on the cross to redeem us;
he made there the one complete and all-sufficient sacrifice
for the sins of the whole world:
he instituted,
and in his holy Gospel commanded us to continue,
a perpetual memory of his precious death
until he comes again:

On the night that he was betrayed he took bread;
and when he had given thanks to you, he broke it,
and gave it to his disciples, saying, Take, eat,

The priest lays his hand on the bread

this is my body which is given for you.
Do this in remembrance of me.

In the same way, after supper he took the cup;
and when he had given thanks to you,
he gave it to them, saying, Drink this, all of you,

The priest lays his hand on the cup

for this is my blood of the new covenant
which is shed for you and for many
for the forgiveness of sins.
Do this, as often as you drink it,
in remembrance of me.

Therefore, Father, with this bread and this cup
we do as Christ your Son commanded:
we remember his passion and death,
we celebrate his resurrection and ascension,
and we look for the coming of his kingdom.

Accept through him this our sacrifice
of praise and thanksgiving;
and as we eat and drink these holy gifts,
grant by the power of the life-giving Spirit
that we may be made one in your holy Church
and partakers of the body and blood of your Son,
that he may dwell in us and we in him:

Through the same Jesus Christ our Lord,
by whom, and with whom, in the unity of the Holy Spirit,
all honour and glory are yours, Almighty Father,
for ever and ever. **Amen.**

25 *The priest says*
As our Saviour Christ has taught us, so we pray

Our Father...⟦ICET 1⟧...**for ever. Amen.**
Save us...trial and] Lead us not into temptation but
or
The Lord's Prayer may be said in the old form.

*THE BREAKING OF THE BREAD
AND THE GIVING OF THE BREAD AND WINE*

26 *As the priest breaks the bread he says*
The bread which we break
is a sharing in the body of Christ.
**We, being many, are one body
for we all share in the one bread.** (1 *Cor.* 10.16, 17)

27 *The priest receives communion.*
Communicants are given the consecrated bread and wine with the words
The body...⟦CF 7(a)⟧...with thanksgiving.
The blood...⟦CF 7(b)⟧...be thankful.
everlasting] eternal TWICE

or

The priest says
Draw near and receive the body of our Lord Jesus Christ which he gave
for you, and his blood which he shed for you. Remember that he died
for you, and feed on him in your hearts by faith with thanksgiving.

Communicants are given the consecrated bread and wine with the words
The body of Christ keep you in eternal life.
The blood of Christ keep you in eternal life.

After receiving the communicant says
Amen.

28 *The following may be sung during the Communion :*
Blessed is he...⟦ICET 5(b)⟧...**the highest.**
Jesus, Lamb of God...⟦ICET 8(a)⟧...**your peace.**
or
Lamb of God...⟦ICET 8(b)⟧...**us peace.**
Other hymns or anthems may be sung.

AFTER COMMUNION

29 *A period of silence may be kept.*

30 *The priest may say*
Father of all,...⟦CF 8⟧...our Lord. **Amen.**
in this hope that we have grasped] firm in the hope you have set before us
so we] so that we

31 *The priest says*
Let us pray.
Almighty God...⟦CF 9⟧ ...**and glory. Amen.**
feeding us with] ADD the spiritual food of

32 *The priest, or the bishop if he is present, says*
The peace of God...⟦CF 10, first half⟧...our Lord.
*On the occasions for which a seasonal blessing is provided it is used in
place of* 'The peace of God...'
And the blessing...⟦CF 10, second half⟧...always. **Amen.**
among] with

33 *The following dismissal may be used :*
Go in peace to love and serve the Lord.
In the name of Christ. Amen.

THE MINISTRY OF THE SACRAMENT:
AN ALTERNATIVE ORDER

THE TAKING OF THE BREAD AND WINE
AND THE GIVING OF THANKS

Stand

23a *The priest takes the bread and wine into his hands. He may say*
Christ our passover has been sacrificed for us;
therefore let us celebrate the feast. (1 *Cor.* 5.7, 8)

24a *The priest says*

  The Lord be with you. *or* The Lord is here.
  And also with you.   **His Spirit is with us.**

Lift up your hearts.
We lift them up to the Lord.

Let us give thanks to the Lord our God.
It is right to give him thanks and praise.

All glory...[as in **Aus5**, no. 20]...**and ever. Amen.**

25a *The priest says here or at 29a*
As our Saviour Christ has taught us, so we pray
Our Father...[ICET 1]...**for ever . Amen.**
Save us...trial and] Lead us not into temptation but
or
The Lord's Prayer may be said in the old form.

THE BREAKING OF THE BREAD
AND THE GIVING OF THE BREAD AND WINE
[Nos. 26a, 27a, and 28a, which follow, are identical to nos. 26, 27, and 28 above]

AFTER COMMUNION

29a *If the Lord's Prayer has not already been said, it is said here. A period of silence may be kept.*

30a *The priest says*
Father, we thank you
that you feed us who have received these holy mysteries
with the spiritual food of the body and blood of our Saviour Jesus Christ.
We thank you for this assurance of your goodness and love,
and that we are living members of his body
and heirs of his eternal kingdom.
Accept this our sacrifice of praise and thanksgiving,
and help us to grow in love and obedience,
that with all your saints we may worship you for ever.
Amen.

31a *All say together*
Father, we offer ourselves to you
as a living sacrifice
through Jesus Christ our Lord.
Send us out in the power of your Spirit
to live and work to your praise and glory. Amen.

〚Nos. 32a and 33a, which follow, are identical to nos. 32 and 33 above〛

THE PROPER PREFACES AND BLESSINGS

Note : Proper prefaces are not used in The Ministry of the Sacrament, An Alternative Order.

34 〚There follow here, under the title of each season or occasion, first a Proper Preface and then a Blessing, and these are printed here in Appendixes C and D respectively〛

THE TEN COMMANDMENTS: FULL FORM
(*Exodus* 20.1–17)

See also pp. ... 〚i.e. no. 14 above〛

35 1 God spoke... 〚CF 2, with variants of **EngA** no. 78B but without brackets〛...your neighbour's.

RESPONSES AFTER FOURTH AND TENTH AS AT NO. 14 ABOVE

SENTENCES WHICH MAY BE USED AT THE OFFERTORY

36¹ 〚The sentences which follow are to be found in Appendix B〛
Other sentences may be said.

WHEN THE CONSECRATED ELEMENTS ARE INSUFFICIENT

37 *If either or both of the consecrated elements are insufficient, the priest returns to the holy table and adds more, saying these words and laying his hand on the bread and/or cup :*

Father,
giving thanks over the bread and the cup
according to the institution of your Son Jesus Christ,
who said, Take, eat, this is my body

and/or
Drink this, this is my blood.

We pray that this bread/wine also may be to us his body/blood,
to be received in remembrance of him.

¹ 〚The Book prints '22' against this (and only this) Appendix, and it has been overridden editorially here to match the other editorial numbering.〛

CHAPTER 5

THE ANGLICAN CHURCH OF CANADA

THE 'Alternative Canadian Liturgy' of 1974 was published in **FAL**, pages 112–118, with the code '**Can1**'. In the years following, the General Synod both encouraged further work in revising this modern language form of the eucharist, and also began a project for a larger *Book of Alternative Services*, finally published in 1985.

The revision of the eucharist led to a draft form being published in 1979 for experimental use.[1] It was then revised in the light of comment, presented to the General Synod in June 1980, authorized in principle by the Synod, further corrected, and published early in 1981. It was entitled *The Holy Eucharist : Third Canadian Order* (**Can3**).[2] This text itself became subject to revision, and a new draft went to General Synod in June 1983. Further comment there led to a meeting between some members of the Doctrine and Worship Committee with the House of Bishops in February 1984, and a definitive text came before the National Executive Council for inclusion in the Book of Alternative Services, being approved on 10 May 1984. It is coded '**Can4**', and goes beyond **Can3** not only in the flexibility of its provisions, but also in the more determined way in which it has used 'inclusive' language. Both rites have a notable relationship with the American rites. **Can4** is edited below with **Can3** shown as an *apparatus*.

In the preparation for the '*BAS*', the Doctrine and Worship Committee decided that a rite in traditional language should also be included. It adopted a re-ordering of **CanR**, similar to that which had been earlier produced by the Toronto diocese, and added as an alternative Eucharistic Prayer a slightly edited one from **Amer1–1**. This rite (**Can1A**) is the only traditional language service in the *BAS*.

THE MODERN LANGUAGE RITE IN THE CANADIAN *BOOK OF ALTERNATIVE SERVICES* 1985 (Can4)

[As with **Can1A** below, the numbering here, including that of the Notes before the service, is editorial. The text is derived from that in *The Holy Eucharist : Third Canadian Order* (1981) (**Can3**), and the **Can3** text is shown throughout by an *apparatus*. References to 'the Book' are to the *Book of Alternative Services*]

---

[1] The Church permits any diocese to authorize the use of any rite, but this draft was put out specifically with a view to its being revised in the light of short-term use.

[2] '*Third*' was used in the title on the assumption that **CanR** was 'first', and **Can1** 'second'. Thus the coding here is '**Can3**', though there is no '**Can2**'.

THE HOLY EUCHARIST

CONCERNING THE LITURGY

1. *The holy table is spread with a clean (white) cloth during the celebration.*

2. *The celebration of the eucharist is the work of the whole People of God. However, throughout this rite the term 'celebrant' is used to describe the bishop or priest who presides at the eucharist.*

Can3: *bishop or priest*] *one*

3. *As chief liturgical officer it is the bishop's prerogative to preside at the Lord's table and to preach the Gospel.*

4. *It is appropriate that other priests who may be present stand with the celebrant at the altar during the eucharistic prayer, and join in the breaking of the bread and in the ministration of communion.*

5. *It is the function of a deacon to read the Gospel and to make ready the table for the celebration, preparing and placing upon it the bread and cup of wine. The deacon may also lead the Prayers of the People.*

6. *Lay persons should normally be assigned the readings which precede the Gospel, and may lead the Prayers of the People. When authority is given by the bishop, they may also assist in the ministration of communion.*

7. *It is desirable that the readings be read from a lectern or pulpit, and that the Gospel be read from the same lectern or pulpit, or in the midst of the congregation. It is desirable that the readings and Gospel be read from a book or books of appropriate size and dignity.*

8. *The leader of the Prayers of the People should use creativity and discretion in the planning of the intercessions and thanksgivings, and scope should be provided for members of the congregation to add their own petitions. The suggested forms are examples; these may be modified as local customs and needs require. The use of silence in the intercessions is optional.*

Can3: *examples*] *examples; only portions of them should be utilized, and*

⟦In **Can3** this note comes later – note 13 follows note 11 below, and this note 8 follows it, to be numbered '12': nos. 9, 10, and 11, are '8', '9', and '10'.⟧

9. *If there is no communion, all that is appointed through the Prayers of the People may be said. (If it is desired to include a confession of sin, the service begins with the Penitential Order.) A hymn or anthem may then be sung, and the offerings of the people received. The service may then be concluded with the Lord's Prayer, and with either the Grace or a blessing, or with the exchange of the Peace. In the absence of a priest, all that is described above, except for the absolution and blessing, may be said by a deacon or, if there is no deacon, by an authorized lay person.*

10. *When a certain posture is particularly appropriate, it is indicated. For the rest of the service local custom may be established and followed. The Great Thanksgiving is a single prayer, the unity of which may be obscured by changes of posture in the course of it.*

11. *During the Great Thanksgiving it is desirable that there be only one chalice on the altar and, if need be, a flagon, decanter, jug, or suitable container of wine from which additional chalices may be filled after the breaking of the bread.*

Can3: *decanter…container*] OM

12. *Care should be taken at the time of the preparation of the gifts to place on the holy table sufficient bread and wine for the communion of the people so that supplementary consecration is unnecessary. However, if the consecrated bread or wine does not suffice for the number of communicants, the celebrant consecrates more of either or both, by saying:*

We thank you, heavenly Father, for your saving love, and we pray you to bless and sanctify this bread (wine) with your Word and Holy Spirit, that it also may be the sacrament of the precious body (blood) of your Son, our Lord Jesus Christ. **Amen.**

Can3: *Care should be…However*] OM

13 *Opportunity is always to be given to every communicant to receive the consecrated bread and wine separately.* ⟦In **Can3** this comes, as '11', after note 11 above which in **Can3** is '10'.⟧

14 *Communion should be given at each celebration of the eucharist from bread and wine consecrated at that liturgy.*

> **Can3**: OMITS

15 *Any remaining consecrated bread and wine (unless reserved for the communion of persons not present) is consumed at the end of the distribution or immediately after the service. This is appropriately done at the credence table or in the sacristy.*

> **Can3**: [This note comes, as '13', after note 8 above, which is there '12']
> *remaining*]   OM
> (*unless…not present*)] *which is not required for purposes of communion*

THE GATHERING OF THE COMMUNITY

1 *All stand.*   *The presiding celebrant greets the community.*

Celebrant   The grace of our Lord Jesus Christ,
      and the love of God,
      and the fellowship of the Holy Spirit,
      be with you all.

People   **And also with you.**

> **Can3**: ADDS   *or the celebrant says,*
> *Celebrant*   Blessed be God: Father, Son, and Holy Spirit.
> *People*   **And blessed be his kingdom,**
>   **now and for ever. Amen.**

or from Easter Day through the Day of Pentecost,

Celebrant   Alleluia. Christ is risen.
People   **The Lord is risen indeed. Alleluia.**

Celebrant   May his grace and peace be with you.
People   **May he fill our hearts with joy.**

2 *The following prayer may be said.*
Celebrant   Almighty God,
All   **to you all hearts are open** … [CF 1] … **our Lord. Amen.**
      whom] you
      hid] hidden

3 *Then may follow an act of praise : one of the following hymns, or a canticle or other hymn. It is appropriate that the hymn Gloria in Excelsis be used during the Christmas season and from Easter Day through the Day of Pentecost, but not during the seasons of Advent and Lent. During Lent it is appropriate that Kyrie Eleison or the Trisagion be used. Other canticles may be found on pages…* [i.e. elsewhere in the Book, in **Can3** after no. 43]

> **Can3**: *an act…hymns, or*]   OM

4 *GLORIA IN EXCELSIS*

Celebrant   Glory to God in the highest,
All   **and peace** … [ICET 4] … **the Father. Amen.**

> **Can3**: *All*] *People*

5 *KYRIE ELEISON*
may be sung in three-fold, six-fold, or nine-fold form.

Kyrie eleison.	*or*	**Lord, have mercy.**
Christe eleison.		**Christ, have mercy.**
Kyrie eleison.		**Lord, have mercy.**

6 *TRISAGION*
may be sung three times or antiphonally, and may include The Gloria Patri.

Holy God,
holy and mighty,
holy immortal One,
have mercy upon us.

Can3: *and may...Patri]* OM
upon] on

7 *THE COLLECT OF THE DAY*

Can3: ADDS *If the Collect of the Day does not immediately follow the opening greeting or acclamation, the presiding celebrant may say,* The Lord be with you. *The people respond,* **And also with you.**

Celebrant   Let us pray.

The community may pray silently. The celebrant then sings or says the collect, after which the people respond, **Amen.**

Can3: *respond]* say

THE PROCLAMATION OF THE WORD

THE READINGS
8 *A first reading as appointed.*

Can3: ADDS AT BEGINNING *On Sundays and major festivals*

Reader   A reading from...
At the conclusion of the passage, the reader says,
The Word of the Lord.
People   **Thanks be to God.**

9 *Silence may be kept. Then shall follow a psalm as appointed. On Sundays and major festivals a second reading as appointed is read.*

Can3: *On Sundays...is read.]* The reading (*or second reading on Sundays and major festivals*).

Reader   A reading from...

At the conclusion of the passage the reader says,
The Word of the Lord.
People   **Thanks be to God.**

10 *Silence may be kept. A psalm, canticle, hymn, or anthem may follow. All stand for the Gospel.*

Reader   The Lord be with you.
People   **And also with you.**

Reader	The Holy Gospel of our Lord Jesus Christ according to . . .
People	**Glory to you, Lord Jesus Christ.**

> **Can3: Glory...Christ] Glory to Christ our Lord.**

At the conclusion of the Gospel, the reader says,
> The Gospel of Christ.

People	**Praise to you, Lord Jesus Christ.**

> **Can3: Praise...Christ] Praise to Christ our Saviour.**

11 *THE SERMON* [[**Can3** adds 'OR HOMILY']]

A silence for reflection may follow.

12 *The Nicene Creed shall be said on major festivals. On Sundays either the Nicene Creed or the Apostles' Creed is appropriate.*

13 *THE NICENE CREED*

The celebrant may invite the people, in these or similar words, to join in the recitation of the Creed.

Celebrant	Let us confess our faith, as we say,

> **Can3: *The celebrant*...as we say,]** OM

All	**We believe...** [[ICET 3]] **...world to come. Amen.**

> **us men] us**
> **[and the Son]]** OM
> **Can3:** BEGINS *Celebrant* We believe in one God.
>   *People* **the Father**

14 *THE APOSTLES' CREED*

The celebrant may invite the people, in these or similar words, to join in the recitation of the Creed.

Celebrant	Let us confess the faith of our baptism, as we say,
All	**I believe...** [[ICET 2]] **...life everlasting. Amen.**

> **Can3:** *The celebrant...Creed]* OM
>   BEGINS *Celebrant* I believe in God,
>   *People* **the Father...**

15 *THE PRAYERS OF THE PEOPLE*

A deacon or lay member of the community leads the Prayers of the People after the following model.

Intercession or thanksgiving may be offered for :

> *the church*
> *the Queen and all in authority*
> *the world*

> the local community
> those in need
> the departed

Can3: *the Queen and*] OM

A short litany may be selected from pages . . . [i.e. elsewhere in the Book]. Other prayers are found on pages . . . [i.e. elsewhere in the Book]. These prayers may be modified in accordance with local need or extempore forms of prayer may be used.

Can3: SUBSTITUTE *Other forms for the Prayers of the People are found on pages . . . [i.e. elsewhere in the booklet; see note here after no. 35.]*

16 CONFESSION AND ABSOLUTION

The following prayers may be used here if the Penitential Rite was not used before the Gathering of the Community, or if penitential intercessions were not used in the Prayers of the People.

The people are invited to confession in these or similar words.

Can3: *The people . . . words*] OM

Celebrant Dear friends in Christ,
God is steadfast in love and infinite in mercy;
he welcomes sinners and invites them to his table.
Let us confess our sins,
confident in God's forgiveness.

Can3: in love . . . in mercy] in his love . . . in his mercy
God's] his

Silence is kept.

17 *Celebrant* Most merciful God,
All **we confess that we have sinned against you
in thought, word, and deed,
by what we have done,
and by what we have left undone.
We have not loved you with our whole heart;
we have not loved our neighbours as ourselves.
We are truly sorry and we humbly repent.
For the sake of your Son Jesus Christ
have mercy on us and forgive us,
that we may delight in your will,
and walk in your ways,
to the glory of your name. Amen.**

18 *Celebrant* Almighty God have mercy . . . [CF 5] . . . our Lord.
People **Amen.**

life eternal} eternal life

19 *THE PEACE*

All stand, and the presiding celebrant addresses the people.

Celebrant	The peace of the Lord be always with you.
People	**And also with you.**

The members of the community, ministers, and people, may greet one another in the name of the Lord.

THE CELEBRATION OF THE EUCHARIST

20 *THE PREPARATION OF THE GIFTS*

It is appropriate that a hymn be sung during the offertory. Representatives of the people may present the gifts of bread and wine for the eucharist (with money and other gifts for the needs and responsibilities of the Church) to the deacon or celebrant before the altar.

21 *THE PRAYER OVER THE GIFTS*

When the gifts have been prepared, the celebrant may say the Prayer over the Gifts, following which the people say, **Amen.**

22 *THE GREAT THANKSGIVING*

One of the following Eucharistic Prayers shall be used.

23 *EUCHARISTIC PRAYER 1*

Celebrant	The Lord be with you.
People	**And also with you.**
Celebrant	Lift up your hearts.
People	**We lift them to the Lord.**
Celebrant	Let us give thanks to the Lord our God.
People	**It is right to give our thanks and praise.**
Celebrant	It is indeed right that we should praise you,

gracious God, for you created all things.
You formed us in your own image:
male and female you created us.
When we turned away from you in sin,
you did not cease to care for us,
but opened a path of salvation for all people.
You made a covenant with Israel,
and through your servants Abraham and Sarah
gave the promise of a blessing to all nations.
Through Moses you led your people
from bondage into freedom;

through the prophets you renewed
your promise of salvation.
Therefore, with them, and with all your saints
who have served you in every age,
we give thanks and raise our voices
to proclaim the glory of your name.

All **Holy, holy, holy Lord,
God of power and might,
heaven and earth are full of your glory.
Hosanna in the highest.**

**Blessed is he who comes in the name of the Lord.
Hosanna in the highest.**

Celebrant Holy God, source of life and goodness,
all creation rightly gives you praise.
In the fulness of time,
you sent your Son Jesus Christ,
to share our human nature,
to live and die as one of us,
to reconcile us to you,
the God and Father of all.

He healed the sick
and ate and drank with outcasts and sinners;
he opened the eyes of the blind
and proclaimed the good news of your kingdom
to the poor and to those in need.
In all things he fulfilled your gracious will.

On the night he freely gave himself to death,
our Lord Jesus Christ took bread:
and when he had given thanks to you,
he broke it, and gave it to his disciples.
and said, 'Take, eat:
this is my body which is given for you.
Do this for the remembrance of me.'

After supper he took the cup of wine;
and when he had given thanks,
he gave it to them, and said,
'Drink this, all of you:
this is my blood of the new covenant,
which is shed for you and for many
for the forgiveness of sins.
Whenever you drink it,
do this for the remembrance of me.'

Gracious God,
his perfect sacrifice destroys the power
of sin and death;
by raising him to life
you give us life for evermore.
Therefore we proclaim the mystery of faith.

All   **Christ has died.**
Christ is risen.
Christ will come again.

or

Celebrant   Therefore we proclaim our hope.
All   **Dying you destroyed our death;**
rising you restored our life,
Lord Jesus, come in glory.

Celebrant   Recalling his death,
proclaiming his resurrection,
and looking for his coming again in glory,
we offer you, Father, this bread and this cup.
Send your Holy Spirit upon us
and upon these gifts,
that all who eat and drink at this table
may be one body and one holy people,
a living sacrifice in Jesus Christ, our Lord.

Through Christ, with Christ, and in Christ,
in the unity of the Holy Spirit,
all glory is yours, almighty Father,
now and for ever.

People   **Amen.**

Can3: **give our thanks] give him thanks** [and so in each Eucharistic
Prayer]
we give thanks and raise] we raise
ate and drank with] was a friend to
his perfect sacrifice...death]
        by the death of your Son
        you have destroyed the power of death,
        and
give us life] have given us life
AFTER 'evermore' ADDS '*Either Celebrant*'
Spirit upon us] Spirit upon us your servants,
and upon these gifts...Christ, our Lord]
        and upon the sacrifice of your Church,
        that we may be a holy people,
        united in the body of your Son
        Jesus Christ our Lord.

The service continues with the Lord's Prayer on page...[i.e. no. 29]

24 *EUCHARISTIC PRAYER 2*

Celebrant	The Lord be with you.
People	**And also with you.**
Celebrant	Lift up your hearts.
People	**We lift them to the Lord.**
Celebrant	Let us give thanks to the Lord our God.
People	**It is right to give our thanks and praise.**

Celebrant
We give you thanks and praise, almighty God,
through your beloved Son, Jesus Christ,
our saviour and redeemer.
He is your living Word,
through whom you have created all things.

By the power of the Holy Spirit
he took flesh of the Virgin Mary
and shared our human nature.
He lived and died as one of us,
to reconcile us to you,
the God and Father of all.

In fulfilment of your will
he stretched out his hands in suffering,
to bring release
to those who place their hope in you;
and so he won for you a holy people.

He chose to bear our griefs and sorrows
and to give up his life on the cross,
that he might shatter the chains
of evil and death
and banish the darkness of sin and despair.
By his resurrection he brings us
into the light of your presence.

Now with all creation we raise our voices
to proclaim the glory of your name.

All
**Holy, holy, holy Lord,
God of power and might,
heaven and earth are full of your glory.
Hosanna in the highest.
Blessed is he who comes in the name of the Lord.
Hosanna in the highest.**

Celebrant
Holy and gracious God,
accept our praise,

through your Son our Saviour Jesus Christ;
who on the night he was handed over
to suffering and death,
took bread and gave you thanks, saying:
'Take, and eat:
this is my body which is broken for you.'
In the same way he took the cup, saying:
'This is my blood which is shed for you.
When you do this, you do it in memory of me.'

Remembering, therefore, his death
and resurrection,
we offer you this bread and this cup,
giving thanks that you have made us worthy
to stand in your presence and serve you.

We ask you to send your Holy Spirit
upon the offering of your holy Church.
Gather into one all who share
in these sacred mysteries,
filling them with the Holy Spirit
and confirming their faith in the truth,
that together we may praise you
and give you glory
through your Servant, Jesus Christ.

All glory and honour are yours,
Father and Son,
with the Holy Spirit
in the holy Church,
now and for ever.

People   **Amen.**

[**Can3** has a rather different Eucharistic Prayer 2, though with similar roots in Hippolytus, and it can be found here in Appendix E.]

The service continues with the Lord's Prayer on page... [i.e. at no. 29]

25 *EUCHARISTIC PRAYER 3*

Celebrant   The Lord be with you.
People   **And also with you.**

Celebrant   Lift up your hearts.
People   **We lift them to the Lord.**

Celebrant   Let us give thanks to the Lord our God.
People   **It is right to give our thanks and praise.**

Here follows one of the proper prefaces on pages...
[The Proper Prefaces which are printed at no. 44 below are to be found in Appendix C.]

All

Holy, holy, holy Lord,
God of power and might,
heaven and earth are full of your glory.
Hosanna in the highest.

Blessed is he who comes in the name of the Lord.
Hosanna in the highest.

Celebrant

We give thanks to you, Lord our God,
for the goodness and love
you have made known to us in creation;
in calling Israel to be your people;
in your Word spoken through the prophets;
and above all in the Word made flesh,
Jesus your Son.
For in these last days you sent him
to be incarnate from the Virgin Mary,
to be the Saviour and Redeemer of the world.
In him, you have delivered us from evil,
and made us worthy to stand before you.
In him, you have brought us
out of error into truth,
out of sin into righteousness,
out of death into life.

On the night he was handed over
to suffering and death,
a death he freely accepted,
our Lord Jesus Christ took bread;
and when he had given thanks to you,
he broke it, and gave it to his disciples,
and said, 'Take, eat:
this is my body, which is given for you.
Do this for the remembrance of me.'

After supper he took the cup of wine;
and when he had given thanks,
he gave it to them, and said,
'Drink this, all of you:
this is my blood of the new covenant,
which is shed for you and for many
for the forgiveness of sins.
Whenever you drink it,
do this for the remembrance of me.'

Therefore, Father, according to his command,

All   **we remember his death,**
we proclaim his resurrection,
we await his coming in glory;

Celebrant   And we offer our sacrifice of praise
and thanksgiving to you, Lord of all;
presenting to you, from your creation,
this bread and this wine.

We pray you, gracious God,
to send your Holy Spirit upon these gifts
that they may be the Sacrament
of the body of Christ
and his blood of the new covenant.
Unite us to your Son in his sacrifice,
that we, made acceptable in him,
may be sanctified by the Holy Spirit.

In the fulness of time,
reconcile all things in Christ,
and make them new,
and bring us to that city of light
where you dwell with all your sons and daughters;
through Jesus Christ our Lord,
the firstborn of all creation,
the head of the Church,
and the author of our salvation;
by whom, and with whom, and in whom,
in the unity of the Holy Spirit,
all honour and glory are yours, almighty Father,
now and for ever.

People   **Amen.**

⟦**Can3** has no comparable Eucharistic Prayer, and the Prayers which follow are
numbered '3', '4', and '5', rather than '4', '5', and '6'.⟧

The service continues with the Lord's Prayer on page ... ⟦i.e. at no. 29⟧

26 EUCHARISTIC PRAYER 4

Celebrant   The Lord be with you.
People   **And also with you.**

Celebrant   Lift up your hearts.
People   **We lift them to the Lord.**

Celebrant   Let us give thanks to the Lord our God.
People   **It is right to give our thanks and praise.**

Celebrant	It is right to give you thanks and praise, O Lord, our God, sustainer of the universe, you are worthy of glory and praise.
People	**Glory to you for ever and ever.**
Celebrant	At your command all things came to be: the vast expanse of interstellar space, galaxies, suns, the planets in their courses, and this fragile earth, our island home; by your will they were created and have their being.
People	**Glory to you for ever and ever.**
Celebrant	From the primal elements you brought forth the human race, and blessed us with memory, reason, and skill; you made us the stewards of creation.
People	**Glory to you for ever and ever.**
Celebrant	But we turn against you, and betray your trust; and we turn against one another. Again and again you call us to return. Through the prophets and sages you reveal your righteous law. In the fulness of time you sent your Son, born of a woman to be our Saviour. He was wounded for our transgressions, and bruised for our iniquities. By his death he opened to us the way of freedom and peace.
People	**Glory to you for ever and ever.**
Celebrant	Therefore, we praise you, joining with the heavenly chorus, with prophets, apostles, and martyrs, and with those in every generation who have looked to you in hope, to proclaim with them your glory, in their unending hymn:
All	**Holy, holy, holy Lord, God of power and might, heaven and earth are full of your glory. Hosanna in the highest. Blessed is he who comes in the name of the Lord. Hosanna in the highest.**

Celebrant	Blessed are you, Lord our God,
	for sending us Jesus, the Christ,
	who on the night he was handed over
	to suffering and death, took bread,
	said the blessing, broke the bread,
	gave it to his friends, and said,
	'Take this and eat it:
	this is my body which is given for you.
	do this for the remembrance of me.'
	In the same way, after supper,
	he took the cup of wine;
	he gave you thanks, and said,
	'Drink this, all of you:
	this is my blood of the new covenant,
	which is shed for you and for many
	for the forgiveness of sins.
	Whenever you drink it,
	do this for the remembrance of me.'
People	**Glory to you for ever and ever.**
Celebrant	Gracious God, we recall the death
	of your Son Jesus Christ,
	we proclaim his resurrection and ascension,
	and we look with expectation for his coming
	as Lord of all the nations.
	We who have been redeemed by him,
	and made a new people by water and the Spirit,
	now bring you these gifts.
	Send your Holy Spirit upon us
	and upon this offering of your church,
	that we who eat and drink at this holy table
	may share the divine life of Christ our Lord.
People	**Glory to you for ever and ever.**
Celebrant	Pour out your Spirit upon the whole earth
	and make it your new creation.
	Gather your Church together
	from the ends of the earth into your kingdom,
	where peace and justice are revealed,
	that we, with all your people,
	of every language, race, and nation,
	may share the banquet you have promised;
	through Christ, with Christ, and in Christ,

all honour and glory are yours,
creator of all.

People **Glory to you for ever and ever. Amen.**

Can3: to give you thanks and praise] and a good and joyful thing, to
give thanks to you.

be our Saviour...he opened to us] fulfil your law, to open to us
Blessed are you...

the blessing] And so Father, we who have been redeemed by him,
and made a new people by water and the Spirit,
now bring you these gifts.
Sanctify them by your Holy Spirit,
to be for us the body and blood of Christ.
On the night he was handed over
to suffering and death,
a death he freely accepted,
our Lord Jesus Christ took bread,
said the blessing
...creator of all] you drink it
do this for the remembrance of me.'
Father, we recall the death of your Son Jesus Christ,
we proclaim his resurrection and ascension,
and we look with expectation for his coming
as Lord of all the nations.

People **Glory to you for ever and ever.**

Celebrant You have counted us worthy, in union with Christ
to offer this sacrifice of praise.
To you be all praise and glory
beyond all times and places, now and for ever.

The service continues with the Lord's Prayer on page... [i.e. no. 29]

27 EUCHARISTIC PRAYER 5

*Other refrains than, '***Glory to you for ever and ever***', may be used
with this prayer or the refrain may be omitted.*

Celebrant	The Lord be with you.
People	**And also with you.**
Celebrant	Lift up your hearts.
People	**We lift them to the Lord.**
Celebrant	Let us give thanks to the Lord our God.
People	**It is right to give our thanks and praise.**
Celebrant	We give you thanks and praise, almighty God,
	for the gift of a world full of wonder,
	and for our life which comes from you.
	By your power you sustain the universe.
People	**Glory to you for ever and ever.**
Celebrant	You created us to love you with all our heart,
	and to love each other as ourselves,
	but we rebel against you by the evil that we do.

In Jesus, your Son,
you bring healing to our world,
and gather us into one great family.
Therefore, with all who serve you
on earth and in heaven,
we praise your wonderful name, as we sing (say):

All **Holy, holy, holy Lord,**
God of power and might,
heaven and earth are full of your glory,
Hosanna in the highest.

Blessed is he who comes in the name of the Lord,
Hosanna in the highest!

Celebrant We give you thanks and praise, loving Father,
because in sending Jesus, your Son, to us
you showed us how much you love us.
He cares for the poor and the hungry.
He suffers with the sick and the rejected.

Betrayed and forsaken, he did not strike back,
but overcame hatred with love.
On the cross
he defeated the power of sin and death.
By raising him from the dead
you show us the power of your love
to bring new life to all your people.

People **Glory to you for ever and ever.**

Celebrant On the night before he gave up his life for us,
Jesus, at supper with his friends,
took bread, gave thanks to you,
broke it, and gave it to them, saying,
'Take this, all of you, and eat it:
this is my body which is given for you.'

After supper, Jesus took the cup of wine,
said the blessing, gave it to his friends,
and said, 'Drink this all of you:
this is the cup of my blood,
the blood of the new and eternal covenant,
which is shed for you and for many,
so that sins may be forgiven.
Do this in memory of me.'

People **Glory to you for ever and ever.**

Celebrant   Gracious God,
with this bread and wine
we celebrate the death and resurrection of Jesus,
and we offer ourselves to you in him.
Send your Holy Spirit on us and on these gifts,
that we may know the presence of Jesus
in the breaking of bread,
and share in the life
of the family of your children.

People   **Glory to you for ever and ever.**

Father, you call us to be your servants;
fill us with the courage and love of Jesus
that all the world may gather in joy
at the table of your kingdom.

We sing your praise, almighty Father,
through Jesus, our Lord,
in the power of the Holy Spirit,
now and for ever.

People   **Glory to you for ever and ever. Amen.**

[Can3, whilst like this Prayer, differs widely. There is no opening rubric. The parts which differ are shown here in such a way that they can be fitted into the Prayer above:

By your power you sustain the universe;
through Jesus, your Son,
you gather us into one great family.
Therefore, with all who serve you
on earth and in heaven,
we praise your wonderful name, as we say,

All
Holy, holy,...[ICET 5(a) and 5(b)]...**highest**

Celebrant
We give you thanks and praise, loving Father,
because you sent Jesus, your son, to us.
He opens our eyes and hearts.
He shows us how much you love us,
and how we can love you,
and love one another.

People
We praise you, we bless you, we thank you.

Celebrant
He heals the sick.
He is a friend to everyone in need.
He forgives those who do wrong,
and teaches us to forgive each other.
He comes to take away sin and hate.
People
We praise you, ...thank you.

Celebrant
On the night...in memory of me.'
Jesus gave his life for us;

therefore we proclaim the mystery of faith.

All
Christ has died.
Christ is risen.
Christ will come again.

Celebrant
Father, you raised Jesus from death to life for us;
Send your Holy Spirit on us,
and on these gifts which we offer you.
Give us a share in your life,
that we may live in the joy of
your family for ever.

People
We praise you, ...thank you.

Celebrant
We are filled with wonder
when we see what you do for us,
through Jesus, our Lord.
In the power of the Holy Spirit,
with the whole company of earth and heaven,
we sing your praise, almighty Father,
now and for ever.

People
Amen.
Come, Lord Jesus,
and fill us with your love.]

The service continues with the Lord's Prayer on page...[i.e. at no. 29]

28 EUCHARISTIC PRAYER 6

Celebrant	The Lord be with you.
People	**And also with you.**
Celebrant	Lift up your hearts.
People	**We lift them to the Lord.**
Celebrant	Let us give thanks to the Lord our God.
People	**It is right to give our thanks and praise.**

Celebrant   It is right to glorify you, Father,
and to give you thanks;
for you alone are God, living and true,
dwelling in light inaccessible
from before time and for ever.
Fountain of life and source of all goodness,
you made all things and fill them with your blessing;
you created them to rejoice
in the splendour of your radiance.
Countless throngs of angels stand before you
to serve you night and day,
and, beholding your presence,
they offer you unceasing praise.
Joining with them, and giving voice
to every creature under heaven,
we acclaim you, and glorify your name,
as we sing (say):

All   **Holy, holy, holy Lord,
God of power and might,
heaven and earth are full of your glory.
Hosanna in the highest.**

**Blessed is he who comes in the name of the Lord.
Hosanna in the highest.**

Celebrant   We acclaim you, holy Lord, glorious in power;
your mighty works reveal your wisdom and love.
You formed us in your own image,
giving the whole world into our care,
so that, in obedience to you, our Creator,
we might rule and serve all your creatures.
When our disobedience took us far from you,
you did not abandon us to the power of death.
In your mercy you came to our help,
so that in seeking you we might find you.

Again and again you called us
into covenant with you,
and through the prophets you taught us
to hope for salvation.
Father, you loved the world so much
that in the fulness of time
you sent your only Son to be our Saviour.
Incarnate by the Holy Spirit, born of the Virgin Mary,
he lived as one of us, yet without sin.
To the poor he proclaimed
the good news of salvation;
to prisoners, freedom; to the sorrowful, joy.
To fulfil your purpose he gave himself up to death;
And, rising from the grave, destroyed death
and made the whole creation new.
And that we might live no longer for ourselves,
but for him who died and rose for us,
he sent the Holy Spirit,
his own first gift for those who believe,
to complete his work in the world,
and to bring to fulfillment the sanctification of all.
When the hour had come
for him to be glorified by you, his heavenly Father,
having loved his own who were in the world,
he loved them to the end:
at supper with them he took bread;
and when he had given thanks to you,
he broke it, and gave it to his disciples,
and said, 'Take, eat:
this is my body, which is given for you.
Do this for the remembrance of me.'
After supper he took the cup of wine;
and when he had given thanks,
he gave it to them, and said,
'Drink this, all of you:
this is my blood of the new covenant,
which is shed for you and for many
for the forgiveness of sins.
Whenever you drink it,
do this for the remembrance of me.'
Father,
we now celebrate the memorial of our redemption,

recalling Christ's death and descent among the dead,
proclaiming his resurrection
and ascension to your right hand,
awaiting his coming in glory;
and offering to you from the gifts you have given us,
this bread, and this cup,
we praise you and we bless you.

All   **We praise you, we bless you,
we give thanks to you,
and we pray to you, Lord our God.**

Celebrant   Father,
we pray that in your goodness and mercy
your Holy Spirit may descend upon us,
and upon these gifts,
sanctifying them and showing them
to be holy gifts for your holy people,
the bread of life and the cup of salvation,
the body and blood of your Son Jesus Christ.
Grant that all who share this bread and this cup
may become one body and one spirit,
a living sacrifice in Christ to the praise of your Name.

Remember, Lord,
your one holy catholic and apostolic Church,
redeemed by the blood of your Christ.
Reveal its unity, guard its faith,
and preserve it in peace.
[Remember (*NN* and) all who minister
in your Church.]
[Remember all your people,
and those who seek your truth.]
[Remember _____.]
[Remember all who have died in the peace of Christ,
and those whose faith is known to you alone;
bring them into the place of eternal joy and light.]
And grant that we may find our inheritance
with the blessed Virgin Mary,
with Partriarchs, Prophets, Apostles and Martyrs
(with _____), and all the saints
who have found favour with you in ages past.

We praise you in union with them
and give you glory

through your Son Jesus Christ our Lord.
Through Christ, and with Christ, and in Christ,
all honour and glory are yours,
almighty God and Father,
in the unity of the Holy Spirit,
for ever and ever.

People　　**Amen.**

29 *THE LORD'S PRAYER*

Celebrant　　As our Saviour taught us, let us pray,
All　　**Our Father in heaven** ... ⟦ICET 1⟧ ... **for ever. Amen.**

or

Celebrant　　And now, as our Saviour Christ has taught us, we are bold
　　　　　　to say,
All　　**Our Father, who art** ... ⟦MAL CF 1⟧ ... **and ever. Amen.**
　　　　in earth] on earth
　　　　them that] those who

Silence

30 *THE BREAKING OF THE BREAD*

*The celebrant breaks the consecrated bread for distribution, and may say
one of the following.*

1. *Celebrant*　　'I am the bread of life', says the Lord.
　　　　　　　'Whoever comes to me will never be hungry;
　　　　　　　whoever believes in me will never thirst.'
　　All　　**Taste and see that the Lord is good;
　　　　happy are they who trust in him!**
　　　　Can3: Whoever ... whoever] He who ... he who

2. *Celebrant*　　We break this bread to share in the body of Christ.
　　All　　**We, being many, are one body,
　　　　for we all share in the one bread.**

　　or

3. *Celebrant*　　Creator of all,
　　　　　　　you gave us golden fields of wheat,
　　　　　　　whose many grains we have gathered
　　　　　　　and made into this one bread.
　　All　　**So may your Church be gathered
　　　　from the ends of the earth
　　　　into your kingdom.**

or

4 *Celebrant* 'I am the bread which has come
down from heaven', says the Lord.

All **Give us this bread for ever.**

Celebrant 'I am the vine, you are the branches'.

All **May we dwell in him, as he lives in us.**

⟦Nos. 5–8 which follow are for high seasons, and are to be found here in Appendix D.
Can3 prints all eight without numbers⟧

31 *THE COMMUNION*

The celebrant invites the people to share in communion and may say

Celebrant The gifts of God for the people of God.
People **Thanks be to God.**

> **Can3**: *and may say*] OM
> *People* **Thanks be to God**] OM

The celebrant and people then receive communion.

> **Can3**: OMITS

The sacrament is given with the following words.

The body of Christ (given for you).
The blood of Christ (shed for you).

or The body of Christ, the bread of heaven.
The blood of Christ, the cup of salvation.

The communicant responds each time, **Amen.**

> **Can3**: ADDS *and then receives*

*During the Breaking of the Bread and the Communion, psalms, hymns,
and anthems such as those on pp...* ⟦i.e. at no. 45⟧ *may be sung.*

> **Can3**: *such as...sung*] *such as the following may be sung. Alleluia is omitted
> during Lent.*
> **(Alleluia) Christ our Passover is sacrificed for us;
> therefore let us keep the feast (Alleluia).**
> **Lamb of God...**⟦ICET 8(b)⟧**...us peace.**
> sins] sin

At the conclusion of the communion, silence may be kept.

> **Can3**: OMITS

32 *PRAYER AFTER COMMUNION*

Celebrant Let us pray.

*Standing the community prays in silence. The celebrant may say the
Prayer after Communion appointed for the day.*

At the conclusion of the prayer the congregation says, **Amen.**

33 *Then the following doxology may be said.*

Celebrant Glory to God
All **whose power, working in us,**
can do infinitely more
than we can ask or imagine.
Glory to God from generation to generation,
in the Church and in Christ Jesus,
for ever and ever. Amen.

Can3: **God from]** him from

34 *Or instead of the Prayer after Communion and the doxology, the*
following may be said.

Celebrant All your works praise you, O Lord.
All **And your faithful servants bless you.**

Gracious God
we thank you for feeding us
with the body and blood of your Son, Jesus Christ.
May we who share his body...⟦CF 8⟧...our Lord.
Amen.

in this hope...grasped] firm in the hope you have set before us
so] so that

Can3: *instead...doxology]* OM
said] used
All your works...**your Son, Jesus Christ]**
Celebrant Bless the Lord for he is gracious,
All **For his mercy endures for ever.**
Celebrant Father of all,
People **We give you thanks and praise**...⟦CF 8 with
variants shown above but reading **'Christ's**
body'⟧...**our Lord. Amen**

35 *THE DISMISSAL*

The celebrant may bless the people.
The deacon, or other leader, dismisses the people, saying in these or similar
words

Can3: *in these or similar words]* OM

Leader Go forth in the name of Christ.
People **Thanks be to God.**

or

Leader Go in peace to love and serve the Lord.
People **Thanks be to God.**

or

Leader Go forth into the world,
rejoicing in the power of the Spirit.
People **Thanks be to God.**

or

| Leader | Let us bless the Lord. |
| People | **Thanks be to God.** |

From Easter Day through the Day of Pentecost, Alleluia *is added to the dismissal and the people's response.*

[[Can3 has an Appendix of 'The Prayers of the People' including three forms, based on **Amer1/1–3/3**, Forms I, VI, and II (this last expanded by provision of substantial prayers in the various sections). Form I is virtually identical to **Can1A**, no. 12, below. The forms are not reprinted here in **Can4**, but are to be found elsewhere in the Book]]

A PENITENTIAL ORDER

36 *This rite is appropriate for use before the eucharist, on Sundays during Lent. It may also be used on other occasions, or as a separate service.*

37 *GREETING*

All stand. The presiding celebrant greets the community.

Celebrant	The grace of our Lord Jesus Christ,
	and the love of God,
	and the fellowship of the Holy Spirit,
	be with you all.
People	**And also with you.**

| Celebrant | Bless the Lord who forgives all our sins. |
| People | **His mercy endures for ever.** |

Can3: *The presiding...***with you]**   OM

38 *The following prayer may be said.*

| Celebrant | Almighty God, |
| All | **to you...**[[CF 1]]**...our Lord. Amen.** |

whom] you
hid] hidden
Can3: OMITS SECTION

39 *THE WORD OF GOD*

A suitable passage of Scripture, such as one of the following may be read.

Exodus 20. 1–17	*Matthew 9. 9–13*	*Luke 15. 11–32*
Deuteronomy 5. 6–21	*Matthew 18. 15–20*	*Luke 19. 1–10*
Isaiah 55. 6–7	*Matthew 25. 31–46*	*John 8. 1–11*
Ezekiel 11. 19–20	*Mark 12. 28–34*	*Romans 6. 3–11*
Matthew 5. 13–16	*Luke 15. 1–7 or 8–10*	*1 John 1. 8–9*

Can3: *may be read]*   OM

Reader   A reading from...

At the conclusion of the passage, the reader says,

The Word of the Lord.

People   **Thanks be to God.**

If this order is used as a separate service, a sermon may follow.

Can3: *If this...may follow]* OM

CONFESSION AND ABSOLUTION

40 *The people are invited to confession in these or similar words.*

Can3: OMITS

Celebrant   Dear friends in Christ,
God is steadfast in love and infinite in mercy;
he welcomes sinners and invites them to his table.
Let us confess our sins,
confident in God's forgiveness.

Can3: *love...mercy] his love...his mercy*
God's] his

Silence is kept.

41 *Celebrant*   Most merciful God,

People   **we confess that we have sinned against you
in thought, word, and deed,
by what we have done,
and by what we have left undone.
we have not loved you with our whole heart;
we have not loved our neighbours as ourselves.
We are truly sorry and we humbly repent.
For the sake of your Son Jesus Christ
have mercy on us and forgive us,
that we may delight in your will,
and walk in your ways,
to the glory of your name. Amen.**

42 *The celebrant stands and says,*

Almighty God have mercy on you,
forgive you all your sins
through the Lord Jesus Christ,
strengthen you in all goodness,
and by the power of the Holy Spirit
keep you in eternal life.

People   **Amen.**

43 *When this order is used before the eucharist, the eucharist begins with an act of praise or the Collect of the Day. When used separately, it concludes with suitable prayers, and the Grace or a blessing.*

> **Can3**: before] *at the beginning of*
> *an act of praise or*] OM
> [**Can3** has an Appendix of 'Canticles'. They are not reprinted here.]

PROPER PREFACES

44 [The Proper Prefaces which are printed here are to be found in Appendix C]

ANTHEMS TO BE SUNG DURING THE BREAKING OF BREAD AND COMMUNION

[This Appendix is absent from **Can3**]

45 *These anthems are of varying length, and should be chosen on the basis of the time required. Some of them may be sung responsively between cantor and congregation or choir as indicated.*

Christ our Passover...[see no. 31, **Can3**]...**keep the feast.**
The bread...[see **EngA**, no. 43, altered]...**the one bread.**
Lamb of God...[ICET 8(b)]...us peace.

[Various similar scriptural anthems follow. There is also provision to use the 'Fraction Sentences' (see no. 30), and particular verses of scripture, with some seasonal suggestions from the Psalms]

THE TRADITIONAL LANGUAGE RITE IN THE CANADIAN *BOOK OF ALTERNATIVE SERVICES* 1985 (Can1A)

[This rite is bound in the *Book of Alternative Services* after **Can4**, and thus follows it here. References to 'the Book' are to the *Book of Alternative Services*. The numbering is editorial.]

THE HOLY EUCHARIST

A FORM IN THE LANGUAGE OF THE BOOK OF COMMON PRAYER 1962
CONCERNING THE SERVICE

Notes found on pages... [i.e. at the beginning of **Can4** on pages 93–94 above] *apply to this service also.*

The celebrant should pick up and hold the bread and the cup at appropriate points in the institution narrative, but the bread should be broken after the Lord's Prayer.

If the consecrated bread or wine is insufficient for the number of communicants, the celebrant consecrates more, saying:

We thank thee, heavenly Father, for thy saving love, and we pray thee to bless and sanctify this bread (wine) with thy Word and Holy Spirit, that it also may be the sacrament of the precious Body (Blood) of thy Son, our Lord Jesus Christ. **Amen.**

THE GATHERING OF THE COMMUNITY

1 *All stand.*   *The presiding celebrant greets the community.*

The grace of our Lord Jesus Christ,
and the love of God,
and the fellowship of the Holy Spirit,
be with you all.

People   **And with thy spirit.**

Or, from Easter Day through the Day of Pentecost:

Celebrant   Alleluia. Christ is risen.
People   **The Lord is risen indeed. Alleluia.**
Celebrant   May his grace and joy be with you.
People   **May he fill our hearts with joy.**

2 *Then may be said by the celebrant alone or with the people:*

Almighty God, unto whom all hearts be open...⟦CF 1⟧
...our Lord. **Amen.**

your...you] thy...thee THROUGHOUT

3 *Then one or more of the following may be said or sung.*

It is appropriate that the hymn Gloria in Excelsis be used during the Christmas season and from Easter Day through the Day of Pentecost, but not during the seasons of Advent and Lent. During Lent it is appropriate that the Kyrie Eleison or the Trisagion be used. The Kyrie Eleison may be sung in three-fold, six-fold or nine-fold form. The Trisagion may be sung three times or antiphonally.

1. *The Summary of the Law:*

Our Lord Jesus Christ said: Hear, O Israel...⟦**MAL** CF 4(b)⟧...the Law and the Prophets.

first] first and great
namely this] unto it
There is...than these] OM

People   **Lord, have mercy upon us, and write both these thy laws in our hearts, we beseech thee.**

2. *The Decalogue (see page...*⟦i.e. no 33 below⟧*)*

3. *Kyrie* :

Lord, have mercy upon us.	*or*	**Kyrie eleison.**
Christ, have mercy upon us.		**Christe eleison.**
Lord, have mercy upon us.		**Kyrie eleison.**

4. *Gloria in Excelsis* :

Glory be to God on high...⟦**MAL** CF 5⟧...**the Father. Amen.**
sins] sin THROUGHOUT
Thou that takest...upon us] OM ⟦See **FAL**, p. 62, footnote⟧

5. *Trisagion*

Holy God,
holy and mighty,
holy immortal One,
have mercy upon us.

4 THE COLLECT OF THE DAY

The celebrant shall say

Let us pray.

The community may pray silently. The celebrant then sings or says the collect, after which the people respond, **Amen.**

THE PROCLAMATION OF THE WORD

THE READINGS

5 *A first reading as appointed.*

Reader A reading from...

At the conclusion of the passage, the reader says,

The Word of the Lord.

People **Thanks be to God.**

6 *Silence may be kept. Then shall follow a psalm as appointed. On Sundays and major festivals a second reading as appointed is read.*

Reader A reading from...

At the conclusion of the passage the reader says,

The Word of the Lord.

People **Thanks be to God.**

7 *Silence may be kept. A psalm, canticle, hymn, or anthem may follow. All stand for the Gospel.*

The Lord be with you

People **And with thy spirit.**

Reader The Holy Gospel of our Lord Jesus Christ according to...

People **Glory be to thee, O Lord.**

At the conclusion of the Gospel, the reader says

The Gospel of Christ.

People **Praise be to thee, O Christ.**

8 *THE SERMON*

A silence for reflection may follow. The Nicene Creed shall be said on major festivals. On Sundays either the Nicene Creed or the Apostles' Creed (page ... [[*i.e. at no. 34.*]]) *is appropriate.*

9 *THE NICENE CREED*

I believe in one God... [[**MAL** CF 6]] **...to come. Amen.**

his Father] the Father
by whom] through whom
us men] us

10 *THE PRAYERS OF THE PEOPLE*

A deacon or lay members of the community may lead the Prayers of the People. Intercessions and thanksgivings may be used according to local custom and need. All or portions of either of the following forms may be used.

11 *Leader*   Let us pray for the Church and the world.
            Almighty and everlasting God... [[as in **CanR**, **LIE**
            pp. 139–140]] ...without end. **Amen.**

            to accept our alms and oblations, and]   OM
            THE SECOND AND THIRD PARAGRAPHS ARE INTERCHANGED
            Ghost] Spirit

or

12 *Leader*   In peace let us pray to the Lord.
   People   **Lord, have mercy.** [[and so after each bidding]]
   Leader   For peace from on high
            and for our salvation,
            let us pray to the Lord.

   Leader   For the peace of the whole world,
            for the welfare of the holy Church of God,
            and for the unity of all,
            let us pray to the Lord.

   Leader   For our bishops,
            and for all the clergy and people,
            let us pray to the Lord.

   Leader   For Elizabeth our Queen,
            for the leaders of the nations,
            and for all in authority,
            let us pray to the Lord.

   Leader   For this city (town, village, etc.)
            for every city and community,
            and for those who live in them in faith,
            let us pray to the Lord.

Leader	For good weather, and for abundant harvests for all to share, let us pray to the Lord.
Leader	For those who travel by land, water, or air, for the sick and the suffering (especially...) for prisoners and captives, and for their safety, health and salvation, let us pray to the Lord.
Leader	For our deliverance from all affliction, strife, and need, let us pray to the Lord.
Leader	For the absolution and remission of our sins and offences, let us pray to the Lord.
Leader	For all who have died (*especially...*) let us pray to the Lord.
Leader	Remembering (.......*and*) all the saints, we commit ourselves, one another, and our whole life to Christ our God.
People	**To thee, O Christ.**
Leader	Almighty God, who hast...⟦St. Chrysostom's as in 1662 Morning prayer, but with 'hear' for 'grant'⟧...life everlasting; for thou, Father, art good and loving, and we glorify thee through thy Son Jesus Christ our Lord, in the Holy Spirit, now and for ever.
People	**Amen.**

13 *CONFESSION AND ABSOLUTION*

A Confession of Sin may be made here if a penitential rite has not been used earlier, or if penitential intercessions were not used in the Prayers of the People. The celebrant or other person may say one or more of the following :

> Hear what comfortable...⟦**MAL** CF 12⟧...for our sins: and not for ours only, but also for the sins of the whole world. (1 *St. John* 2.1, 2)
>
> travail] labour
> so God] God so
> everlasting] eternal
> all men] all
> Jesus Christ] Christ Jesus ⟦see **FAL**, p. 422, footnote⟧
> any man] anyone

14 *Then shall be said :*

> Let us humbly confess our sins to Almighty God.

or　　Ye that do...⟦**MAL** CF 9⟧...confession to Almighty God.
　　　　a new life] the new life

15 *Silence is kept. The celebrant and people say together:*

    Almighty God...⟦MAL CF 10⟧...our Lord. Amen.

    Judge] and judge
    men] people
    bewail] confess
    Provoking...against us] OM
    The remembrance...intolerable.] OM
    Have mercy upon us] OMIT ONCE

16 *Celebrant*   Almighty God...⟦**MAL** CF 11⟧...our Lord. **Amen.**

THE PEACE

17 *Celebrant*   The peace of the Lord be always with you;
   People   **And with thy spirit.**

Then all may greet one another in the name of the Lord.

THE CELEBRATION OF THE EUCHARIST
THE PREPARATION OF THE GIFTS

18 *During the Offertory a hymn, psalm or anthem may be sung. Representatives of the people may present the gifts of bread and wine for the Eucharist, with money and other gifts for the needs and responsibilities of the church, to the deacon or celebrant before the altar.*

THE PRAYER OVER THE GIFTS

19 *When the gifts have been prepared, the celebrant may say the Prayer over the Gifts, following which the people say,* **Amen.**

THE GREAT THANKSGIVING

20 *One of the following Eucharistic Prayers shall be used.*

21 *Eucharistic Prayer A*

⟦There follows the Eucharistic Prayer of **CanR**, **LIE** nos. 34–39, pages 140–142, without any rubrics, except as follows:

In the opening dialogue: '*Celebrant*'/'*People*'
Thereafter: '*Celebrant*'/'*All*'
Re Proper Prefaces: '*Here follows one of the Proper Prefaces on pages...*
   ⟦i.e. no. 35 below – the Proper Prefaces are described here in Appendix C⟧
After 'he hath commanded':
   '*All*   **We praise thee, we bless thee, we thank thee,**
         and we pray to thee, Lord our God.
   Celebrant   And we entirely desire...'⟧

The service continues with the Lord's Prayer on page... ⟦i.e. at no. 23⟧

or

22 *Eucharistic Prayer B*

⟦The Dialogue, Preface, Sanctus, and Benedictus Qui Venit are exactly as in Eucharistic Prayer A above. The Prayer proceeds:⟧

  Celebrant   All glory be to thee, O Lord our God, who didst make us in thine own image; and, of thy tender mercy, didst give thine only Son Jesus Christ to take our nature upon him, and to suffer death upon the Cross for our redemption. He made there a full and perfect sacrifice for the whole world; and did institute, and in his holy Gospel command us to continue, a perpetual memory of that his precious death and sacrifice, until his coming again.

Who, in the same night that he was betrayed, took bread; and when he had given thanks to thee, he broke it, and gave it to his disciples, saying, 'Take, eat, this is my Body, which is given for you. Do this in remembrance of me.'

Likewise, after supper, he took the cup; and when he had given thanks, he gave it to them, saying, 'Drink this, all of you; for this is my Blood of the New Covenant, which is shed for you, and for many, for the remission of sins. Do this, as oft as ye shall drink it, in remembrance of me.'

Wherefore, O Lord and heavenly Father, we thy people do celebrate and make, with these thy holy gifts which we now offer unto thee, the memorial thy Son hath commanded us to make; having in remembrance his blessed passion and precious death, his mighty resurrection and glorious ascension; and looking for his coming again with power and great glory.

And we most humbly beseech thee, O merciful Father, to hear us, and, with thy Word and Holy Spirit, to bless and sanctify these gifts of bread and wine, that they may be unto us the Body and Blood of thy dearly-beloved Son Jesus Christ.

All **We praise thee, we bless thee, we thank thee, and we pray to thee, Lord our God.**

Celebrant And we earnestly desire thy fatherly goodness to accept this our sacrifice of praise and thanksgiving, whereby we offer and present unto thee, O Lord, our selves, our souls and bodies. Grant, we beseech thee, that all who partake of this Holy Communion may worthily receive the most precious Body and Blood of thy Son Jesus Christ, and be filled with thy grace and heavenly benediction; and also that we and all thy whole Church may be made one body with him, that he may dwell in us, and we in him; through the same Jesus Christ our Lord;

By whom, and with whom, and in whom, in the unity of the Holy Spirit all honour and glory be unto thee, O Father Almighty, world without end. **Amen.**

23 *Celebrant*   And now, as our Saviour Christ hath taught us, we are bold
to say:

All   **Our Father, who art...⟦MAL CF 1⟧...and ever.
Amen.**

in earth] on earth

Silence

THE BREAKING OF THE BREAD

24 *Then the celebrant breaks the consecrated bread. Then may be said:*

All   **We do not...⟦MAL CF 13⟧...he in us. Amen.**
our sinful...blood, and that] OM

THE COMMUNION

25 *The celebrant and people receive the Communion in both kinds. At the
distribution the minister says to each communicant:*

    The Body...⟦**MAL** CF 15⟧...with thanksgiving).

    The Blood...⟦**MAL** CF 16⟧...be thankful).

    preserve] (preserve IN EACH SET OF WORDS

or   The Body of Christ, the bread of heaven.
The Blood of Christ, the cup of salvation.

The communicant responds each time, **Amen.**

26 *During the Breaking of the Bread and the Communion, psalms, hymns and
anthems such as the following may be sung or said:*

Celebrant   (Alleluia!) Christ our Passover is sacrificed for us;

People   **Therefore, let us keep the feast. (Alleluia!)**
O Lamb of God...⟦MAL CF 14⟧...thy peace.
sins] sin

At the conclusion of the Communion, silence may be kept.

PRAYER AFTER COMMUNION

27 *Celebrant*   Let us pray
*The celebrant may say the Prayer after Communion appointed for the day.
At the conclusion of the prayer the congregation says,* **Amen.**

28 *Then the following doxology may be said.*

Celebrant   Glory to God
All   **whose power, working in us,**
can do infinitely more
than we can ask or imagine.
Glory to God from generation to generation,
in the Church and in Christ Jesus,
for ever and ever. Amen.

29 *If Eucharistic Prayer A has been used, the following prayer may be said instead of the Prayer after Communion and the doxology.*

    All   **Almighty and everliving...⟦CanR no. 45, LiE p. 143⟧ ...Spirit, be all honour and glory, world without end. Amen.**

30 *If Eucharistic Prayer B has been used, the following prayer may be said instead of the Prayer after Communion and the doxology.*

    All   **We most heartily thank thee,**
                almighty and everliving God,
                that thou dost graciously feed us,
                in these holy mysteries
                ...⟦MAL CF 18⟧...without end. Amen.

and dost assure] assuring
very members] living members
incorporate in the mystical body of thy Son] of his mystical Body
by the merits...dear Son] OM
most humbly] humbly
Ghost] Spirit

31 *The celebrant may bless the people*

    Celebrant   The peace of God, which passeth...⟦CF 10⟧...always. **Amen.**

among] amongst

THE DISMISSAL

32 *Then the deacon or the celebrant says*

                Go forth in the name of Christ.
    People   **Thanks be to God.**
    or
    Leader   Go in peace...⟦as in **Can4**, no. 35⟧... *response.*

THE DECALOGUE

33 God spake these words...⟦**MAL** CF 3, omitting bracketed portions⟧... **we beseech thee.**

I am the Lord thy God] ADD who brought thee out of the land of Egypt, out of the house of bondage
Six days...Sabbath of the Lord thy God] OM
false witness] ADD against thy neighbour

THE APOSTLES' CREED

34 ⟦The text in bold type follows the text in 1662 Morning Prayer.⟧

PROPER PREFACES

35 ⟦The Proper Prefaces which are printed here are described in Appendix C⟧

CHAPTER 6

THE EPISCOPAL CHURCH IN THE UNITED STATES OF AMERICA

THE programme for a definitive new Book of Common Prayer in ECUSA was laid out in **FAL** on page 129, and duly came to pass. The Standing Liturgical Commission produced a complete draft, published in limp blue covers, on 2 February 1976 (and known, because of the day, as the 'groundhog' Book). The 1976 General Convention at Minneapolis accepted it in principle in the House of Deputies on 17 September. Voting was by orders and dioceses – clergy 107 to 3 (3 divided), and laity 90 to 12 (9 divided). The Bishops voted on 20 September for certain amendments – particularly to delete the *Filioque* which the Deputies had restored, and to print 'Amen' at the end of the eucharistic prayers in capitals. The next day the Deputies refused the first change, and accepted the second, and the Bishops then climbed down over the *Filioque*, and the Book was accepted for use from Advent 1976 as an alternative to the 1928 BCP. It was duly published, as the 'Proposed' Book of Common Prayer, in February 1977.

At the 1979 Convention, in Denver, on 11 September the House of Bishops sent the Book to the Deputies to be 'adopted and declared as the Book of Common Prayer' (with 4 votes recorded against). On 14 September the Deputies, voting by orders and dioceses, concurred – clergy 107 to 1 (2 divided); laity 99 to 2 (3 divided) – and 'Proposed' was eliminated from the title-page. The 1928 Book was thus discontinued, except for limited further use of 'liturgical texts from the 1928 [BCP]' under prescribed conditions. The new eucharistic rites are retouched forms of **Amer1**, **Amer2**, and **Amer3**, in **FAL**. Exclusive language has been purged, and many other minor changes made. The Book has been officially translated into French and Spanish.

THE RITES FROM THE AMERICAN *BOOK OF COMMON PRAYER* 1977 (Amer1–1, Amer2–2, Amer3-3)

[The numbering below is editorial. Considerable reference is made to forms published in **FAL**. The BCP titles at the foot of pages distinguish between, e.g., '*Penitential Order I*' and '*Holy Eucharist I*', and that is followed here. '1976' indicates the draft Book, but the capitalized '*AMEN*' at the end of the eucharistic prayers (and only there), which was not in '1976', has not been distinguished here under the editorial conventions. American spelling has been retained.]

THE HOLY EUCHARIST

THE LITURGY FOR THE PROCLAMATION OF THE WORD OF GOD AND CELEBRATION OF THE HOLY COMMUNION

1 〚After this general title comes first 'An Exhortation' hardly changed from that at no. 43 in **FAL.** Then comes 'Decalogue I', i.e. a Decalogue in traditional form with traditional responses. Then 'A Penitential Order: Rite One': this has opening greetings as at nos. 3–4 below, then the option of using either or both of the Exhortation and the Decalogue, then a choice of sentences as in **FAL**, no. 46 (but with the Lord's Summary of the Law first); the deacon or celebrant calls the worshippers to confess their sins, which they do with either no. 18 below or the confession (very slightly altered) from 1662 Morning Prayer; the Absolution is as at no. 49 in **FAL**; final rubrics provide for a deacon to say 'us' 'our' in the Absolution, and for continuing into the eucharist – or for the conclusion when the Penitential Order stands on its own.〛

2 ## CONCERNING THE CELEBRATION

It is the bishop's prerogative, when present, to be the principal celebrant at the Lord's Table, and to preach the Gospel.

At all celebrations of the Liturgy, it is fitting that the principal celebrant, whether bishop or priest, be assisted by other priests, and by deacons and lay persons.

It is appropriate that the other priests present stand with the celebrant at the Altar, and join in the consecration of the gifts, in breaking the Bread, and in distributing Communion.

A deacon should read the Gospel and may lead the Prayers of the People. Deacons should also serve at the Lord's Table, preparing and placing on it the offerings of bread and wine, and assisting in the ministration of the Sacrament to the people. In the absence of a deacon, these duties may be performed by an assisting priest.

Lay persons appointed by the celebrant should normally be assigned the reading of the Lessons which precede the Gospel, and may lead the Prayers of the People.

Morning or Evening Prayer may be used in place of all that precedes the Peace and the Offertory, provided that a lesson from the Gospel is always included, and that the intercessions conform to the directions given for the Prayers of the People.

Additional Directions are on page... 〚i.e. no. 108 〛

THE HOLY EUCHARIST: RITE ONE 〚Amer1–1〛
THE WORD OF GOD

3 *A hymn, psalm, or anthem may be sung.*

4 *The people standing, the Celebrant may say*

>   Blessed be God: Father, Son, and Holy Spirit.

People   **And blessed be his kingdom, now and for ever. Amen.**

In place of the above, from Easter Day through the Day of Pentecost

Celebrant   Alleluia. Christ is risen.
People   **The Lord is risen indeed. Alleluia.**

In Lent and on other penitential occasions

Celebrant   Bless the Lord who forgiveth all our sins;
People   **His mercy endureth for ever.**

5 *The Celebrant says*

Almighty God, unto whom... [CF 1] ...Christ our Lord. **Amen.**
your...you] thy...thee THROUGHOUT

Then the Ten Commandments (page... [i.e. at no. 1 above]) may be said, or the following

Hear what our... [**MAL** CF 4(a)] ...and the Prophets.

6 *Here is sung or said*

Lord, have mercy upon us.   Kyrie eleison.
Christ, have mercy upon us.   *or*   **Christe eleison.**
Lord, have mercy upon us.   Kyrie eleison.

or this

Holy God,
Holy and Mighty,
Holy Immortal One,
Have mercy upon us.

7 *When appointed, the following hymn or some other song of praise is sung or said, in addition to, or in place of, the preceding, all standing*

Glory be to God on high... [**MAL** CF 5] ...**Father. Amen.**
in earth] on earth
Jesu Christ] Jesus Christ
Thou that takest away...mercy upon us] OM [see **FAL**, p. 62, footnote 1]

THE COLLECT OF THE DAY

8 *The Celebrant says to the people*

>   The Lord be with you.

People   **And with thy spirit.**
Celebrant   Let us pray.

9 *The Celebrant says the Collect.*

People   **Amen.**

THE LESSONS

10 *The people sit. One or two Lessons, as appointed, are read, the Reader first saying*

A Reading (Lesson) from _____

A citation giving chapter and verse may be added.

After each Reading, the Reader may say
The Word of the Lord.

People **Thanks be to God.**

or the Reader may say Here endeth the Reading (Epistle).

Silence may follow.

11 *A Psalm, hymn, or anthem may follow each Reading.*

12 *Then, all standing, the Deacon or a Priest reads the Gospel, first saying*
The Holy Gospel of our Lord Jesus Christ according to __

People **Glory be to thee, O Lord.**

After the Gospel, the Reader says
The Gospel of the Lord.

People **Praise be to thee, O Christ.**

13 THE SERMON

14 *On Sundays and other Major Feasts there follows, all standing*

THE NICENE CREED

We believe... ⟦ICET 3⟧ **...world to come. Amen.**

men] OM
[and the Son]] OM BRACKETS (1976: OM ENTIRE)

or this

I believe... ⟦MAL CF 6⟧ **...world to come. Amen.**

The giver] **and Giver**

THE PRAYERS OF THE PEOPLE

15 *Intercession is offered according to the following form, or in accordance with the directions on page...* ⟦i.e. no. 85⟧

16 *The Deacon or other person appointed says*

Let us pray for the whole state of Christ's Church and the world.

After each paragraph of this prayer, the People may make an appropriate response, as directed.

Almighty and everliving God, who in thy holy Word hast taught us to make prayers, and supplications, and to give thanks for all men: Receive these our prayers which we offer unto thy divine Majesty, beseeching thee to inspire continually the Universal Church with the spirit of truth, unity, and concord; and grant that all those who do confess thy holy Name may agree in the truth of thy holy Word, and live in unity and godly love.

Give grace, O heavenly Father, to all bishops and other ministers [especially _____], that they may, both by their life and doctrine, set forth thy true and lively Word, and rightly and duly administer thy holy Sacraments.

And to all thy people give thy heavenly grace, and especially to this congregation here present; that, with meek heart and due reverence, they may hear and receive thy holy Word, truly serving thee in holiness and righteousness all the days of their life.

We beseech thee also so to rule the hearts of those who bear the authority of government in this and every land [especially _____], that they may be led to wise decisions and right actions for the welfare and peace of the world.

Open, O Lord, the eyes of all people to behold thy gracious hand in all thy works, that, rejoicing in thy whole creation, they may honor thee with their substance, and be faithful stewards of thy bounty.

And we most humbly beseech thee, of thy goodness, O Lord, to comfort and succor [_____ and] all those who, in this transitory life, are in trouble, sorrow, need, sickness, or any other adversity.

Additional petitions and thanksgivings may be included here.

And we also bless thy holy Name for all thy servants departed this life in thy faith and fear [especially _____], beseeching thee to grant them continual growth in thy love and service; and to grant us grace so to follow the good examples of [_____ and of] all thy saints, that with them we may be partakers of thy heavenly kingdom.

Grant these our prayers, O Father, for Jesus Christ's sake, our only Mediator and Advocate. **Amen.**

If there is no celebration of the Communion, or if a priest is not available, the service is concluded as directed on page. . . ⟦i.e. no. 108⟧

CONFESSION OF SIN

17 *A Confession of Sin is said here if it has not been said earlier. On occasion, the Confession may be omitted.*

The Deacon or Celebrant says the following, or else the Exhortation on page. . . ⟦see no. 1 ⟧

Ye who do. . .⟦**MAL** CF 9⟧. . .to Almighty God, devoutly kneeling.
and take this holy sacrament to your comfort] OM

or this

Let us humbly confess our sins unto Almighty God.

Silence may be kept.

18 *Minister and People*

Almighty God...⟦MAL CF 10⟧...Christ our Lord. Amen.

or this

Most merciful God,
we confess that we have sinned against thee
in thought, word, and deed,
by what we have done,
and by what we have left undone.
We have not loved thee with our whole heart;
we have not loved our neighbors as ourselves.
We are truly sorry and we humbly repent.
For the sake of thy Son Jesus Christ,
have mercy on us and forgive us;
that we may delight in thy will,
and walk in thy ways,
to the glory of thy Name. Amen.

19 *The Bishop when present, or the Priest, stands and says*

Almighty God...⟦**MAL** CF 11⟧...our Lord. **Amen.**

all them that] all those who

20 *A Minister may then say one or more of the following sentences, first saying*

Hear the Word of God to all who truly turn to him.

Come unto me, all ye that travail...⟦**MAL** CF 12⟧...Christ the righteous; and he is the perfect offering for our sins, and not for ours only, but for the sins of the whole world.   (1 *John* 2. 1–2)

So God] God so
Hear also what St. Paul saith]   OM
Jesus Christ] Christ Jesus ⟦see **FAL**, page 422, footnote 1⟧
Hear also what St. John saith]   OM

21 *THE PEACE*

All stand. The Celebrant says to the people

            The peace of the Lord be always with you.
People   **And with thy spirit.**

Then the Ministers and People may greet one another in the name of the Lord.

THE HOLY COMMUNION

22 *The Celebrant may begin the Offertory with one of the sentences on pages* ... ⟦*i.e. at no. 41*⟧, *or with some other sentence of Scripture.*

23 *During the Offertory, a hymn, psalm, or anthem may be sung.*

24 *Representatives of the congregation bring the people's offerings of bread and wine, and money or other gifts, to the deacon or celebrant. The people stand while the offerings are presented and placed on the Altar.*

25 *THE GREAT THANKSGIVING*
An alternative form will be found on page ... ⟦*i.e. no. 39*⟧

26 *EUCHARISTIC PRAYER I*
The people remain standing. The Celebrant, whether bishop or priest, faces them and sings or says

	The Lord be with you.
People	**And with thy spirit.**
Celebrant	Lift up your hearts.
People	**We lift them up unto the Lord.**
Celebrant	Let us give thanks unto our Lord God.
People	**It is meet and right so to do.**

Then, facing the Holy Table, the Celebrant proceeds

It is very meet, right, and our bounden duty, that we should at all times, and in all places, give thanks unto thee, O Lord, holy Father, almighty, everlasting God.

Here a Proper Preface is sung or said on all Sundays, and on other occasions as appointed.

⟦The Proper Prefaces, which come at no 42, are to be found in Appendix C⟧.

Therefore with Angels and Archangels, and with all the company of heaven, we laud and magnify thy glorious Name; evermore praising thee, and saying,

Celebrant and People
Holy, holy, holy, Lord God of Hosts:
Heaven and earth are full of thy glory.
Glory be to thee, O Lord Most High.
Here may be added
Blessed is he that cometh in the name of the Lord.
Hosanna in the highest.
The people kneel or stand.

Then the Celebrant continues

All glory be to thee, Almighty God, our heavenly Father, for that thou, of thy tender mercy, didst give thine only Son Jesus Christ to suffer death upon the cross for our redemption; who made there, by his one oblation of himself once offered, a full, perfect, and sufficient sacrifice, oblation, and satisfaction, for the sins of the whole world; and did institute, and in his holy Gospel command us to continue, a perpetual memory of that his precious death and sacrifice, until his coming again. *At the following words concerning the bread, the Celebrant is to hold it, or lay a hand upon it; and at the words concerning the cup, to hold or place a hand upon the cup and any other vessel containing wine to be consecrated.* For in the night in which he was betrayed, he took bread; and when he had given thanks, he brake it, and gave it to his disciples, saying, 'Take, eat, this is my Body, which is given for you. Do this in remembrance of me.'

Likewise, after supper, he took the cup; and when he had given thanks, he gave it to them, saying, 'Drink ye all of this; for this is my Blood of the New Testament, which is shed for you, and for many, for the remission of sins. Do this, as oft as ye shall drink it, in remembrance of me.'

Wherefore, O Lord and heavenly Father, according to the institution of thy dearly beloved Son our Savior Jesus Christ, we, thy humble servants, do celebrate and make here before thy divine Majesty, with these thy holy gifts, which we now offer unto thee, the memorial thy Son hath commanded us to make; having in remembrance his blessed passion and precious death, his mighty resurrection and glorious ascension; rendering unto thee most hearty thanks for the innumerable benefits procured unto us by the same.

And we most humbly beseech thee, O merciful Father, to hear us; and, of thy almighty goodness, vouchsafe to bless and sanctify, with thy Word and Holy Spirit, these thy gifts and creatures of bread and wine; that we, receiving them according to thy Son our Savior Jesus Christ's holy institution, in remembrance of his death and passion, may be partakers of his most blessed Body and Blood.

And we earnestly desire thy fatherly goodness mercifully to accept this our sacrifice of praise and thanksgiving; most humbly beseeching thee to grant that, by the merits and death of thy Son Jesus Christ, and through faith in his blood, we, and all thy whole Church, may obtain remission of our sins, and all other benefits of his passion.

And here we offer and present unto thee, O Lord, our selves, our souls and bodies, to be a reasonable, holy, and living sacrifice unto thee; humbly beseeching thee that we, and all others who shall be partakers of this Holy Communion, may worthily receive the most precious Body and Blood of thy Son Jesus Christ, be filled with thy grace and heavenly benediction, and made one body with him, that he may dwell in us, and we in him.

And although we are unworthy, through our manifold sins, to offer unto thee any sacrifice, yet we beseech thee to accept this our bounden duty and service, not weighing our merits, but pardoning our offenses, through Jesus Christ our Lord;

By whom, and with whom, in the unity of the Holy Ghost, all honor and glory be unto thee, O Father Almighty, world without end. **Amen.**

27 And now, as our Savior Christ hath taught us, we are bold to say,

People and Celebrant

Our Father, who art...⟦MAL CF 1⟧...and ever. Amen.

in earth] on earth
them that] those who
the power] and the power

28 *THE BREAKING OF THE BREAD*

The Celebrant breaks the consecrated Bread.

A period of silence is kept.

29 *Then may be sung or said*

[Alleluia.] Christ our Passover is sacrificed for us;
Therefore let us kéep the feast. [Alleluia.]

In Lent, Alleluia is omitted, and may be omitted at other times except during Easter Season.

30 *The following or some other suitable anthem may be sung or said here*

O Lamb of God...⟦MAL CF 14⟧...grant us thy peace.

31 *The following prayer may be said. The People may join in saying this prayer*

We do not presume...⟦**MAL** CF 13⟧...he in us. **Amen.**

that our sinful...precious blood, and]   OM

32 *Facing the people, the Celebrant may say the following Invitation*

The Gifts of God for the People of God.

and may add Take them in remembrance that Christ died for you, and feed on him in your hearts by faith, with thanksgiving.

33 *The ministers receive the Sacrament in both kinds, and then immediately deliver it to the people.*

The Bread and the Cup are given to the communicants with these words

The Body...⟦**MAL** CF 15(a)⟧...with thanksgiving.
The Blood...⟦**MAL** CF 15(b)⟧...be thankful.

or with these words

The Body (Blood) of our Lord Jesus Christ keep you in everlasting life. [**Amen.**]

or with these words

The Body of Christ, the bread of heaven. [**Amen.**]
The Blood of Christ, the cup of salvation. [**Amen.**]

During the ministration of Communion, hymns, psalms, or anthems may be sung.

34 *When necessary, the Celebrant consecrates additional bread and wine, using the form on page ...⟦i.e. at no. 108⟧*

35 *After Communion, the Celebrant says*

Let us pray.

The People may join in saying this prayer

Almighty and everliving God...⟦**MAL** CF 18⟧...world without end. **Amen.**

vouchsafe to] OM
who have duly received these] in these
which is the blessed] the blessed
by the merits...of thy dear Son] OM
most humbly] humbly

36 *The Bishop when present, or the Priest, gives the blessing*

The peace of God...⟦**MAL** CF 19⟧...always. **Amen.**

or this

The blessing of God Almighty, the Father, the Son, and the Holy Spirit, be upon you and remain with you for ever. **Amen.**

37 *The Deacon, or the Celebrant, may dismiss the people with these words*

　　　　　　Let us go forth in the name of Christ.
People　　**Thanks be to God.**

or the following
Deacon　　Go in peace to love and serve the Lord.
People　　**Thanks be to God.**
or this

Deacon　　Let us go forth into the world, rejoicing in the power of the Spirit.

People　　**Thanks be to God.**
or this

Deacon　　Let us bless the Lord.
People　　**Thanks be to God.**

38 *From the Easter Vigil through the Day of Pentecost* 'Alleluia, alleluia' *may be added to any of the dismissals.*

The People respond **Thanks be to God. Alleluia, alleluia.**

ALTERNATIVE FORM OF THE GREAT
THANKSGIVING

39 *EUCHARISTIC PRAYER II*

The people remain standing. The Celebrant, whether bishop or priest, faces them and sings or says

	The Lord be with you.
People	**And with thy spirit.**
Celebrant	Lift up your hearts.
People	**We lift them up unto the Lord.**
Celebrant	Let us give thanks unto our Lord God.
People	**It is meet and right so to do.**

Then, facing the Holy Table, the Celebrant proceeds

It is very meet, right, and our bounden duty, that we should at all times, and in all places, give thanks unto thee, O Lord, holy Father, almighty, everlasting God.

Here a Proper Preface is sung or said on all Sundays, and on other occasions as appointed.

Therefore with Angels and Archangels, and with all the company of heaven, we laud and magnify thy glorious Name; evermore praising thee, and saying,

Celebrant and People

Holy, holy, holy, Lord God of Hosts:
Heaven and earth are full of thy glory.
Glory be to thee, O Lord Most High.

Here may be added

Blessed is he that cometh in the name of the Lord.
Hosanna in the highest.

The People kneel or stand.

Then the Celebrant continues

All glory be to thee, O Lord our God, for that thou didst create heaven and earth, and didst make us in thine own image; and, of thy tender mercy, didst give thine only Son Jesus Christ to take our nature upon him, and to suffer death upon the cross for our redemption. He made there a full and perfect sacrifice for the whole world; and did institute, and in his holy Gospel command us to continue, a perpetual memory of that his precious death and sacrifice, until his coming again.

At the following words concerning the bread, the Celebrant is to hold it, or lay a hand upon it; and at the words concerning the cup, to hold or place a hand upon the cup and any other vessel containing wine to be consecrated.

For in the night in which he was betrayed, he took bread; and when he had given thanks to thee, he broke it, and gave it to his disciples, saying, 'Take, eat, this is my Body, which is given for you. Do this in remembrance of me.'

Likewise, after supper, he took the cup; and when he had given thanks, he gave it to them, saying, 'Drink this, all of you; for this is my Blood of the New Covenant, which is shed for you, and for many, for the remission of sins. Do this, as oft as ye shall drink it, in remembrance of me.'

Wherefore, O Lord and heavenly Father, we thy people do celebrate and make, with these thy holy gifts which we now offer unto thee, the memorial thy Son hath commanded us to make; having in remembrance his blessed passion and precious death, his mighty resurrection and glorious ascension; and looking for his coming again with power and great glory.

And we most humbly beseech thee, O merciful Father, to hear us, and, with thy Word and Holy Spirit, to bless and sanctify these gifts of bread and wine, that they may be unto us the Body and Blood of thy dearly-beloved Son Jesus Christ.

And we earnestly desire thy fatherly goodness to accept this our sacrifice of praise and thanksgiving, whereby we offer and present unto thee, O Lord, our selves, our souls and bodies. Grant, we beseech thee, that all who partake of this Holy Communion may worthily receive the most precious Body and Blood of thy Son Jesus Christ, and be filled with thy grace and heavenly benediction; and also that we and all thy whole Church may be made one body with him, that he may dwell in us, and we in him; through the same Jesus Christ our Lord;

By whom, and with whom, and in whom, in the unity of the Holy Ghost all honor and glory be unto thee, O Father Almighty, world without end. **Amen.**

40 And now, as our Savior Christ hath taught us, we are bold to say,

Continue with the Lord's Prayer, page ... [[i.e. no. 27]].

41   OFFERTORY SENTENCES

One of the following, or some other appropriate sentence of Scripture, may be used

[The Offertory Sentences which are printed here are to be found in Appendix B]

42   PROPER PREFACES

[The Proper Prefaces which are printed here are to be found in Appendix C]

43 ## DECALOGUE: CONTEMPORARY

Hear the commandments of God to his people: I am... [CF 2, without bracketed sections]...covet anything that belongs to your neighbor.

[The response after each commandment is '**Amen. Lord have mercy.**']
your God] your God who brought you out of bondage
graven image] idol
You shall not bow down to them nor worship them] OMIT
take,...in vain] invoke with malice...
to keep holy the sabbath day] the Sabbath Day and keep it holy
bear] be a

44 ## A PENITENTIAL ORDER: RITE TWO

[As with the traditional form for Rite One (no. 1 above) the opening greetings of the liturgy are printed first, and the order then follows no. 1 closely: – permitting the Exhortation (see no. 1), the Decalogue (no. 43 above, and printed on the facing verso in the American Book), the sentences of scripture (with CF 3, slightly amended, first), then the text as at nos 59 and 60 below, and two closing rubrics corresponding to the last two in the Penitential Order: Rite One (see no. 1 above).]

45 ## CONCERNING THE CELEBRATION

[This is identical to no. 2 above. In the book it occupies the left-hand page, facing the beginning of Rite Two.]

THE HOLY EUCHARIST: RITE TWO [Amer2–2]
THE WORD OF GOD

46 *A hymn, psalm, or anthem may be sung.*

47 *The people standing, the Celebrant says*

Blessed be God: Father, Son, and Holy Spirit.

People **And blessed be his kingdom, now and for ever. Amen.**

In place of the above, from Easter Day through the Day of Pentecost

Celebrant Alleluia. Christ is risen.

People **The Lord is risen indeed. Alleluia.**

In Lent and on other penitential occasions

Celebrant Bless the Lord who forgives all our sins;

People **His mercy endures for ever.**

48 *The Celebrant may say*

Almighty God, to you... [CF 1]...our Lord. **Amen.**

whom] you

49 *When appointed, the following hymn or some other song of praise is sung or said, all standing*

Glory to God...⟦ICET 4⟧...**God the Father. Amen.**

50 *On other occasions the following is used*

Lord, have mercy...⟦as at no. 6 above, Kyries (omitting 'upon us') or Trisagion⟧...**Have mercy upon us.**

THE COLLECT OF THE DAY

51 *The Celebrant says to the people*

	The Lord be with you.
People	**And also with you.**
Celebrant	Let us pray.

52 *The Celebrant says the Collect.*

People	**Amen.**

THE LESSONS

53 *The people sit. One or two Lessons, as appointed, are read, the Reader first saying*

A Reading (Lesson) from _____ .

A citation giving chapter and verse may be added.

After each Reading, the Reader may say

	The Word of the Lord.
People	**Thanks be to God.**

or the Reader may say Here ends the Reading (Epistle).

Silence may follow.

54 *A Psalm, hymn, or anthem may follow each Reading.*

55 *Then, all standing, the Deacon or a Priest reads the Gospel, first saying*

	The Holy Gospel of our Lord Jesus Christ according to _____ .
People	**Glory to you, Lord Christ.**

After the Gospel, the Reader says

	The Gospel of the Lord.
People	**Praise to you, Lord Christ.**

56 THE SERMON

On Sundays and other Major Feasts there follows, all standing

57 *THE NICENE CREED*

We believe...⟦ICET 3⟧...**world to come. Amen.**

men] OM
[and the Son]] OM BRACKETS (1976: OM ENTIRE)

58 *THE PRAYERS OF THE PEOPLE*

Prayer is offered with intercession for

The Universal Church, its members, and its mission
The Nation and all in authority
The welfare of the world
The concerns of the local community
Those who suffer and those in any trouble
The departed (with commemoration of a saint when appropriate)

See the forms beginning on page ...⟦i.e. no. 84⟧

If there is no celebration of the Communion, or if a priest is not available, the service is concluded as directed on page ...⟦i.e. no. 108⟧

59 *CONFESSION OF SIN*

A Confession of Sin is said here if it has not been said earlier. On occasion, the Confession may be omitted.

One of the sentences from the Penitential Order on page ...⟦i.e. no. 44⟧ *may be said.*

The Deacon or Celebrant says

Let us confess our sins against God and our neighbor.

Silence may be kept.

Minister and People

Most merciful...⟦as at no. 18 above but with '**you**'/'**your**'⟧...**your Name. Amen.**

60 *The Bishop when present, or the Priest, stands and says*

Almighty God have mercy on you, forgive you all your sins through our Lord Jesus Christ, strengthen you in all goodness and by the power of the Holy Spirit keep you in eternal life. **Amen.**

61 *THE PEACE*

All stand. The Celebrant says to the people

The peace of the Lord be always with you.

People   **And also with you.**

Then the Ministers and People may greet one another in the name of the Lord.

THE HOLY COMMUNION

62 *The Celebrant may begin the Offertory with one of the sentences on
page ..., or with some other sentence of Scripture.*

⟦The Offertory Sentences which come at no. 82 are to be found here in Appendix B⟧

63 *During the Offertory, a hymn, psalm, or anthem may be sung.*

64 *Representatives of the congregation bring the people's offerings of bread and
wine, and money or other gifts, to the deacon or celebrant. The people stand
while the offerings are presented and placed on the Altar.*

65 *THE GREAT THANKSGIVING*

Alternative forms will be found on page ... ⟦*i.e. no. 76* ⟧ *and following.*

66 *EUCHARISTIC PRAYER A*

*The people remain standing. The Celebrant, whether bishop or priest, faces
them and sings or says*

	The Lord be with you.
People	**And also with you.**
Celebrant	Lift up your hearts.
People	**We lift them to the Lord.**
Celebrant	Let us give thanks to the Lord our God.
People	**It is right to give him thanks and praise.**

Then, facing the Holy Table, the Celebrant proceeds

It is right, and a good and joyful thing, always and everywhere to give
thanks to you, Father Almighty, Creator of heaven and earth.

*Here a Proper Preface is sung or said on all Sundays, and on other
occasions as appointed.*

⟦The Proper Prefaces which come at no. 83 are to be found here in Appendix C⟧

Therefore we praise you, joining our voices with Angels and Archangels
and with all the company of heaven, who for ever sing this hymn to
proclaim the glory of your Name:

Celebrant and People

**Holy, holy, holy Lord, God of power and might,
heaven and earth are full of your glory.
    Hosanna in the highest.
Blessed is he who comes in the name of the Lord.
    Hosanna in the highest.**

The people stand or kneel.

Then the Celebrant continues

Holy and gracious Father: In your infinite love you made us for yourself; and, when we had fallen into sin and become subject to evil and death, you, in your mercy, sent Jesus Christ, your only and eternal Son, to share our human nature, to live and die as one of us, to reconcile us to you, the God and Father of all.

He stretched out his arms upon the cross, and offered himself, in obedience to your will, a perfect sacrifice for the whole world.

At the following words conerning the bread, the Celebrant is to hold it, or lay a hand upon it ; and at the words concerning the cup, to hold or place a hand upon the cup and any other vessel containing wine to be consecrated.

On the night he was handed over to suffering and death, our Lord Jesus Christ took bread; and when he had given thanks to you, he broke it, and gave it to his disciples, and said, 'Take, eat: This is my Body, which is given for you. Do this for the remembrance of me.'

After supper he took the cup of wine; and when he had given thanks, he gave it to them, and said, 'Drink this, all of you: This is my Blood of the new Covenant, which is shed for you and for many for the forgiveness of sins. Whenever you drink it, do this for the remembrance of me.'

Therefore we proclaim the mystery of faith:

Celebrant and People

Christ has died.
Christ is risen.
Christ will come again.

The Celebrant continues

We celebrate the memorial of our redemption, O Father, in this sacrifice of praise and thanksgiving. Recalling his death, resurrection, and ascension, we offer you these gifts.

Sanctify them by your Holy Spirit to be for your people the Body and Blood of your Son, the holy food and drink of new and unending life in him. Sanctify us also that we may faithfully receive this holy Sacrament, and serve you in unity, constancy, and peace; and at the last day bring us with all your saints into the joy of your eternal kingdom.

All this we ask through your Son Jesus Christ. By him, and with him, and in him, in the unity of the Holy Spirit all honor and glory is yours, Almighty Father, now and for ever. **Amen.**

67 And now, as our Savior Christ has taught us, we are bold to say,

As our Savior Christ has taught us, we now pray,

People and Celebrant

Our Father, who art...⟦as at no. 27 above⟧...**ever and ever. Amen.**

Our Father...⟦ICET 1⟧...**for ever. Amen.**

68 *THE BREAKING OF THE BREAD*

The Celebrant breaks the consecrated Bread.

A period of silence is kept.

Then may be sung or said

[Alleluia.] Christ our Passover is sacrificed for us;
Therefore let us keep the feast. [Alleluia.]

In Lent, Alleluia is omitted, and may be omitted at other times except during Easter Season.

In place of, or in addition to, the preceding, some other suitable anthem may be used.

69 *Facing the people, the Celebrant says the following Invitation*

The Gifts of God for the People of God.

and may add Take them in remembrance that Christ died for you, and feed on him in your hearts by faith, with thanksgiving.

70 *The ministers receive the Sacrament in both kinds, and then immediately deliver it to the people.*

The Bread and the Cup are given to the communicants with these words

The Body (Blood) of our Lord Jesus Christ keep you in everlasting life. **[Amen.]**

or with these words

The Body of Christ, the bread of heaven. **[Amen.]**
The Blood of Christ, the cup of salvation. **[Amen.]**

During the ministration of Communion, hymns, psalms, or anthems may be sung.

71 *When necessary, the Celebrant consecrates additional bread and wine, using the form on page* ...⟦i.e. at no. 108 below⟧

72 *After Communion, the Celebrant says*

Let us pray.

Celebrant and People

**Eternal God, heavenly Father,
you have graciously accepted us as living members**

of your Son our Savior Jesus Christ,
and you have fed us with spiritual food
in the Sacrament of his Body and Blood.
Send us now into the world in peace,
and grant us strength and courage
to love and serve you
with gladness and singleness of heart;
through Christ our Lord. Amen.

or the following

Almighty and everliving God,
we thank you for feeding us with the spiritual food
of the most precious Body and Blood
of your Son our Savior Jesus Christ;
and for assuring us in these holy mysteries
that we are living members of the Body of your Son,
and heirs of your eternal kingdom.
And now, Father, send us out
to do the work you have given us to do,
to love and serve you
as faithful witnesses of Christ our Lord.
To him, to you, and to the Holy Spirit,
be honor and glory, now and for ever. Amen.

73 *The Bishop when present, or the Priest, may bless the people.*

74 *The Deacon, or the Celebrant, dismisses them with these words*

	Let us go forth in the name of Christ.
People	**Thanks be to God.**
or this	
Deacon	Go in peace to love and serve the Lord.
People	**Thanks be to God.**
or this	
Deacon	Let us go forth into the world, rejoicing in the power of the Spirit.
People	**Thanks be to God.**
or this	
Deacon	Let us bless the Lord.
People	**Thanks be to God.**

75 *From the Easter Vigil through the Day of Pentecost* 'Alleluia, alleluia' *may be added to any of the dismissals.*

The People respond **Thanks be to God. Alleluia, alleluia.**

ALTERNATIVE FORMS OF THE GREAT THANKSGIVING

76 EUCHARISTIC PRAYER B

The people remain standing. The Celebrant, whether bishop or priest, faces them and sings or says

	The Lord be with you.
People	**And also with you.**
Celebrant	Lift up your hearts.
People	**We lift them to the Lord.**
Celebrant	Let us give thanks to the Lord our God.
People	**It is right to give him thanks and praise.**

Then, facing the Holy Table, the Celebrant proceeds

It is right, and a good and joyful thing, always and everywhere to give thanks to you, Father Almighty, Creator of heaven and earth.

Here a Proper Preface is sung or said on all Sundays, and on other occasions as appointed.

Therefore we praise you, joining our voices with Angels and Archangels and with all the company of heaven, who for ever sing this hymn to proclaim the glory of your Name:

Celebrant and People

Holy, holy...⟦ICET 5(a) and 5(b)⟧...**in the highest.**

The people stand or kneel.

Then the Celebrant continues

We give thanks to you, O God, for the goodness and love which you have made known to us in creation; in the calling of Israel to be your people; in your Word spoken through the prophets; and above all in the Word made flesh, Jesus, your Son. For in these last days you sent him to be incarnate from the Virgin Mary, to be the Savior and Redeemer of the world. In him, you have delivered us from evil, and made us worthy to stand before you. In him, you have brought us out of error into truth, out of sin into righteousness, out of death into life.

At the following words concerning the bread, the Celebrant is to hold it, or lay a hand upon it ; and at the words concerning the cup, to hold or place a hand upon the cup and any other vessel containing wine to be consecrated.

On the night before he died for us, our Lord Jesus Christ took bread; and when he had given thanks to you, he broke it, and gave it to his disciples, and said, 'Take, eat: This is my Body, which is given for you. Do this for the remembrance of me.'

After supper he took the cup of wine; and when he had given thanks, he gave it to them, and said, 'Drink this, all of you: This is my Blood of the new Covenant, which is shed for you and for many for the forgiveness of sins. Whenever you drink it, do this for the remembrance of me.'

Therefore, according to his command, O Father,

Celebrant and People

We remember his death,
We proclaim his resurrection,
We await his coming in glory;

The Celebrant continues

And we offer our sacrifice of praise and thanksgiving to you, O Lord of all; presenting to you, from your creation, this bread and this wine.

We pray you, gracious God, to send your Holy Spirit upon these gifts that they may be the Sacrament of the Body of Christ and his Blood of the new Covenant. Unite us to your Son in his sacrifice, that we may be acceptable through him, being sanctified by the Holy Spirit. In the fullness of time, put all things in subjection under your Christ, and bring us to that heavenly country where, with [_____ and] all your saints, we may enter the everlasting heritage of your sons and daughters; through Jesus Christ our Lord, the firstborn of all creation, the head of the Church, and the author of our salvation.

By him, and with him, and in him, in the unity of the Holy Spirit all honor and glory is yours, Almighty Father, now and for ever. **Amen.**

77 And now, as our Savior Christ has taught us, we are bold to say,

As our Savior Christ has taught us we now pray,

Continue with the Lord's Prayer on page ... [i.e. no. 67 above]

78 EUCHARISTIC PRAYER C

In this prayer, the lines in italics are spoken by the People.[1]

The Celebrant, whether bishop or priest, faces them and sings or says

The Lord be with you.
And also with you.

Lift up your hearts.
We lift them to the Lord.

Let us give thanks to the Lord our God.
It is right to give him thanks and praise.

---

[1] [This use of italics is unusual in the Book, and it accounts for the paucity of rubrics in this prayer.]

Then, facing the Holy Table, the Celebrant proceeds

God of all power, Ruler of the Universe, you are worthy of glory and praise.

Glory to you for ever and ever.

At your command all things came to be: the vast expanse of interstellar space, galaxies, suns, the planets in their courses, and this fragile earth, our island home.

By your will they were created and have their being.

From the primal elements you brought forth the human race, and blessed us with memory, reason, and skill. You made us the rulers of creation. But we turned against you, and betrayed your trust; and we turned against one another.

Have mercy, Lord, for we are sinners in your sight.

Again and again, you called us to return. Through prophets and sages you revealed your righteous Law. And in the fullness of time you sent your only Son, born of a woman, to fulfill your Law, to open for us the way of freedom and peace.

By his blood, he reconciled us.
By his wounds, we are healed.

And therefore we praise you, joining with the heavenly chorus, with prophets, apostles, and martyrs, and with all those in every generation who have looked to you in hope, to proclaim with them your glory, in their unending hymn:

Celebrant and People

Holy, holy...[[ICET 5(a) and 5(b)]]...**in the highest.**

The Celebrant continues

And so, Father, we who have been redeemed by him, and made a new people by water and the Spirit, now bring before you these gifts. Sanctify them by your Holy Spirit to be the Body and Blood of Jesus Christ our Lord.

At the following words concerning the bread, the Celebrant is to hold it, or lay a hand upon it ; and at the words concerning the cup, to hold or place a hand upon the cup and any other vessel containing wine to be consecrated.

On the night he was betrayed he took bread, said the blessing, broke the bread, and gave it to his friends, and said, 'Take, eat: This is my Body, which is given for you. Do this for the remembrance of me.'

After supper, he took the cup of wine, gave thanks, and said, 'Drink this, all of you: This is my Blood of the new Covenant, which is shed for you and for many for the forgiveness of sins. Whenever you drink it, do this for the remembrance of me.'

Remembering now his work of redemption, and offering to you this sacrifice of thanksgiving,

**We celebrate his death and resurrection,
as we await the day of his coming.**

Lord God of our Fathers; God of Abraham, Isaac, and Jacob; God and Father of our Lord Jesus Christ: Open our eyes to see your hand at work in the world about us. Deliver us from the presumption of coming to this Table for solace only, and not for strength; for pardon only, and not for renewal. Let the grace of this Holy Communion make us one body, one spirit in Christ, that we may worthily serve the world in his name.

Risen Lord, be known to us in the breaking of the Bread.

Accept these prayers and praises, Father, through Jesus Christ our great High Priest, to whom, with you and the Holy Spirit, your Church gives honor, glory, and worship, from generation to generation. **Amen.**

79 And now, as our Savior Christ has taught us, we are bold to say,   As our Savior Christ has taught us, we now pray,

Continue with the Lord's Prayer on page ... ⟦i.e. no. 67 above⟧

80 *EUCHARISTIC PRAYER D*

The people remain standing. The Celebrant, whether bishop or priest, faces them and sings or says

	The Lord be with you.
People	**And also with you.**
Celebrant	Lift up your hearts.
People	**We lift them to the Lord.**
Celebrant	Let us give thanks to the Lord our God.
People	**It is right to give him thanks and praise.**

Then, facing the Holy Table, the Celebrant proceeds

It is truly right to glorify you, Father, and to give you thanks; for you alone are God, living and true, dwelling in light inaccessible from before time and for ever.

Fountain of life and source of all goodness, you made all things and fill them with your blessing; you created them to rejoice in the splendor of your radiance.

Countless throngs of angels stand before you to serve you night and day; and, beholding the glory of your presence, they offer you unceasing praise. Joining with them, and giving voice to every creature under heaven, we acclaim you, and glorify your Name, as we sing (say),

Celebrant and People

Holy, holy...⟦ICET 5(a) and 5(b)⟧...**in the highest.**

The people stand or kneel.

Then the Celebrant continues

We acclaim you, holy Lord, glorious in power. Your mighty works reveal your wisdom and love. You formed us in your own image, giving the whole world into our care, so that, in obedience to you, our Creator, we might rule and serve all your creatures. When our disobedience took us far from you, you did not abandon us to the power of death. In your mercy you came to our help, so that in seeking you we might find you. Again and again you called us into covenant with you, and through the prophets you taught us to hope for salvation.

Father, you loved the world so much that in the fullness of time you sent your only Son to be our Savior. Incarnate by the Holy Spirit, born of the Virgin Mary, he lived as one of us, yet without sin. To the poor he proclaimed the good news of salvation; to prisoners, freedom; to the sorrowful, joy. To fulfill your purpose he gave himself up to death; and, rising from the grave, destroyed death, and made the whole creation new.

And, that we might live no longer for ourselves, but for him who died and rose for us, he sent the Holy Spirit, his own first gift for those who believe, to complete his work in the world, and to bring to fulfillment the sanctification of all.

At the following words concerning the bread, the Celebrant is to hold it, or lay a hand upon it; and at the words concerning the cup, to hold or place a hand upon the cup and any other vessel containing wine to be consecrated.

When the hour had come for him to be glorified by you, his heavenly Father, having loved his own who were in the world, he loved them to the end; at supper with them he took bread, and when he had given thanks to you, he broke it, and gave it to his disciples, and said, 'Take, eat; This is my Body, which is given for you. Do this for the remembrance of me.'

After supper he took the cup of wine; and when he had given thanks, he gave it to them, and said, 'Drink this, all of you: This is my Blood of the new Covenant, which is shed for you and for many for the forgiveness of sins. Whenever you drink it, do this for the remembrance of me.'

Father, we now celebrate this memorial of our redemption. Recalling Christ's death and his descent among the dead, proclaiming his resurrection and ascension to your right hand, awaiting his coming in glory; and offering to you, from the gifts you have given us, this bread and this cup, we praise you and we bless you.

Celebrant and People

We praise you, we bless you,
we give thanks to you,
and we pray to you, Lord our God.

The Celebrant continues

Lord, we pray that in your goodness and mercy your Holy Spirit may descend upon us, and upon these gifts, sanctifying them and showing them to be holy gifts for your holy people, the bread of life and the cup of salvation, the Body and Blood of your Son Jesus Christ.

Grant that all who share this bread and cup may become one body and one spirit, a living sacrifice in Christ, to the praise of your Name.

Remember, Lord, your one holy catholic and apostolic Church, redeemed by the blood of your Christ. Reveal its unity, guard its faith, and preserve it in peace.

[Remember (*NN.* and) all who minister in your Church.]
[Remember all your people, and those who seek your truth.]
[Remember ＿＿＿＿ .]
[Remember all who have died in the peace of Christ, and those whose faith is known to you alone; bring them into the place of eternal joy and light.]

And grant that we may find our inheritance with [the Blessed Virgin Mary, with patriarchs, prophets, apostles, and martyrs, (with ＿＿＿＿) and] all the saints who have found favor with you in ages past. We praise you in union with them and give you glory through your Son Jesus Christ our Lord.

Through Christ, and with Christ, and in Christ, all honor and glory are yours, Almighty God and Father, in the unity of the Holy Spirit, for ever and ever. **Amen.**

81 And now, as our Savior Christ has taught us, we are bold to say,

As our Saviour Christ has taught us, we now pray,

Continue with the Lord's Prayer on p.... [i.e. at no. 67]

82 OFFERTORY SENTENCES

⟦The Offertory Sentences which follow here are to be found in Appendix B⟧

83 PROPER PREFACES

⟦The Proper Prefaces which follow here are to be found in Appendix C⟧

THE PRAYERS OF THE PEOPLE (Amer1-1, 2-2, 3-3)[1]

84 ⟦The Prayers of the People are adapted forms of those in **FAL**, pages 156–167. They are presented here solely by *apparatus* to save space, and reference must be had to **FAL** to recover the full text. The symbols □ ■ do not recur here.⟧

85 ⟦No. 107 in **FAL** – opening rubrics⟧

and all its members] its members, and its mission
If a confession...or VII.]⟧   OMIT AND INSERT:
   Any of the forms which follow may be used.
   Adaptations or insertions suitable to the occasion may be made.
   Any of the forms may be conformed to the language of the Rite being used. ⟦'Thou', etc., are not then italicized in the text.⟧
   A bar in the margin indicates petitions which may be omitted. ⟦This bar then replaces the asterisks in **FAL**.⟧
to the Season] to the occasion, or the season
When a briefer...omitted]   OMIT

86 ⟦Nos 108, 109, 110 in **FAL** – now entitled '*FORM 1*'⟧

mankind] peoples
* For the good earth...]   NO BAR IN MARGIN
in the air, or through outer space] or in the air [or through outer space]
widows] the widowed
suffering] the suffering
⟦After this petition add an additional one with bar 'For...'⟧
oppressed] the oppressed, for the unemployed and the destitute
* For deliverance...]   NO BAR IN MARGIN
* That we may end...]   NO BAR IN MARGIN
communion of Saints] communion of [......and of all the] saints
⟦In place of nos. 109 and 110 in **FAL** read;
   Silence
   The Celebrant adds a concluding Collect.⟧

87 ⟦Nos. 111 and 112 in **FAL** – '*FORM II*'⟧

⟦'Brothers' is omitted from the invitation throughout⟧
among men]   OM
found of] found by
thanksgiving] *thanksgivings*
Give thanks, brothers, for God's great goodness]   OMIT
And pray] Pray
Priest] *Celebrant*

88 ⟦Nos. 113, 114, 115 in **FAL** are omitted, and '*FORM III*' corresponds to Nos. 116, 117, and 118⟧

After the Priest's invitation to prayer]   OMIT
stewards] ministers
peace and justice among men] **justice and peace on the earth**
courage] grace
we may be blest in all our works] **our works may find favor in your sight**
your light] **light perpetual**
for ever]   OMIT
all your saints] your saints
⟦No. 118 is replaced by: '*The People may add their own petitions.*
       The Celebrant adds a concluding Collect.'⟧

[1] ⟦This odd coding indicates that the Prayers of the People are intended for use with all three rites, and the title at the foot of the page in the Book of Common Prayer shows this.⟧

89 *FORM IV* ⟦This corresponds to nos. 119 and 120 in **FAL**, but is much changed, so is reprinted here entire⟧

Deacon or other leader
Let us pray for the Church and for the world.

Grant, Almighty God, that all who confess your Name may be united in your truth, live together in your love, and reveal your glory in the world.

⟦Here and after each paragraph are the rubric '*Silence*' and the versicle and response 'Lord, in your mercy **Hear our prayer.**'⟧

Guide the people of this land, and of all the nations, in the ways of justice and peace; that we may honor one another and serve the common good.

Give us all a reverence for the earth as your own creation, that we may use its resources rightly in the service of others and to your honor and glory.

Bless all those whose lives are closely linked with ours, and grant that we may serve Christ in them, and love one another as he loves us.

Comfort and heal all those who suffer in body, mind, or spirit; give them courage and hope in their troubles, and bring them the joy of your salvation.

We commend to your mercy all who have died, that your will for them may be fulfilled; and we pray that we may share with all your saints in your eternal kingdom.

The Celebrant adds a concluding Collect.

90 ⟦Nos. 121, 122, 123 in **FAL** – '*FORM V*'⟧

* For all who fear] NO BAR IN MARGIN
his Christ] you, Lord Christ
you, Lord] you
* For the mission] NO BAR IN MARGIN
people] peoples
all men] every person
⟦After this petition add an additional one (with bar)'|For all who live and work in this
    community [especially...],'⟧
the labours of men] all human labor
mankind] the world
from famine] from poverty, famine
for those who are present, and for those who are absent] ADD SQUARE BRACKETS
faith of Christ] communion of your Church, and those whose faith is known to you
    alone
The Priest says this doxology] *The Celebrant adds a concluding Collect, or the following
    Doxology*
or else he concludes...for ever. **Amen.**] OMIT

91 ⟦Nos. 130, 131, 132 and 133 in **FAL** – '*FORM VI*'⟧

⟦After first and last lines of text in no. 130 add '*Silence*'⟧
For Bishops...our Bishop(s)];] For [*N.* our presiding Bishop, and *N.*(*N.*) our
    Bishop(s); and for] all bishops and other ministers;
Those present] *The People*
⟦After first line of no. 131 add '*Silence*' and again after 'eternal kingdom'⟧
⟦After last line of no. 132 add '**through Jesus Christ our Lord. Amen.**'⟧
Priest concludes the prayers] *Celebrant concludes*

92   THE COLLECT AT THE PRAYERS

⟦This section corresponds to nos. 134 and 135 in **FAL**, with similar opening rubrics, and eight collects printed, which include the first five in **FAL**, and three other general ones. In the first and fourth from **FAL** '*thy*' (italicized) replaces 'your'⟧

93 COMMUNION UNDER SPECIAL CIRCUMSTANCES

⟦This is omitted here in accordance with the editorial principles governing this volume⟧

AN ORDER FOR CELEBRATING
THE HOLY EUCHARIST (Amer3–3)

94　*This rite requires careful preparation by the Priest and other participants.*

95　*It is not intended for use at the principal Sunday or weekly celebration of the Holy Eucharist.*

THE PEOPLE AND PRIEST

96　*GATHER IN THE LORD'S NAME*

97　*PROCLAIM AND RESPOND TO THE WORD OF GOD*
The proclamation and response may include readings, song, talk, dance, instrumental music, other art forms, silence. A reading from the Gospel is always included.

98　*PRAY FOR THE WORLD AND THE CHURCH*

99　*EXCHANGE THE PEACE*
Either here or elsewhere in the service, all greet one another in the name of the Lord.

100　*PREPARE THE TABLE*
Some of those present prepare the table; the bread, the cup of wine, and other offerings, are placed upon it.

101　*MAKE EUCHARIST*
The Great Thanksgiving is said by the Priest in the name of the gathering, using one of the eucharistic prayers provided.

The people respond – **Amen**!

102　*BREAK THE BREAD*

103　*SHARE THE GIFTS OF GOD*
The Body and Blood of the Lord are shared in a reverent manner; after all have received, any of the Sacrament that remains is then consumed.

104　*When a common meal or Agapé is part of the celebration, it follows here.*

105　　　　AT THE GREAT THANKSGIVING
In making Eucharist, the Celebrant uses one of the Eucharistic Prayers from Rite One or Rite Two, or one of the following forms

106　*FORM 1*

Celebrant	The Lord be with you.
People	**And also with you.**
Celebrant	Lift up your hearts.
People	**We lift them to the Lord.**

Celebrant	Let us give thanks to the Lord our God.
People	**It is right to give him thanks and praise.**

The Celebrant gives thanks to God the Father for his work in creation and his revelation of himself to his people;

Recalls before God, when appropriate, the particular occasion being celebrated;

Incorporates or adapts the Proper Preface of the day, if desired.

If the Sanctus is to be included, it is introduced with these or similar words

And so we join the saints and angels in proclaiming your glory, as we sing (say),

Celebrant and People
Holy, holy...⟦ICET 5(a) and 5(b)⟧...**in the highest.**

The Celebrant now praises God for the salvation of the world through Jesus Christ our Lord.

The Prayer continues with these words

And so, Father, we bring you these gifts. Sanctify them by your Holy Spirit to be for your people the Body and Blood of Jesus Christ our Lord.

At the following words concerning the bread, the Celebrant is to hold it, or lay a hand upon it; and at the words concerning the cup, to hold or place a hand upon the cup and any other vessel containing wine to be consecrated.

On the night he was betrayed he took bread, said the blessing, broke the bread, and gave it to his friends, and said, 'Take, eat: This is my Body, which is given for you. Do this for the remembrance of me.'

After supper, he took the cup of wine, gave thanks, and said, 'Drink this, all of you; This is my Blood of the new Covenant, which is shed for you and for many for the forgiveness of sins. Whenever you drink it, do this for the remembrance of me.'

Father, we now celebrate the memorial of your Son. By means of this holy bread and cup, we show forth the sacrifice of his death, and proclaim his resurrection, until he comes again.

Gather us by this Holy Communion into one body in your Son Jesus Christ. Make us a living sacrifice of praise.

By him, and with him, and in him, in the unity of the Holy Spirit all honor and glory is yours, Almighty Father, now and for ever. **Amen.**

07 *FORM 2*

Celebrant	The grace of our Lord Jesus Christ and the love of God and the fellowship of the Holy Spirit be with you all.
People	**And also with you.**
Celebrant	Lift up your hearts.
People	**We lift them to the Lord.**

⟦Then the Form follows Form 1 above, in both text and rubrics, as far as the rubric after the Benedictus Qui Venit. This rubric ('*The Celebrant now praises...*') is followed immediately by the rubric and text of the narrative of institution ('*At the following words...*') as in Form 1.⟧

...the remembrance of me.'

Recalling now his suffering and death, and celebrating his resurrection and ascension, we await his coming in glory.

Accept, O Lord, our sacrifice of praise, this memorial of our redemption.

Send your Holy Spirit upon these gifts. Let them be for us the Body and Blood of your Son. And grant that we who eat this bread and drink this cup may be filled with your life and goodness.

The Celebrant then prays that all may receive the benefits of Christ's work, and the renewal of the Holy Spirit.

The Prayer concludes with these or similar words

All this we ask through your Son Jesus Christ. By him, and with him, and in him, in the unity of the Holy Spirit all honor and glory is yours, Almighty Father, now and for ever. **Amen.**

ADDITIONAL DIRECTIONS

108 ⟦The rites above are followed in the American Book of Common Prayer by four pages of 'Directions', largely corresponding to those printed out in **FAL**. The first ten are a reduced form of nos. 136 to 140 in **FAL**, concerning the Preparation and the Ministry of the Word, providing guidance about the use of the Gloria Patri with psalms, variant forms of the Kyries, the omission of the Gloria in Excelsis in Lent etc. as far as provision for when there is no communion. There are then four Directions about the Peace, notices, and the preparation of the bread and wine, corresponding to nos. 141 in **FAL**, but with minor alterations. No. 142 has disappeared totally, and no. 143 is represented by a permission to use the Agnus Dei (ICET 8(b) is printed out) at the Breaking of the Bread. The first provisions of no. 144 have disappeared, but those at the top of page 171 reappear almost *verbatim*. To the third is added '*In the absence of sufficient deacons and priests, lay persons licensed by the bishop according to the canon may administer the Chalice.*' No. 145 is reproduced as follows:

If the consecrated Bread or Wine does not suffice for the number of communicants, the celebrant is to return to the Holy Table, and consecrate more of either or both, by saying

Hear us, O heavenly Father, and with thy (your) Word and Holy Spirit bless and sanctify this bread (wine) that it, also, may be the Sacrament of the precious Body (Blood) of thy (your) Son Jesus Christ our Lord, who took bread (the cup) and said, 'This is my Body (Blood).' **Amen.**

or else the celebrant may consecrate more of both kinds, saying again the words of the Eucharistic Prayer, beginning with the words which follow the Sanctus, and ending with the Invocation (in the case of Eucharistic Prayer C, ending with the narrative of the Institution).

Nos. 146 and 147 are barely altered, though the final provision about the use of 'Alleluia' (which is now in the text of the rites) is omitted. No. 148 has disappeared.

Following these 'Directions', though still under the general heading, is a section sub-headed '*Disciplinary Rubrics*'. These carry forward the provision traditional in the 1928 Prayer Book (and its predecessors) to cover cases where persons are to be restrained from presenting themselves for communion.⟧

CHAPTER 7

THE CHURCH OF THE PROVINCE OF THE WEST INDIES

FAL RECORDS on page 172 that a somewhat traditional draft of a revised eucharistic liturgy was rejected by the Provincial Synod in 1972. The Liturgical Commission therefore worked on a more modern rite, using the ICET texts of 1970–1, addressing God as 'you' throughout (though with 'thou' form alternatives in some well-loved parts), and providing two wholly new eucharistic prayers (which drew freely on the new Roman Catholic prayers). Five forms of intercession were provided in an appendix. This rite, called the '1975 Experimental Rite', was accepted by the Provincial Synod in February 1975.[1] Comments were to be submitted to the Commission from each diocese by the end of 1975. However, the printing and distribution took too long, and the House of Bishops extended the period of experiment to the next meeting of the Provincial Synod in 1978. Submissions were duly made.

The Liturgical Commission then presented a revised and enriched rite to the 1978 Synod. The main change was the increase to eight forms of intercession, and, although the eucharistic prayers were virtually unchanged, a range of acclamations was added to them. The Peace and other parts had more alternatives included also. The rite was then published in the substantial book *Revised Services CPWI* (1980). This rite is presented below under the code '**WIndR**'.

THE RITE FROM THE BOOK '*REVISED SERVICES FOR THE CHURCH OF THE PROVINCE OF THE WEST INDIES*' 1980 (WInd1)

[The numbering is editorial. The capitalization of the original has been followed. In sections 36 and 37 the eucharistic prayers have not been 'lined out' as they are in the original, where there is some inconsistency of practice.]

---

[1] Technically, the 1959 rite, **WInd**, is 'experimental' as it has never officially replaced 1662.

THE HOLY EUCHARIST
THE PREPARATION

1 *At the entry of the Ministers a psalm, canticle, or hymn may be sung.*

2 *OPENING SENTENCES*

The president greets the congregation with one of the following :

[The Seasonal and other Sentences which follow are to be found in Appendix D]

3 *President*   Blessed be God: Father, Son and Holy Spirit.
Alleluia! Alleluia!

All   **And blessed be His Kingdom, now and for ever.
Amen.
Alleluia! Alleluia!**

4 *The following may be said by the President and people :*
All

**Blessed Lord and Father, we have assembled in your name and
in fellowship with one another; Enable us by your grace to offer
the sacrifice of praise and thanksgiving; to proclaim and respond
to your holy word. Teach us to pray for your world and your
Church. Grant that we, confessing our sins, may worthily offer
to you our souls and bodies as a living sacrifice and eat and drink
of your spiritual food in this Holy Sacrament. Amen.**

5 *The following may also be said :*

Collect for Purity
All
Almighty God, to you... [CF 1] **...our Lord. Amen.**
whom] you

6 *Here may follow :*

The Kyries

Lord, have mercy.
Lord, have mercy.

Christ, have mercy.
Christ, have mercy.

Lord, have mercy.
Lord, have mercy.

*In place of the above form, the Ninefold or the Threefold Kyrie may be
said or sung.*

7 *Here may follow :*
Gloria in Excelsis
Glory to God ... ⟦ICET 4⟧ ... **the Father. Amen.**

8 *The Collect of the day shall be said or sung.*
President   Let us pray.
At the end of the collect the people respond :
             Amen.

THE MINISTRY OF THE WORD

9 *A READING FROM THE OLD TESTAMENT OR THE APOCRYPHA*
Reader   A reading from the Word of God written in _____

At the end of the reading :
Reader   This is the Word of the Lord
or   Here ends the reading.
All   **Thanks be to God.**

10 *A psalm, hymn or canticle may be sung.*

11 *A READING FROM THE NEW TESTAMENT*
Reader   A reading from the Word of God written in _____

At the end of the reading :
Reader   This is the Word of the Lord.
or   Here ends the reading.
All   **Thanks be to God.**

12 *A psalm, hymn or canticle may be sung.*

13 *A READING FROM THE GOSPEL*
Reader   The Lord be with you.
All   **And also with you.**
Reader   A Reading from the Holy Gospel according to _____
All   **Glory to Christ our Saviour.**
At the end of the reading :
Reader   This is the Gospel of Christ.
All   **Praise to Christ our Lord.**

14 *THE SERMON*

15 *Here may follow the Nicene Creed or the Apostles' Creed.*
THE NICENE CREED
We believe ... ⟦ICET 3 with 1971 variants⟧ ... **to come. Amen.**

seen and unseen] seen or unseen
[and the Son]]   OM

THE APOSTLES' CREED
I believe...⟦ICET 2⟧...**life everlasting. Amen.**

16 *THE PRAYERS*

Intercession

The prayers of the Church are offered in one of the following forms, the Leader to indicate the form of Intercession and appropriate directions to be used.

17 *Form A*
Extempore prayer may be offered, but shall include prayers for the world, the Church and the local community.

18 *Form B*

Leader	Father, we pray for your holy Catholic Church;
All	**That we all may be one.**
Leader	Grant that every member of the Church may truly and humbly serve you;
All	**That your Name may be glorified by all people.**
Leader	We pray for all Bishops, Priests, and Deacons;
All	**That they may be faithful ministers of your Word and Sacraments.**
Leader	We pray for all who govern and hold authority in the nations of the world;
All	**That there may be justice and peace on the earth.**
Leader	Give us grace to do your will in all that we undertake;
All	**That our works may find favour in your sight.**
Leader	Have compassion on those who suffer from any grief or trouble;
All	**That they may be delivered from their distress.**
Leader	Give to the departed eternal rest;
All	**Let light perpetual shine upon them.**
Leader	We praise you for your saints who have entered into joy;
All	**May we also come to share in your heavenly kingdom.**
Leader	Let us pray for our own needs and those of others.

Silence may be kept.

All
Almighty God, to whom our needs are known before we ask, help us to ask only what accords to your will; and the good things

which we dare not, or in our blindness cannot ask, grant us for the sake of your Son, Jesus Christ our Lord. Amen.

19 *Form C*

Leader

With all our heart and all our mind let us pray to the Lord, saying, 'Lord, have mercy.'

Leader

For the peace from above, for the loving kindness of God, and for the salvation of our souls:

Let us pray to the Lord.

All   **Lord, have mercy.**

Leader

For the peace and welfare of the world, for the witness and work of the Church, and for the unity of all peoples:

Let us pray to the Lord.

All   **Lord, have mercy.**

Leader

For our Bishops and all ministers of God's Word and Sacraments, that they may be filled with truth and love and be found without fault at the Lord's coming:

Let us pray to the Lord.

All   **Lord, have mercy.**

Leader

For the leaders of the nations and for those in authority among us, that they may serve justice and promote the freedom and dignity of all peoples:

Let us pray to the Lord.

All   **Lord, have mercy.**

Leader

For the victims of hunger, fear, injustice and oppression, and for all who labour in the cause of human liberation and fulfilment:

Let us pray to the Lord.

All   **Lord, have mercy.**

Leader

For the sick, the suffering, the sorrowful, and the dying; and for all who remember and care for them:

Let us pray to the Lord.

All   **Lord, have mercy.**

Leader

For deliverance from the ravages of hurricane, earthquake, drought or flood, and for a just and proper use of God's creation:
Let us pray to the Lord.

All   **Lord, have mercy.**

Leader

For ourselves and all who confess the name of Christ, that we may show forth the excellencies of Him who called us out of darkness into His marvellous light:
Let us pray to the Lord.

All   **Lord, have mercy.**

Leader

That with all His servants who have served Him here and are now at rest we may enter into the fullness of His unending joy:
Let us pray to the Lord.

All   **Lord, have mercy.**

Silence may be kept.

All

O Lord our God, accept the fervent prayers of your people in the multitude of your mercies. Look with compassion on us and all who turn to you for help; for you are gracious O Lord of love, and to you we give glory, Father, Son, and Holy Spirit, now and for ever. Amen.

20 *Form D*

Leader

Our Heavenly Father has promised through our Lord Jesus Christ to hear us when we pray in faith. Let us therefore pray for the Church and the World, and let us thank God for His goodness.

Silence may be kept.

Leader

We pray for the Church of God in every place; especially for this Diocese, our Bishop _____, and all the people of God.

All

Strengthen your Church to carry forward the work of Christ; that we and all who confess your Name may unite in truth, live together in your love, and reveal your glory to the world.

Leader

We pray for our country and for all the nations of the world, especially
_____; and for all people in their various callings.

All

**Direct this nation and all nations in the ways of justice and truth.
Give wisdom to all in positions of public trust and authority; that
they may promote the prosperity, godliness and peace of your
people everywhere.**

Leader

We pray for our own community, for this parish, for our families,
friends, and all who live and work with us.

All

**Give grace to all our friends and neighbours in Christ, that we
may serve Him in one another and grow together in His love.**

Leader

We pray for the poor, the sick, the unemployed, the handicapped; all
who have requested our prayers and all who seek the prayers of the
Church in their time of trouble.

All

**Give healing and strength to all who suffer in body, mind or
spirit. Give them courage and hope in their troubles and sustain
all those who remember and care for them.**

Leader

We commemorate the departed, especially _____.

All

**We commend all people to your unfailing love, that in them your
will may be fulfilled; and we rejoice at the faithful witness of
your saints in every age, praying that we may share with them
in your eternal kingdom.**

All

**Accept these prayers, O Lord our God, for the sake of your Son,
our Saviour Jesus Christ. Amen.**

21 *Form E*

Leader

Let us pray for the fellowship of the Church of Christ, and for all God's
creatures.

Leader

With all who confess the name of Jesus, as Lord and Saviour, we offer
our prayers and praises, in Spirit and in truth.

Father in Heaven,

All   **Hear our prayer.**

Leader

With Jesus Christ, our Great High Priest, who ever lives to intercede for us, we uphold all ministers of God's Word and Sacraments, that they may fulfill their high calling in the Faith.

Father in Heaven,

All   **Hear our prayer.**

Leader

We pray for the unfailing guidance of the Holy Spirit on those who are called to interpret and expound the will of the Lord to others.

Father in Heaven,

All   **Hear our prayer.**

Leader

We pray for all organizations, within the fellowship of the Body of Christ, that their work may edify the people of God, and bear faithful witness to the Gospel.

Father in Heaven,

All   **Hear our prayer.**

Leader

We pray for all persons who do not share our confession of faith, that with courage, truth and love we may work together with them, and promote the common good.

Father in Heaven,

All   **Hear our prayer.**

Leader

For the leaders of our country, and all who make decisions on our behalf, that they may be filled with the fruit of the Spirit, to direct our affairs in righteousness and peace,

Father in Heaven,

All   **Hear our prayer.**

Leader

For our Judges, Magistrates and all who administer justice, that in all things they may seek to do your will, and to protect the rights and freedom of your people.

Father in Heaven,

All   **Hear our prayer.**

Leader

In our schools, and in all other places of learning, may true knowledge, sound wisdom, and godly discipline ever be found.

Father in Heaven,

All   **Hear our prayer.**

Leader

To the poor, the hungry, the unemployed, the persecuted immigrants, and the victims of racial oppression, may God in Christ help us all to bring relief and just protection.

Father in Heaven,

All **Hear our prayer.**

Leader

To all who suffer now from pain and disease, from human discomfort and misery, may God in Christ bring healing and joy, for the renewal of their faith.

Father in Heaven,

All **Hear our prayer.**

Leader

That we may use aright the fullness of the Earth, that our pursuits in science, and the advancement of our skills, may ever be in service of that true humanity, which is created in the image of God,

Father in Heaven,

All **Hear our prayer.**

Leader

That we may never become slaves of money, or of the lust for power, but may rather strive for victory through the power of love,

Father in Heaven,

All **Hear our prayer.**

Leader

That with all who belong to the communion of saints, both living and departed, we may ever rejoice in the blessed assurance of that hope, which has been won for us in Christ,

Father in Heaven,

All **Receive these our prayers in the name of your dear Son, even Jesus Christ our Lord. Amen.**

22 *Form F*

After the Priest's invitation to prayer, he shall say:

Let us pray for the Church and for all men according to their needs.

Lord in your love

All **Hear our prayer.**

⟦After this '*All*' comes above each response, but is omitted here⟧

Leader

Bless and inspire all members of the clergy, especially _____, our Archbishop; _____, our Bishop; and _____, our Priest(s).

That their lives may be examples of their teaching, and that they may rightly and faithfully administer your holy Sacraments.

Leader
Guide and protect all Heads of State and all who bear rule, especially those in this land: our (President), the Prime Minister, and all members of Parliament.

That our people may be godly and peacefully governed.

Leader
Direct those who administer justice; and strengthen those who guard and protect the land.

That our people may dwell in peace.

Leader
Reveal the common good to those in positions of public trust and to decision-makers in industry and commerce.

That freedom and dignity may prevail among us.

Leader
Enlighten with your Spirit all places of education and learning.

That the whole world may be filled with the knowledge of your truth.

Leader
Comfort and help _____, and all others in any trouble, sorrow, need, sickness, or any other adversity.

Help us to help them, O Lord.

Leader
Remember our brothers and sisters, especially _____, and all others who have died in your faith and fear.

Grant them peace and eternal life.

Leader
We thank you, heavenly Father, for the witness of the Blessed Virgin Mary, Mother of Jesus, our Lord and Saviour; for the holy Patriarchs, Prophets, Apostles and Martyrs; and all the Saints who have been good examples in their several generations.

Priest
And finally let us pray for our own needs and those of others.

A period of silence may be kept.

Priest
Accept our prayers and intercessions, Father, according to your wisdom, for the sake of your Son, Jesus Christ.

All   **Amen.**

23 *Form G*

In the course of the silence after each bidding, the people offer their own prayers, either silently or aloud.

Leader
I ask your prayers for God's people throughout the world; for our Bishop _____; for this gathering; and for all ministers and people.
Pray for the Church.

Silence

Leader
I ask your prayers for peace; for goodwill among nations; and for the well-being of all people.
Pray for justice and peace.

Silence

Leader
I ask your prayers for the poor, the sick, the hungry, the oppressed, and those in prison.
Pray for those in any need or trouble.

Silence

Leader
I ask your prayers for all who seek God, or a deeper knowledge of him.
Pray that they may find and be found by him.

Silence

Leader
I ask your prayers for the departed (especially _____).
Pray for those who have died.

Silence

Members of the congregation may ask the prayers or the thanksgivings of those present.
I ask your prayers for _____.
I ask your thanksgiving for _____.

Silence

Leader
Praise God for those in every generation in whom Christ has been honoured (especially _____ whom we remember today).
Pray that we may have grace to glorify Christ in our own day.

Silence

The President adds a concluding Collect.

24 *Form H*

Leader

Let us pray for the Church and for the world.

Grant, Almighty God, that all who confess your Name may be united in your truth, live together in your love, and reveal your glory in the world.

Silence

Leader   Lord, in your mercy
All   **Hear our prayer.**

⟦The rubric '*Silence*' and the versicle and response are repeated in this form after each paragraph, including the last one.⟧

Leader

Guide the people of this land, and of all the nations, in the ways of justice and peace; that we may honour one another and serve the common good.

Leader

Give us all a reverence for the earth as your own creation, that we may use its resources rightly in the service of others and to your honour and glory.

Leader

Bless all whose lives are closely linked with ours, and grant that we may serve Christ in them, and love one another as he loves us.

Leader

Comfort and heal all those who suffer in body, mind, or spirit; give them courage and hope in their troubles, and bring them the joy of your salvation.

Leader

We commend to your mercy all who have died, that your will for them may be fulfilled; and we pray that we may share with all your saints in your eternal kingdom.

The President adds a concluding Collect.

PENITENCE

25 *The President shall introduce the Act of Penitence.*

President

If we say we have no sin, we deceive ourselves, and the truth is not in us. If we confess our sins, God is faithful and just, and will forgive our sins and cleanse us from all unrighteousness.

A period of silence shall be kept.

26 *President*   Let us therefore confess our sins.

All

Almighty God, our Heavenly Father, we have sinned against you and one another, in thought, word and deed, and in what we have left undone. We are sorry and repent of all our sins. For your Son, our Lord Jesus Christ's sake, forgive us all that is past, and grant that we may serve you in newness of life to the glory of your Name.

THE ABSOLUTION

27 *President*   Almighty God, have mercy...⟦CF 5⟧...our Lord.

  All   **Amen.**

THE GREETING OF PEACE

28 *One of the following forms shall be said:*

29 *Form A*

  President

  We are the Body of Christ. By the one Spirit we were all baptized into one body.

  All

  Let us then pursue the things that make for peace and build up the common life.

30 *Form B*

  President

  If you are offering your gift at the altar, and there remember that your brother has something against you,

  All

  Leave your gift there before the altar and go; first be reconciled to your brother, and then come and offer your gift.

31 *Form C*

  President

  The Kingdom of God is justice, peace, and joy, inspired by the Holy Spirit.

  All

  They who thus serve Christ are acceptable to God and approved by others.

32 *The President shall then greet the congregation.*

  President   The peace of the Lord be always with you.

  All   **And also with you.**

  The President and people shall exchange the Peace.

33 *Notices and Banns may be given.*

THE PRESENTATION OF THE OFFERINGS

34 *When the offerings are presented at the altar, either 'A' or 'B' shall be said:*

A

President
Through your goodness, Lord,
we have this bread and wine to offer,
the fruit of the earth and the work of human hands.
They will become our spiritual food.
All
**All things come from you, O Lord,
and of your own do we give you.
Blessed be God for ever. Amen.**

B

President　　Father,
All
**We offer to you these gifts
which you have given us;
this bread, this wine, this money.
With them we offer ourselves, our lives, and our work,
to become through your Holy Spirit
a reasonable, holy, and lively sacrifice.
As this bread and wine
become the Body and Blood of Christ,
so may we and all your people
become channels of your love;
through the same Christ our Lord. Amen.**

THE EUCHARISTIC PRAYER

35 *President*　　The Lord be with you.
　　All　　**And also with you.**
　　President　　Lift up your hearts.
　　All　　**We lift them up to the Lord.**
　　President　　Let us give thanks to the Lord our God.
　　All　　**It is right to give him thanks and praise.**
　　President
It is right, and a good and joyful thing, always and everywhere to give
you thanks, Father Almighty, everlasting God:

The Proper Preface shall follow :

⟦The Proper Prefaces which are printed here are to be found in Appendix C⟧

Therefore we praise you, joining our voices with angels and archangels and with all the company of heaven, who forever sing this hymn to proclaim the glory of your Name:

All

Holy, holy, holy Lord, God of power and might;
heaven and earth are full of your glory.
Hosanna in the highest.
Blessed is he who comes in the name of the Lord.
Hosanna in the highest.

Either ' A' or ' B' shall now be said :

36 *A*

President

All Holy and glorious Father, our Creator God, we give you thanks because in your loving wisdom you brought all things into being, and are truly worthy of praise from every creature you have made.

Again and again we have turned away from you; yet in every age your steadfast love has called us to return, to live in union with you: for it is your eternal purpose to put new life into all things and make them holy.

Through your Son, Jesus Christ, who took our human nature upon Him you have redeemed the world from the bondage of sin: and by the power of your Holy Spirit you have gathered a people to yourself, to make known in every place His perfect offering which He made to the glory of your Name.

Hear us, therefore, Father, through your Son, Jesus Christ our Lord; And grant that these gifts of bread and wine may be unto us His Body and Blood.

For, on the night that He was betrayed He took bread, and when he had given thanks to you, He broke it and gave it to his disciples and said: 'Take this, and eat it: This is my Body which is given for you. Do this for the remembrance of me.'

And after supper He took the cup of wine: and when He had given thanks, he gave it to them and said: 'Drink this, all of you: This is my Blood of the New Covenant, which is shed for you and for many for the forgiveness of sins. Whenever you drink it, do this for the remembrance of me.'

President

Let us proclaim the mystery of our faith.

One of the following Acclamations shall be said :

All

Christ has died.
Christ is risen.
Christ will come again.

or

Jesus is Lord.
He has reconciled us to himself:
Christ makes all things new.

or

Christ is Lord.
Through His death we were made children of God:
He is our hope of glory.

President

And so, Heavenly Father, rejoicing in His Holy Incarnation; His Blessed Passion and His Perfect Sacrifice made once for all upon the Cross; His Mighty Resurrection from the dead; His Glorious Ascension into heaven; and looking for His Coming in glory; we offer to you this Bread and this Cup.

We pray that you will accept this sacrifice of praise and thanksgiving; and grant that all who eat and drink of the Body and Blood of your Son, our great High Priest, may be renewed by your Holy Spirit, and be one Body, one Spirit, in Him.

Let faith and love increase in us. Unite us with all Bishops, all other ministers of your Word and Sacraments, and with the whole people of God, living and departed, whom you have made for yourself.

Confirm us in holiness, that we may be found ready to join the company of the Blessed Virigin Mary, the Holy Apostles, and all your saints, when our Lord Jesus Christ comes again: Forever giving you thanks and praise through Him from whom all good things do come.

With Him and in Him and through Him, by the power of the Holy Spirit, we worship you, Father Almighty, with all who stand before you in earth and heaven, in songs of everlasting praise:

All

Blessing and honour and glory and power
Be yours for ever and ever. Amen.

37 *B*

President

Holy and gracious Father, all creation rightly gives you praise. All life, all holiness, comes from you through your Son, Jesus Christ our Lord, whom you sent to share our human nature, to live and die as one of us, to reconcile us to you, the God and Father of all.

We therefore bring you these gifts, and we ask you to make them holy by the power of your Spirit, that they may become the Body and Blood of your Son, our Saviour Jesus Christ, who offered Himself in obedience to your will, the Perfect Sacrifice for all mankind.

On the night he was betrayed, he took bread, and when he had given thanks to you, He broke it and gave it to his disciples and said: Take this and eat it: This is my Body which is given for you. Do this for the remembrance of me.'

After supper he took the cup of wine and when he had given thanks He gave it to them and said: 'Drink this, all of you: This is my Blood of the new Covenant, Which is shed for you and for many for the forgiveness of sins. Do this, whenever you drink it, for the remembrance of me.'

One of the following Acclamations shall be said:

All

When we eat this Bread and drink this Cup, we proclaim the death of Christ until he comes again.

or

Christ has died.
Christ is risen.
Christ will come again.

or

Christ Jesus is Lord.
He has set us free from the law of sin and death:
In his name alone is our salvation.

President

Father, calling to mind the death your Son endured for our salvation; His Glorious Resurrection and Ascension; His continual intercession for us in heaven; and looking for His coming again in glory, we offer you, in thanksgiving, this holy and life-giving sacrifice.

Look with favour on your Church's offering, and grant that we who eat and drink these holy gifts may be filled with your Holy Spirit and become one body in Christ, and serve you in unity, constancy and peace.

May He make us a perpetual offering to you and enable us, in communion with blessed Mary and the whole company of heaven, to share in the inheritance of your saints.

With Him, and in Him, and through Him, by the power of the Holy Spirit, we worship you, Father Almighty, with all who stand before you in earth and heaven in songs of everlasting praise:

All

Blessing and honour and glory and power
Be yours for ever and ever. Amen.

38　*THE LORD'S PRAYER*

President　　As our Saviour has taught us, so we pray:

All　　　　**Our Father...⟦ICET 1⟧...for ever. Amen.**

THE BREAKING OF THE BREAD

39　*President*

We break this bread to share in the body of Christ.

All

Though we are many, we are one body, because we all share in one bread.

40　*The Agnus Dei may follow here.*

THE COMMUNION

41　*The Invitation*

One of the following forms shall be used:

42　*Form A*

President

My brothers and sisters in Christ, draw near and receive His Body which He gave for you, and His blood which He shed for you. Remember that He died for you, and feed on Him in your hearts by faith with thanksgiving.

All

Grant us, gracious Lord, that we may so eat the flesh of your dear Son, Jesus Christ and drink His blood, that we may evermore dwell in Him and He in us. Amen.

43　*Form B*

President

The Gifts of God for the People of God.

All

Our souls will feast and he satisfied, and we will sing glad songs of praise to Him.

44　*Form C*

President

Draw near and receive the Body and Blood of our Saviour Jesus Christ with faith and thanksgiving.

45 *All*

**We do not presume to approach your Table, most merciful
Father, trusting in our own righteousness, for we are not worthy
even to gather together the crumbs which fall from your Table.
Yet in your boundless and most gracious favour towards us, you
are ready to welcome us who come to your Table in penitence
and faith. Grant, O Lord of Grace and Love, that we may so eat
of this Bread – the Body of your dear Son Jesus Christ, and drink
of this Cup – which is his Blood, that with bodies, minds, and
souls made clean from every stain of sin, we may from hence-
forth live in him, and he in us. Amen.**

46 *The Agnus Dei may follow here.*
Lamb of God... ⟦ICET 8(b)⟧ ... us peace.

sins] sin THROUGHOUT

47 *During the administration, the Ministers say to each communicant :*
The Body of Christ given for you.
The Blood of Christ shed for you.
and the communicant replies, each time : **Amen.**

THE DISMISSAL

Post Communion
Either

48 *All*

**Almighty Father,
we thank you for feeding us
with the Body and Blood of your Son, Jesus Christ.
May we who share His Body... ⟦CF 8⟧ ... our Lord. Amen.**

we whom the Spirit lights] we upon whom your Spirit shines
Keep us...grasped] Help us to continue in faithful witness to your Word.

Or

49 **Eternal God and Heavenly Father,
we thank you for feeding us
with the Body and Blood of your Son Jesus Christ.
Send us now into the world in peace,
and grant us strength and courage
to love and serve you and our fellow men
with gladness and singleness of heart,
through your Son Jesus Christ our Lord. Amen.**

Dismissal

50 *The President (or the Bishop, if present) may say this Blessing :*
The Blessing... ⟦CF 10⟧ ... always. **Amen.**

51 *A hymn may be sung.*

| 52 *President* | Go in peace and serve the Lord. |
| *All* | **In the name of Christ. Amen.** |

APPENDICES TO THE LITURGY

53 *APPENDIX 1*

⟦This is 'The Litany for Ordinations' and is omitted here⟧

54 *APPENDIX 2*

WHEN THE CONSECRATED ELEMENTS ARE INSUFFICIENT

If either or both of the consecrated elements are likely to prove insufficient, the President returns to the holy table and adds more, with these words:

Having given thanks to you, Father, over the bread and the cup according to the institution of your son, Jesus Christ, on the night that he was betrayed; we pray that you will accept the praise and thanksgiving we offer through him who said, 'Take, eat; this is my Body' (*and/or* 'Drink this; this is my Blood'), and grant that this bread/wine also may be to us his Body/Blood and be received in remembrance of him.

55 *APPENDIX 3*

COMMUNION ANTHEM
Jesus, Lamb of God...⟦ICET 8(a)⟧...**your peace.**

56 *APPENDIX 4*

⟦This is 'A Penitential Order' and is omitted here⟧

57 *APPENDIX 5*

CONCERNING THE CELEBRATION

The President or Celebrant at the Celebration of the Eucharist shall be a duly ordained Priest or Bishop of the Anglican Communion.

It is the bishop's prerogative, when present, to be the principal celebrant at the Lord's Table, and to preach the Gospel.

At all celebrations of the Liturgy, it is fitting that the principal celebrant, whether bishop or priest, be assisted by other priests, and by deacons and lay persons.

It is appropriate that the other priests present stand with the celebrant at the Altar, and join in the consecration of the gifts, in breaking the Bread, and in distributing Communion.

A deacon should read the Gospel and may lead The Prayers. Deacons should also serve at the Altar, preparing and placing on it the offerings of bread and wine, and assisting in the ministration of the Sacrament to the people. In the absence of a deacon, these duties may be performed by an assisting priest or, with the permission of the bishop, by a duly accredited lay person.

Lay persons appointed by the celebrant should normally be assigned the reading of the Lessons which precede the Gospel, and may lead The Prayers.

Morning or Evening Prayer may be used in place of all that precedes the Greeting of Peace, provided that a lesson from the Gospel is always included, and that the intercessions conform to the directions given for The Prayers.

⟦A lengthy rubric then provides for a deacon distributing communion to the worshippers from previously consecrated elements.⟧

It is desirable that the Lessons be read from a lectern or pulpit, and that the Gospel be read from the same lectern, or from the pulpit, or from the midst of the congregation. It is desirable that the Lessons and Gospel be read from a book or books of appropriate size and dignity.

CHAPTER 8

THE PROVINCES OF
SOUTH AMERICA

THE Province of Brazil had Portuguese-language rites from 1967 and 1972 published in translation in **MAL** and **FAL** (**Braz** and **BrazR**). There has been a further revision of **BrazR** in the years since 1980 and a new Prayer Book was authorized by the Provincial Synod in July 1984, which will contain it. The book will be published in February 1986.

The Spanish-speaking dioceses of Southern South America were formed into a new autonomous Province of the Southern Cone of South America in April 1983. They are still at a very early stage of developing provincial common bonds, and no provincial liturgy is as yet in view. In most dioceses, the 1973 Chile rite (**ChilR** to be found in **FAL**) is in use. In Southern Argentina the Spanish version of the ECUSA Prayer Book, mentioned on page 127 above, is used. This was produced for the Central American and Caribbean dioceses of 'Province IX' of ECUSA.

The Falkland Islands were separated in 1976 from the mainland dioceses, and are under the Archbishop of Canterbury's jurisdiction, and follow Church of England liturgical uses.

CHAPTER 9

THE CHURCH OF THE PROVINCE OF WEST AFRICA

THE Province of West Africa includes dioceses in Ghana, Guinea, Gambia, Liberia and Sierra Leone, and these have different liturgical backgrounds. Nevertheless, following the 1978 Lambeth Conference, the Provincial Liturgy Committee (of which the members are mostly diocesan bishops) recommended a eucharistic liturgy to the Standing Committee of the Province in February 1980, and this was authorized for use for three years, and printed a year later with that authorization included (as shown below). A simpler version came into use in the diocese of Gambia, and there are variants in printings in other dioceses. In December 1983 the Provincial Synod extended the three-year experimental period for another three years. The rite draws heavily upon traditional Anglican material, though in a 'you' form of address to God. In Sierra Leone it has been translated into Temne and Mende.

THE EXPERIMENTAL LITURGY OF THE CHURCH OF THE PROVINCE OF WEST AFRICA 1980 (WAfr)

〚The rite is published in a printed booklet. The numbering is original to it. The rubrics for '*Silence*' are usually printed in capitals in the original, but have been altered here. Various corrections of printers' errors have been made here. The Gambian version omits sections 7, 8, 9, 10, 12 (the bracketed words), 28, 30, 31, 40, 46 (the longer form), 47, and 51, and has tiny rubrical alterations in a few places also. The rite is numbered accordingly.〛

EUCHARISTIC LITURGY

(*Authorised for experimental use until 1983*)

THE PREPARATION

1 (*Where there is no celebration of the Holy Eucharist, this Order, as far as the Prayers, may be used as an Order of Morning Worship on Sundays.*)

THE WORD AND THE PRAYERS

2 (*As the Ministers come to the Lord's Table the people stand. A hymn, a canticle, a psalm or an anthem may be sung. The Bible from which the Lessons are to be read is carried in and put on the Table or the Lectern. The Celebrant of the Eucharist carries the vessels.*)

3 (*The Celebrant may say*):
> The Lord be with you.

All: **And also with you.**

4 (*One of the Seasonal Greetings may be used*):
> 〚The Seasonal Sentences, which are printed here, are to be found in Appendix D.〛

5 *Celebrant*: Let us pray:

> ### THE COLLECT FOR PURITY
>
> *All*: **Almighty God... 〚CF 1〛... our Lord. Amen.**
> **magnify] praise**

One of the following is said or sung.
Either

6 *All*: **Glory to God... 〚ICET 4〛... God the Father. Amen.**
sin] sins
on] upon

Or

7 *All*: **Holy God, Holy and Mighty, Holy and Immortal, have mercy upon us.**
(*May be repeated three times*)

Or

8 *Celebrant*: Worthy is the Lamb that has been slain to receive the power, and the riches, and wisdom, and might, and honour, and glory, and blessing.

All: **Unto the Lamb be the glory!**

Celebrant: Unto Him that sits on the throne and unto the Lamb, be blessing, and honour, and glory and dominion for ever and ever.

All: **Unto the Lamb be the glory!**

Celebrant: Worthy are you, for you were slain, and you purchased for God with your precious blood men of every tribe and tongue, and people, and nation.

All: **Unto the Lamb be glory! Salvation to our God who sits on the throne, and to the Lamb. Blessing and glory and wisdom, and thanksgiving, and honour and power, and might, be to our God for ever and ever. Amen.** (*Revelation* 5. 9; & 13)

Either

9 ### THE TEN COMMANDMENTS

Celebrant : 1. Hear the commandments which God has given to His people, and take them to heart. I am the Lord your God: you shall have no other gods but me.

All : **Lord have mercy upon us, we pray you.**

Celebrant : 2. You shall not make for yourself any idol.

⟦This then follows CF 2 without the bracketed parts (except in no. 9) in the format shown above.

take...in vain] dishonour
to keep...day] the Sabbath day and keep it holy.
bear...witness] give...evidence against your neighbour   as far as no. 10⟧

...covet anything that belongs to your neighbour.

All : **Lord, have mercy upon us, we pray you.**

(*Exodus* 20. 2–17)

(*The responses after the first nine commandments are optional. Silence may be kept after each commandment.*)

Or

10 ### OUR LORD'S SUMMARY OF THE LAW

Celebrant : Our Lord Jesus Christ said: The first commandment is, Hear O Israel: the Lord our God is the only Lord; love... ⟦CF 3⟧...greater than these. (*Mark* 12. 29–31)

All : **Lord, have mercy upon us and incline our hearts to keep this Law.**

This...commandment] OM AND INCLUDE RESPONSE IN THIS PLACE AS WELL AS AFTER THE SUMMARY

THE NEW COMMANDMENT

Celebrant : Our Lord Jesus Christ said: A new commandment I give you: that you love one another; even as I have loved you, so you are to love one another.   (*John* 13. 34)

All : **Lord, have mercy upon us, and stamp all these your Laws in our hearts, we pray you.**

Or

11 ### THE KYRIES

All : **Lord, have mercy   Kyrie eleison**
Lord, have mercy   Kyrie eleison
Lord, have mercy   Kyrie eleison

All:	Christ, have mercy	Christe eleison
	Christ, have mercy	Christe eleison
	Christ, have mercy	Christe eleison
All:	Lord, have mercy	Kyrie eleison
	Lord, have mercy	Kyrie eleison
	Lord, have mercy	Kyrie eleison

12   *THE EXHORTATION*

Celebrant: My brothers and sisters (having heard the commandments of God), let us examine ourselves in silence; let us seek God's grace to draw near to Him in penitence and faith.

13 *A short period of silence is kept*

14 *Celebrant:* Let us confess our sins to God firmly resolved to obey God's commandments and to live in love and peace with our neighbours.

THE CONFESSION

15 *All:* **Heavenly and eternal Father, we confess that we have sinned against you and our neighbours. We have walked in darkness rather than light; we have called upon the name of Christ, but have not departed from our sins. Have mercy upon us, we pray you; for the sake of Jesus Christ forgive us all our sins. Cleanse us by your Holy Spirit; quicken our consciences and enable us to forgive others; lead us out from darkness to walk as children of light; through Jesus Christ our Lord. Amen.**

16 *Celebrant:* Hear the gracious Words of Comfort Our Saviour says to all who truly turn to Him.

(One or more of the following Scriptural passages shall then be said by the Celebrant.)

Come to me, all who labour and are heavy-laden, and I will give you rest.   *(Matthew* 11. 28)

For God loved the world so much that he gave His only begotten Son, so that everyone who believes in Him may not die but have eternal life   *(John* 3. 16)

Hear what St. Paul says:
This is a true saying, to be completely accepted and believed: Christ Jesus came into the world to save sinners.

               (1 *Timothy* 1. 15)

Hear what St. John says:
If anyone does sin, we have someone who pleads with the
Father on our behalf – Jesus Christ, the righteous one. And
Christ Himself is the means by which our sins are forgiven.

(1 *John* 2. 1)

17 *A short silence is kept. Then the Celebrant or the Bishop if he is present,
pronounces*

THE ABSOLUTION
Almighty God...⟦CF 5⟧...our Lord.

All :   **Amen. Thanks be to God.**

forgives...repent] pardons...repent, and are themselves forgiving
life eternal] eternal life

18 *Celebrant :*   The Lord be with you.

All :   **And also with you.**

Celebrant :   Let us pray.

Here shall follow

THE COLLECT(S) OF THE DAY
THE MINISTRY OF THE WORD
THE OLD TESTAMENT LESSON

19 *Reader :*   Hear the Word of God, as it is written in, *Book*, in
the..........*chapter*, beginning at the..........*verse*.

After reading the passage, he says :

This is the Word of God

All :   **Thanks be to you, O God, for your holy Word.**

20 *A canticle, psalm or a hymn may be said or sung.*

21   ### THE EPISTLE

Reader :   Hear the Word of God as it is written in the *Letter*
of......in the......*chapter*, beginning at the......*verse*.

After reading the Epistle he says :

This is the Word of God.

All :   **Thanks be to God.**

22 *A canticle, psalm, or a hymn may be said or sung.*

23   ### THE GOSPEL (all stand)

Celebrant,   Hear the Gospel of Christ according to..........in
Deacon/   the..........*chapter*, beginning at the..........*verse*
Reader :

All :   **Glory to Christ our Saviour.**

After reading the Gospel, he says:

This is the Gospel of Christ.

All: **We praise you Christ, for your Holy Gospel.**

24   *THE SERMON*

25 *A psalm, hymn or a canticle may be said/sung; or a period of silence may be kept.*

26 *THE NICENE CREED (said or sung by all standing)*

We believe...⟦ICET 3, 1971 text⟧...**to come. Amen.**
[and the Son]] OMIT BRACKETS

Silence may be kept

27   *NOTICES*

28   *THE COLLECTION*

(An anthem, canticle, psalm, hymn or chorus may be sung while the Collection is being received.)

THE PRAYERS

Either

29   *THE FIRST LITANY*

Celebrant: Let us pray.
Almighty God, you have taught us to make prayers, and to give thanks for all men: hear us when we pray. May it please you to inspire continually the universal Church with the spirit of truth, unity and concord. Lord, in your mercy.

All: **Graciously, hear our prayer.**

Celebrant: May it please you to grant that all those who confess your Holy Name may agree in the truth of your Holy Word, and bear witness to it with courage and perseverance. Lord, in your mercy.

All: **Graciously, hear our prayer.**

Celebrant: May it please you to lead the nations in the paths of justice, peace and righteousness. Lord, in your mercy.

All: **Graciously, hear our prayer.**

Celebrant: May it please you to guide with your pure and peace-giving wisdom, those who hold authority in the affairs of men; especially *N.* our President and all those who rule over us; that men may honour one another and seek the common good. Lord, in your mercy.

All: **Graciously, hear our prayer.**

Celebrant : May it please you to give grace to all bishops, priests, deacons and other ministers; especially *N.* our Archbishop and *N.* our Bishop; that by their lives and doctrine they may proclaim your true and living Word, and rightly and duly administer your holy sacraments. Lord, in your mercy.

All : **Graciously, hear our prayer.**

Celebrant : May it please you to guide and prosper all those who are labouring for the spread of your Gospel among the nations; enlighten with your Holy Spirit all places of education, healing and learning. Lord, in your mercy.

All : **Graciously, hear our prayer.**

Celebrant : May it please you to give your heavenly grace to all your people in their various vocations and ministries, and especially this congregation; that they may faithfully bear witness in their daily lives to the Holy Word that they have received and serve you in holiness all the days of their life. Lord, in your mercy.

All : **Graciously, hear our prayer.**

Celebrant : May it please you out of the abundance of your mercy to comfort and heal all those who suffer in body, mind or spirit; all those under the tyranny of oppressors; all those who are in prison; all those who have lost their faith; give them courage in their troubles and bring them the joy of your salvation. Lord, in your mercy.

All : **Graciously, hear our prayer.**

Celebrant : And now we praise you for all your servants who have departed this life in your faith and fear; we beg you to give us grace that we may all share in your eternal kingdom. Lord, in your mercy.

All : **Graciously, hear our prayer.**

Or

30   *THE SECOND LITANY*

Celebrant : Let us pray.
For the peace that is from above and for the salvation of our souls, let us pray to the Lord.

All : **Lord, have mercy.**

Celebrant: For the welfare of God's people; for the unity of the Church, and for love to live together as brethren and to reveal God's glory in the world; let us pray to the Lord.

All: **Lord, have mercy.**

Celebrant: For our bishops, priests and deacons, especially *N.* our Archbishop and *N.* our bishop; that with a good heart and a pure conscience they may fulfil their ministry; let us pray to the Lord.

All: **Lord, have mercy.**

Celebrant: For our rulers and all in authority in our land; that they may govern us according to the will of God; let us pray to the Lord.

All: **Lord, have mercy.**

Celebrant: For the sick, the suffering, the sorrowful the dying; let us pray to the Lord.

All: **Lord, have mercy.**

Celebrant: For the poor, the hungry, orphans and widows and those who suffer persecution for their faith; let us pray to the Lord.

All: **Lord, have mercy.**

Celebrant: For ourselves and all who confess the name of Christ; that we may show forth the excellence of Him who called us out of darkness into His marvellous light; let us pray to the Lord.

All: **Lord, have mercy.**

Celebrant: For all who have served God here and now rest in the sleep of peace, and for the faithful witness of the saints in every age; that with them we may enter into the fulness of His unending joy; let us pray to the Lord.

All: **Lord, graciously have mercy. Amen.**

Celebrant: Almighty and eternal God, the fountain of all wisdom, who knows our needs before we ask, and our ignorance in making our requests before you; have compassion on our weakness; may it please you to give us, because of the blood of your Son Jesus Christ, those things, which because of our blindness we cannot ask, and because of our unworthiness we dare not ask; through the same Jesus Christ our Lord and Saviour.

All: **Amen.**

Or

31   *THE BIDDING PRAYER*

(*During the periods of silence after each bidding the people may offer their own prayers either silently or aloud.*)

Celebrant :   Let us pray for all people and for the Church throughout the world.

             Silence

Celebrant :   I ask your prayers for the holy Church of God: that she may be filled with truth and love, and be found without fault at the day of our Lord's coming.

             Silence

             Lord, in your mercy.

All :   **Hear our prayer.**

〚The rubric '*Silence*' and the versicle and response are repeated in the same words after each of the following paragraphs.〛

Celebrant :   I ask your prayers for *N.* our Archbishop, for *N.* our own bishop(s), for all bishops, priests, deacons and other ministers, and for all the holy people of God.

Celebrant :   I ask your prayers for all who fear God and believe in the Lord Jesus Christ, that our divisions may cease, and that we may be one as Christ and the Father are one.

Celebrant :   I ask your prayers for the mission of the Church: that in faithful witness she may preach the Gospel to all mankind.

Celebrant :   I ask your prayers for those who do not yet believe in Jesus Christ; those who oppose His Gospel and for those who have lost their faith: that they may receive the light of the Gospel.

Celebrant :   I ask your prayers for the peace of the world: that a spirit of respect and forbearance may grow among nations and peoples.

Celebrant :   I ask your prayers for the leaders of our nation, and those in positions of public trust; especially . . . : that they may serve justice and promote the dignity, freedom and welfare of every person.

Celebrant :   I ask your prayers for all who live in our community; for a blessing upon all human labour, and for the right use of the resources of creation: that the world may be freed from poverty, famine and disaster.

Celebrant : I ask your prayers for the poor, the persecuted, the sick and all who suffer; for refugees, prisoners and all who are in danger: that they may be relieved and protected.

Celebrant : I ask your prayers for this congregation; for those who are present and those who are absent: that we may be delivered from hardness of heart and show forth Christ's glory in all that we do.

Celebrant : I ask your prayers for our enemies and those who wish us harm; for all whom we have injured or offended, and for ourselves: the forgiveness of our sins and for the grace of the Holy Spirit to amend our lives.

Celebrant : I ask your prayers for all who have commended themselves to our prayers; for our families, friends and neighbours: that being freed from anxiety, they may live in health, joy and peace.

Celebrant : I ask your prayers for all who have died in the fellowship of Christ's Church; for those whose faith is known to God alone: that with the saints in every age, they may have rest in that place where there is no grief or pain, but life eternal.

Celebrant : And now rejoicing in the fellowship of all the saints, let us commend ourselves and one another and all our life to Christ our God.

All : **For yours is the majesty, O Father, Son and Holy Spirit; yours is the kingdom and the power and the glory, now and forever. Amen.**

32 *If there is no Communion, the Lord's Prayer, the Grace or Benediction may be said or sung.*

THE COMMUNION

33 *(All stand) The Celebrant says the Offertory Sentences*

Celebrant : We who are many are one loaf, one body, for we all share in the one loaf. (1 *Corinthians* 10. 17)

How good and pleasant it is when brothers live together in unity. (*Psalm* 133. 1)

All : **We will offer in His dwelling an oblation with great gladness: we will sing and speak praises to the Lord.**
(*Psalm* 27. 7)

THE PEACE

34 *Celebrant :* The peace of the Lord be always with you.

People : **And also with you.**

THE TAKING OF THE BREAD AND WINE

35 *An anthem, canticle, hymn or psalm is now sung ; an offering for the poor may be taken ; the bread and wine are brought and placed on the holy table.*

36 (*All stand*): *The Celebrant says :*

Holy Father, who through the blood of your dear Son has consecrated for us a new and living way to your throne of grace; unworthy as we are, we come to you through Him, and we pray you to accept and use these our gifts for your glory. All that is in heaven and earth is yours, and out of the abundance do we give you.

All : **Amen.**

Silence

37 *All :* **Be present, (be present), O Jesus, our good High Priest, as you were with your disciples and make yourself known to us in the breaking of bread; You who live and reign with the Father and the Holy Spirit, one God, world without end. Amen.**

THE THANKSGIVING

38 *Celebrant :* The Lord is here.

All : **His Spirit is with us.**

Celebrant : Lift up your hearts.

All : **We lift them to the Lord.**

Celebrant : Let us give thanks to the Lord our God.

All : **It is right to give Him thanks and praise.**

Celebrant : It is not only right, it is our duty and joy, at all times and in all places to give you thanks and praise, Holy Father, Heavenly King, almighty and eternal God, through Jesus Christ your only Son our Lord; through whom you brought the universe into being, and made man in your own image, and when we had fallen into sin, you made Him to be the firstfruits of a new creation.

(*Then follows a preface proper to the Season or Occasion*)

[The Proper Prefaces, which are printed here, are to be found in Appendix C]

Celebrant : Therefore with angels and archangels, and with all the company of heaven, we proclaim your great and glorious name, for ever praising you and saying:

All : **Holy, holy, holy, Lord, God of power and might, Heaven and earth are full of your glory, Hosanna in the highest.**

39 *Celebrant :*   You are truly blessed and truly holy, heavenly Father, who out of your tender love towards mankind gave your only Son Jesus Christ to take our nature upon Him and to suffer death upon the cross for our redemption, who by that one offering of Himself; made a full, perfect and sufficient sacrifice for the sins of the whole world; and who instituted, and in His holy Gospel commanded us to commemorate His precious death perpetually until His coming again; who on the night He was betrayed, took bread and when He had given you thanks, He broke it and gave it to His disciples, saying:

> Take, eat; this is my Body which is given for you. Do this in remembrance of me.

Again, after supper He took the cup, and when He had given you thanks, He gave it to them, saying:

> Drink this, all of you; for this is my Blood of the new Covenant, which is shed for you and for many, for the forgiveness of sins. Do this, as often as you drink it, in 'remembrance of me.

All :   **Your death, Lord, we commemorate, your resurrection we confess, and your second coming we await. Praise to you, O Christ.**

Celebrant :   Therefore, Father, in remembrance of the precious death and passion, the mighty resurrection and glorious ascension of your Son our Lord, we your servants, as He has commanded do this in remembrance of Him, until His coming again. Accept this our sacrifice of thanks and praise, for the perfect redemption that you have obtained for us in Him.

All :   **We give you thanks, we praise you, we glorify you, O Lord our God.**

Celebrant :   And we most humbly pray you merciful Father, to sanctify us and, these your gifts of bread and wine, with your Holy Spirit, that the bread which we break may become the communion of the Body of Christ, and the Cup which we bless the communion of the blood of Christ. Grant that being united with Him we may all attain to the unity of faith, and may grow up in all things to Him who is the Head, even Christ, our Lord. With Him, and in Him, and through Him, by the power of the Holy Spirit, with all who stand before you on earth and in heaven, we worship you, Father Almighty, in songs of everlasting praise:

All : **Blessing and honour and glory and power be yours for ever and ever. Amen.**

Silence may be kept

Or

40 *Celebrant :* And so, Father, we who have been redeemed by Him, and made a new people by water and the Spirit, now bring before you these gifts. Sanctify them by your Holy Spirit to be the Body and Blood of Jesus Christ our Lord. On the night He was betrayed He took bread, said the blessing, broke the bread, and gave it to His disciples saying:

> Take, eat; This is my Body which is given for you. Do this for the remembrance of me.

After supper, He took the cup of wine, gave thanks, and gave it to them saying:

> Drink this, all of you: This is my Blood of the new Covenant, which is shed for you and for many for the forgiveness of sins. Whenever you drink it, do this for the remembrance of me.

Remembering now His work of redemption, and offering to you this sacrifice of thanksgiving.

All : **We celebrate His death and resurrection, as we await the day of His coming.**

Celebrant : Lord God of our Fathers, God of Abraham, Isaac and Jacob, God and Father of our Lord Jesus Christ: open our eyes to see your hand at work in the world about us. Deliver us from the presumption of coming to this Table for solace only, and not for strength; for pardon only, and not for renewal. Let the grace of the Holy Communion make us one body, one spirit in Christ, that we may worthily serve the world in His name.

All : **Risen Lord, be known to us in the breaking of bread.**

Celebrant : Accept these prayers and praises, Father, through Jesus Christ our great High Priest, to whom, with you and the Holy Spirit, your Church gives honour, glory and worship, from generation to generation.

All : **Amen.**

Silence may be kept

41 *All :*   **We do not presume... ⟦CF 6⟧...He in us. Amen.**

THE BREAKING OF THE BREAD

42 *Celebrant :*   We break this bread to share in the Body of Christ.

All :   **Though we are many, we are one body, because we all share in one loaf.**   (1 *Corinthians* 10. 16 & 17)

Celebrant :   The cup which we bless,

All :   **is it not the sharing of the Blood of Christ?**

THE GIVING OF THE BREAD AND THE CUP

43   *THE LORD'S PRAYER*

All :   **Our Father in heaven... ⟦ICET 1, with 1971 variants⟧ ...for ever. Amen.**

44 *The Celebrant with those assisting him first receive the consecrated elements, during which the people may say or sing :*

Jesus, Lamb of God... ⟦ICET 8(a)⟧ ...your peace.
(*John* 1.29 & 1 *Peter* 1.18–20)

45 *Celebrant :*   Draw near with faith. Receive the Body of our Lord Jesus Christ which He gave for you, and His Blood which He shed for you. Remember that He died for you, and feed on Him in your hearts by faith with thanksgiving.

46 *At the administration the ministers say to each communicant :*
The body of our Lord Jesus Christ: the bread of life
or The body of Christ.
The blood of our Lord Jesus Christ: the true vine
or The blood of Christ.

The communicant replies each time
Amen
and then receives.

(*During the communion, anthems, canticles, hymns or psalms may be sung quietly.*)

AFTER COMMUNION

One of the following prayers may be said
Either

47 *Celebrant :*   Almighty God, our heavenly Father, who has accepted us as your children in your beloved Son Jesus Christ our Lord, and has fed us with the spiritual food of His most precious Body and Blood, giving us the forgiveness of sins and the promise of eternal life. We thank and praise you

for these inestimable benefits and we offer and present ourselves entirely to you, to be a holy and living sacrifice, which is our reasonable service. Grant us grace to adapt ourselves no longer to the pattern of this present world, but let our minds be remade and our whole nature transformed that we may be able to discern your will and know what is good, acceptable and perfect; so that we may obey you here on earth, that we may at last rejoice with all your saints in your heavenly kingdom; through Jesus Christ our Lord, who lives and reigns with you and the Holy Spirit, one God, for ever. **Amen.**

Or

48 *All :*　　**Father, we offer ourselves to you as a living sacrifice through Jesus Christ our Lord. Send us out in the power of your Holy Spirit to live and work to your praise and glory. Amen.**

49 *The Celebrant or the Bishop, if he is present, may say this or the appropriate seasonal blessing :*

The peace of God... ⟦CF 10⟧ ...you always.

All :　　**Amen.**

50　　*THE DISMISSAL*

Celebrant :　Go in peace and serve the Lord.

All :　　**In the name of Christ. Amen.**

SEASONAL BLESSINGS

⟦The Seasonal Blessings, which are printed here, are to be found in Appendix D⟧

51 *A hymn, part of Psalm 103, the Nunc Dimittis, an anthem or a canticle may be sung, during which the Bible, the Communion vessels and the gifts of the people are carried out. The Ministers and people depart.*

ADDITIONAL DIRECTIONS

1 *It is provided in the Province of West Africa that only those who have been episcopally ordained priest shall consecrate the Holy Sacrament of the Lord's Supper. Every confirmed person should, after careful preparation, communicate regularly and frequently.*

2 *The Holy Table is spread with a clean white cloth during the Celebration.*

3 *Where it is impracticable to carry the Bible and Communion vessels in procession to the Lectern and Holy Tables, then everything should be set in order before the service starts.*

4 *Posture – Local custom about standing, kneeling, sitting and bowing heads may be established and followed in Sections : 2, 3, 4, 5, 6, 7, 8, 9, 10, 11, 12, 14, 15, 16, 17, 18, 29, 30, 31, 32, 33, 37, 38, 39, 40, 41, 42, 43, 46, 47, 48, 49, 50.*

5   *Section 6 may be said or sung after Section 47 or Section 48. Traditionally the Gloria in Excelsis Deo is omitted in Lent, Passiontide, Advent and at Funerals.*

6   *Sections 3–32 may be taken from the Prayer Desk.*

7   *It is desirable that the Lessons be read from the lectern or pulpit. If the Gospeller is the Preacher, he goes to the pulpit during the Gradual, reads the Gospel, then preaches the sermon. If he is not, the preacher goes to the pulpit during the Gradual and the Gospeller to the lectern or traditional place for reading the Gospel. It is an ancient custom for the Deacon to read the Gospel.*

8   *Sections 29–31 may be led by the Celebrant, one of the priests or deacons present or by a layman from the midst of the congregation.*

9   *Section 34 – The Peace. The Celebrant may accompany the words of the Peace with handclasp or a double handshake, both words and the action may be passed through the congregation.*

10 *Section 38 – The Thanksgiving : At the words of Institution, the Celebrant lays his right hand on the bread and the cup respectively.*

11 *Section 42 – The Breaking of Bread : The Celebrant breaks the bread and blesses the cup.*

12 *Opportunity is always given to every communicant to receive the consecrated bread and wine separately. But the Sacrament may be received in both kinds simultaneously, in a manner approved by the Bishop. The Communion may be received either kneeling or standing.*

13 *Hymns, Notices, Offerings of the People : Points are indicated for the singing of Psalms, hymns, canticles or anthems ; for notices, the Collection and presentation of the offerings of the people and the placing of the bread and wine on the Holy Table ; if occasion requires, there are other points at which they may occur.*

14 *Seasonal Material – Sections 2, 38 and 49 : The Seasonal Greetings and proper Prefaces are obligatory ; but the Seasonal Blessings are optional.*

15 *If the consecrated bread and wine is inadequate for the number of communicants, the Celebrant is to return to the Holy Table and consecrate more of either or both, by saying :*

> Hear us, heavenly Father, and with your Word and Holy Spirit bless and sanctify this Bread/Wine, that it/they also may be the precious Body/Blood of your Son Jesus Christ our Lord who took the Bread/Cup and said: 'this is my Body/Blood'. **Amen.**

16 *If any consecrated elements remain apart from any that may be required for the Communion of the sick, or for the distribution of Communion by a Deacon when no priest is available, the Celebrant, other ministers and communicants reverently eat and drink the elements, either after Section 46 or Section 50.*

17 *After Section 51, the Celebrant or another minister may request that silence be observed. He then adds this prayer :*

> Visit, we pray you, Lord, this your family, who have been made holy by your sacred mysteries; and as by your grace we receive the healing gifts of salvation, so may we retain them by your protecting power; through Jesus Christ our Lord. **Amen.**

CHAPTER 10

THE CHURCH OF THE PROVINCE OF NIGERIA

THE dioceses of Nigeria were detached from the Province of West Africa and became a separate Province in 1979. The general use throughout the country had been the 1662 Book of Common Prayer, translated into different local languages where necessary. The Province produced its own liturgy in late 1983, authorized for an experimental use for three years, and published in a substantial booklet form. It owes much to **EngA**, but is clearly adapted for the Nigerian context.

THE LITURGY OF THE CHURCH OF NIGERIA 1983 (Nig)

⟦The numbering is original to the rite. Rubrics are in red in the original.⟧

DIRECTIONS

1. *The President or Celebrant must be an episcopally ordained Priest of our Church or of any Church in Communion with Canterbury.*
2. *When the Bishop is present, it is appropriate that he should act as President. He pronounces the Absolution and the Blessing and receives the elements in both kinds first.*
3. *Every confirmed person should, after careful preparation, communicate regularly and frequently.*
4. *It is the duty of every parishioner to contribute generously, according to his means, to the maintenance of the worship of God, to the spread of the Gospel, and to works of charity.*
5. *The Minister and Churchwardens decide on the disposal of the offertory alms. If they disagree, the Ordinary shall make the decision.*
6. *The Holy Table, at the time of the Communion, is to have a fair linen cloth on it.*
7. *If any of the consecrated Bread and Wine remains, it is to be consumed reverently by the President/Celebrant (and by other communicants if necessary). This may be done either when all have communicated, or after the Blessing – in which case the consecrated elements are to remain, covered with a linen cloth, on the Holy Table from the time of the Communion until after the Blessing.*
8. *The President is to say or sing the Service audibly and clearly.*

THE ORDER FOR HOLY COMMUNION OR THE EUCHARIST

THE PREPARATION

1 *A Hymn may be sung.*

2 *President :*   The Lord be with you.

   All :   **And also with you.**

Or Easter Day to Pentecost

President : Alleluia! Christ is risen.
All : **He is risen indeed. Alleluia!**

3 *Collect for purity*
All : **Almighty God... ⟦CF 1⟧ ...our Lord. Amen.**
hid] hidden

4 *KYRIE ELEISON may be said.*
Lord, have mercy.
Lord, have mercy.
Christ, have mercy.
Christ, have mercy.
Lord, have mercy.
Lord, have mercy.

5 *GLORIA IN EXCELSIS (Standing)*
Glory to God... ⟦ICET 4⟧ ...the Father. Amen.

6 *President :* Let us pray.
The President says THE COLLECT.

THE MINISTRY OF THE WORD

7 *Sit*
OLD TESTAMENT READING
At the end the reader may say
This is the word of the Lord.
All : **Thanks be to God.**

8 *A PSALM may be used.*

9 *Sit*
NEW TESTAMENT READING (EPISTLE)
At the end the reader may say
This is the word of the Lord.
All : **Thanks be to God.**

10 *A CANTICLE OR A HYMN may be used as GRADUAL.*

11 *Stand*
THE GOSPEL When it is announced
All : **Glory to Christ our Saviour.**
At the end the reader says :
This is the Gospel of Christ.
All : **Praise to Christ our Lord.**

12 *Sit*
THE SERMON

13 *Stand*
   THE NICENE CREED
   All :   **We believe**...⟦ICET 3⟧...**world to come. Amen.**
              incarnate from] incarnate of
              [and the Son]] OM BRACKETS
14 *Banns of marriage may be published and necessary announcements may*
   be made before the service, after the Creed, before the Offertory, or at
   the end of the service, as may be convenient.

PRAYERS OF PENITENCE

15 *SUMMARY OF THE LAW*
   Minister :   Our Lord Jesus Christ said: The first commandment is
                  this: Hear, O Israel, the Lord our God is the only...
                  ⟦CF 3⟧...greater than these.
                  This is the first commandment] OM
   All :   **Amen. Lord, have mercy.**

16 *OR THE COMMANDMENTS*
   Minister :   Our Lord Jesus Christ said...⟦The Commandments with
                  New Testament additions, as in **EngA**, section 78A, on
                  pages 23–24 above⟧...fulfilling of the law.
   All :   **Amen. Lord, have mercy.**

17 *The Minister may say :*
                  God so loved the world that he gave his only Son Jesus
                  Christ to save us from our sins, to be our advocate in
                  heaven, and to bring us to eternal life.

   Or   *One or more of these SENTENCES*

                  Hear the words of comfort...⟦CF 4⟧...propitiation for
                  our sins.   (1 *John* 2.1)
                  does sin] sins

   A brief pause.

18 *Minister :*   Let us confess our sins, in penitence and faith, firmly
                  resolved to keep God's commandments and to live in love
                  and peace with all men.

19 *All :*   **Almighty God, our heavenly Father,**
                  we have sinned against you and against our fellow
                       men,
                  in thought and word and deed,
                  through negligence, through weakness,
                  through our own deliberate fault.

We are truly sorry, and repent of all our sins.
For the sake of your Son Jesus Christ, who died for us,
forgive us all that is past;
and grant that we may serve you in newness of life
to the glory of your name. Amen.

20 *President:*   Almighty God... ⟦CF 5⟧ ...Christ our Lord. Amen.

21 *All may say:* **We do not presume**... ⟦CF 6⟧ ...**he in us. Amen.**

THE INTERCESSION

22 *INTERCESSIONS AND THANKSGIVINGS are led by the President, or by others. One of the forms below, or other suitable words, may be used.*

23 *This form may be used*
> *with the insertion of specific subjects between the paragraphs;*
> *as a continuous whole with or without brief biddings.*
> *Not all paragraphs need be used on every occasion. Individual names may be added at the places indicated. This response may be used before or after each paragraph.*

Minister: Lord, in your mercy,
All: **Hear our prayer.**

Minister: Let us pray for the Church and for the world, and let us thank God for his goodness.

Almighty God, our heavenly Father, you promised through your Son Jesus Christ to hear us when we pray in faith.

Strengthen *N* our Archbishop, *N* our bishop and all your Church in the service of Christ; that those who confess your name may be united in your truth, live together in your love, and reveal your glory in the world.

Bless and guide our rulers; give wisdom to all in authority; and direct this and every nation in the ways of justice and of peace; that men may honour one another, and seek the common good.

Give grace to us, our families and friends, and to all our neighbours; that we may serve Christ in one another, and love as he loves us.

Comfort and heal all those who suffer in body, mind, or spirit...; give them courage and hope in their troubles; and bring them the joy of your salvation.

Hear us as we remember those who have died in the faith
of Christ...; according to your promises, grant us with
them a share in your eternal kingdom.

Rejoicing in the fellowship of (*N* and of) all your saints,
we commend ourselves and all Christian people to your
unfailing love.

Merciful Father,

All :　　　　**Accept these prayers for the sake of your Son, our
Saviour Jesus Christ. Amen.**

24 OR *A*[1]

Minister:　　Let us pray for the whole Church of God in Christ Jesus,
and for all men according to their needs.

O God, the creator and preserver of all mankind,
we pray for men of every race, and in every kind of need:
　　make your ways known on earth,
your saving power among all nations.
(Especially we pray for...)
Lord, in your mercy,

All :　　　　**Hear our prayer.**

Minister :　We commend to your fatherly goodness all who
are anxious or distressed in mind or body;
comfort and relieve them in their need;
give them patience in their sufferings
and bring good out of their troubles.
(Especially we pray for...)
Merciful Father,

All :　　　　**Accept these prayers for the sake of your Son, our
Saviour Jesus Christ. Amen.**

25 OR *B*

Minister :　In the power... [The Litany as in **EngA**, section 81B, on
pages 26–28 above, with the changes shown below]...
Christ our Lord. Amen.

Hear our prayers O Lord our God. *All*] *All :* **Hear our prayers O Lord
our God**
Guard and strengthen...honour and glory] Bless your servant the
President of this nation and guide him with your heavenly wisdom
Endue the High Court...understanding] Endue with grace, wisdom and
understanding the State Governors, the Federal Ministers, State
Commissioners, Members of National and State Assemblies, natural
rulers and all in authority in this land.
Bless those who administer the law] Bless the Judges and Magistrates
and all who administer the law

---

[1] [This is as **EngA**, 81A, but without the middle paragraph, possibly through oversight.]

THE MINISTRY OF THE SACRAMENT
THE PEACE
26 *Stand*
The President says either of the following or other suitable words.

Christ is our peace.
He has reconciled us to God
in one body by the cross.
We meet in his name and share his peace.

Or   We are the body of Christ.
In the one Spirit we were all baptized into one body.
Let us then pursue all that makes for peace
and builds up our common life.

He then says

The peace of the Lord be always with you
All :   **And also with you.**

27 *The President may say*
Let us offer one another a sign of peace.
And all may exchange a sign of peace : African fraternal or traditional embrace or double handclasp.

THE PREPARATION OF THE GIFTS

28 *A Hymn or Choruses with or without musical accompaniment and dancing may follow as the bread and wine are placed on the holy table and the offerings of the people collected and/or presented.*
These words may be used.
All :   **Yours, Lord, is the greatness, the power,**
the glory, the splendour, and the majesty;
for everything in heaven and on earth is yours.
All things come from you,
and of your own do we give you.

THE EUCHARISTIC PRAYER
THE TAKING OF THE BREAD AND CUP AND THE GIVING OF THANKS

29 *The President takes the bread and cup into his hands and replaces them on the holy table.*
President :   The Lord be with you.
All :   **And also with you.**
President :   Lift up your hearts.
All :   **We lift them to the Lord.**

President :   Let us give thanks to the Lord our God.
All :   **It is right to give him thanks and praise.**
President :   It is indeed right...⟦as in **EngA**, section 38, on page 9 above⟧..., a people for your own possession.

PROPER PREFACES, when appropriate (Section 44)

Therefore with angels and archangels,
and with all the company of heaven,
we proclaim your great and glorious name,
for ever praising you and saying:

All :   **Holy, holy, holy Lord,**
God of power and might,
heaven and earth are full of your glory.
Hosanna in the highest.

This ANTHEM may also be used.

Blessed is he who comes in the name of the Lord.
Hosanna in the highest.

President :   Accept our praises, heavenly Father,...⟦as in **EngA**, section 38, on pages 10–11 above⟧...**for ever and ever. Amen.**
Silence may be kept.

THE COMMUNION

THE BREAKING OF THE BREAD AND THE GIVING OF THE BREAD AND CUP

30 *THE LORD'S PRAYER*

President :   As our Saviour taught us, so we pray.
All :   **Our Father in heaven**...⟦ICET 1⟧...**for ever. Amen.**
Save us...trial and] Lead us not into temptation but

31 *The President breaks the consecrated bread, saying*

We break this bread
to share in the body of Christ.

All :   **Though we are many, we are one body,**
because we all share in one bread.

32 *Either here or during the distribution, one of the following anthems may be said.*

Lamb of God...⟦ICET 8(b)⟧...grant us peace.
Or   Jesus, Lamb of God...⟦ICET 8(a)⟧...give us your peace.

33 *Before the distribution, the President says*

Draw near with faith, receive the body of our Lord Jesus Christ which he gave you, and his blood which he shed for you.

Eat and drink in remembrance that he died for you,
and feed on him your hearts by faith with thanksgiving.

34 *The President and people receive the communion. At the distribution the minister says to each communicant*

The body of Christ keep you in eternal life.
The blood of Christ keep you in eternal life.

Or

The body of Christ.
The blood of Christ.

The communicant replies each time,

Amen.

and then receives.

35 *During the distribution hymns and anthems may be sung.*

36 *If either or both of the consecrated elements be likely to prove insufficient, the President himself returns to the holy table and adds more, saying these words:*

Father... [as in **EngA**, section 48, on page 18 above]
...in remembrance of Him.

37 *Any consecrated bread and wine which is not required for purposes of communion is consumed at the end of the distribution or after the service.*

AFTER COMMUNION

38 *AN APPROPRIATE SENTENCE may be said and a hymn may be sung.*

39 *Either or both of the following prayers or other suitable prayers are said.*

President: Father of all... [CF 8]...Christ our Lord. Amen.

in this hope that we have grasped] firm in the hope you have set before us

Or

40 *All:* **Almighty God...[CF 9]...praise and glory. Amen.**

41 *The President may say this or an alternative BLESSING*

The peace of God...[CF 10]...always. Amen.

42 *A HYMN may be sung during the recession of the minister.*

43 *President:* Go in peace to love and serve the Lord.

All: **In the name of Christ. Amen.**

Or

President: Go in the peace of Christ.

All: **Thanks be to God.**

APPENDIX

44 *PROPER PREFACES*

[There follow Proper Prefaces which are to be found here in Appendix C.]

CHAPTER 11

THE CHURCH OF THE PROVINCE OF TANZANIA

AFTER three years of use of **Tan** (printed in **FAL**), the text was marginally revised by the Provincial Liturgical and Theological Committee, and approved in this form by the Provincial Standing Committee in February 1977 ('**TanR**'). An English-language translation was published in 1980, but the Swahili text is authoritative.[1]

THE REVISED TANZANIAN LITURGY 1977 (TanR)

⟦This is shown simply as a list of alterations from **Tan**, with **FAL** section numbers.⟧
1   Before no. 1 is a cross-heading 'THE PREPARATION'.
3   A sixfold Kyrie is printed, and a Swahili rubric permits a ninefold when sung.
4   The confession is in the plural '**We confess**...'.
6   The Te Deum is now printed out after the Gloria in Excelsis (but in an appendix in 1662 form in the English).
7   Following is a cross-heading 'THE MINISTRY OF THE WORD OF GOD'.
8   The omissions of 1973 are again omitted.
15   The Apostles' Creed (ICET 2) is now printed out after the Nicene Creed (but in an appendix in the English) – and **FAL** was in error (see Corrigenda).
18   The rubric reads: '*Then follows a SHORT SENTENCE and/or a HYMN and the OFFERING is collected here or after the INTERCESSIONS.*'
19   The rubric at no. 21 is included after the first line of rubric.
24   Add: '*The collection is taken if not done before the INTERCESSION. Then the Minister says:* Yours, Lord, is the greatness, the power, the majesty and the glory; for all in heaven and on earth is yours. All things come from you, and of your own do we give you.'
26   After Sanctus: '*When sung, may be added:* **Blessed**... ⟦ICET 5(b)⟧...**highest.**'
There is now provision of Proper Prefaces. These are shown here in Appendix C.
The Acclamations come one paragraph lower down (not in the English version) through error in the original Swahili.
The anamnesis ('Therefore...intercession for us') is revised:
Therefore, Father, with this bread and this cup, we do this as commanded by your Son Jesus Christ, in remembrance of him. We proclaim his perfect sacrifice made for us once for all upon the cross, and celebrate the redemption he won for us.[2] We thank you, Father, for his mighty resurrection and ascension into heaven, where he is always interceding for us. And we look for his coming again in glory.
27   No. 29 comes before 27 and 28. The second half of the Minister's words at 27 are printed for congregational use including: '**Because there is one bread.**'
31   The rubric reads: '*Then the Minister says:*'
32   The rubric reads: '*The Minister receives the Holy Communion. When he administers Communion to the people he says:*' The previous separate rubrics disappear.
34   There is a cross-heading before no. 34 'THANKSGIVING' ('AFTER COMMUNION' in the English).
36   No. 37 is promoted to come before 36.

Appendices: the first has supplementary consecration (by the part of the narrative of institution) and others the Proper Prefaces, the Ten Commandments (CF 2), and (in the English) Te Deum and the Apostles' Creed (see 6 and 15 above).

[1] Thus 1974 ICET texts are printed in the English version, but the Swahili original is unchanged. There are two differences in no. 26 noted above.
[2] English: 'and celebrate our salvation'.

CHAPTER 12

THE REST OF AFRICA

THE Church of the Province of South Africa published in 1975 *Liturgy 1975*, a thick paperback book, containing offices and the eucharist. The eucharist was published in **FAL** as '**SAfr2**'.[1] The emphasis since 1975 for the Liturgical Committee has been on the provision of other services, and further supplementary material. There are plans to revise the material and draw it together into a more definitive book in 1986.

The Church of the Province of Central Africa, which in the past had used the Book of Common Prayer of South Africa, in 1976 authorized an adapted form of **SAfr2** is known as *Ukaristia 1976*. It draws from **Eng3** for the confession, first intercession, and the post-Communion Prayer (CF8); it omits the first two intercessions, and First Eucharistic Prayer of **SAfr2**; and amends its rubrics and text elsewhere also.

The Church of the Province of Kenya is only now approaching first steps in writing its own eucharistic liturgy. 1662 is still the main use in the Province. In 1975 the Provincial Synod authorized for a three-year experiment a book entitled *Modern English Services*. This included a very literal rendering of 1662 communion service into a 'you' form of address to God, with the 1971 ICET texts and the form of the Decalogue in **EngA**, 78B, as an alternative to the traditional text.

The Church of the Province of Uganda is also still using 1662 though some vernacular uses include parts of 1928. **EngA** has been used a little. In 1980 there was published a booklet of modernized English services, roughly comparable to those of Kenya mentioned above, under the title *Come and Worship*. This has its own rendering of 1662 throughout, even to the point of not having ICET texts for the Lord's Prayer and other common forms. It is not in widespread use in churches. There is little prospect of eucharistic revision in the near future.

The Church of the Province of Burundi, Rwanda and Zaire was detached from the larger previous province, which included Uganda, in 1980. There are no specifically provincial uses, but the French-speaking dioceses of Zaire tend to use the French version of the American Book of Common Prayer of 1977, though for vernacular use there are some versions of **EngA** available, and Zaire prefers ASB to 1662 for English-language services.

The Church of the Province of the Sudan was formed in 1976. The main eucharistic use continues to be that of 1662.

There is nothing to report from the Province of the Indian Ocean.

[1] This text was edited in **FAL** from a duplicated document of the Liturgical Committee and had more tiny errors than other texts. (See **FAL** corrigendum sheet.)

CHAPTER 13

THE CHURCHES OF PAKISTAN AND NORTH AND SOUTH INDIA

The Church of Pakistan continues the uses of the Churches which united in 1970. There is nothing to hand to report beyond what is contained in **FAL**, page 263.

The Church of South India has continued to use the modern English liturgy (**CSIR**) which was authorized in 1972 (and published in **FAL**). It has been republished unaltered in 1982 in a joint publication by the I.S.P.C.K. containing **CSIR**, the fourth edition of the North India rite (see below), and 'The Holy Qurbana' of the Malankara Mar Thoma Syrian Church.

The Church of North India has continued to produce new editions of its liturgy. The 1973 and 1974 editions were published (as **CNI**) in **FAL**, and these were followed by new editions in 1978, 1980, and 1983. The 1980 fourth edition was that in the joint publication mentioned above, and the fifth edition (authorized by the Synod Executive Committee in April 1983) is shown below (and coded as '**CNIR**') by its variants from **CNI**. The ICET texts of 1971 are still used (with **Eng3** variants in the Lord's Prayer).

THE LITURGY OF THE CHURCH OF NORTH INDIA
REVISED 1983 (CNIR)

No. 1: *Or he may use...section 47)*]   OMIT
No. 7: *read] pray in the words of*
No. 8: *An Old Testament lesson] A reading from the Old Testament*
No. 14: *used] said or sung*
No. 16: family of man] family of mankind
Let us pray to the Lord] Heavenly Father, we pray
every man] every one
who work on the land...in commerce] engaged in agriculture, industry and commerce, for all labourers and craftsmen
oppressed, the sick] oppressed, the unemployed, the sick
others who exercise] who have
their fellow-men] other people
For... our Moderator and] For your whole Church in our country; for its Councils and leaders, especially for...our Moderator,...Moderator of the Church of South India and...Metropolitan of the Mar Thoma Church, for

⟦After 'joy of your kingdom' the versicle and response are added, then the paragraph 'Hasten...' is printed in bold and allocated to '*All*'⟧

any particular need in society] (*pray for any...society*)
men may honour] we may all honour

The Church throughout the world...this diocese and for] your whole
Church in our country and throughout the world...
especially the Church of North India;
for its Councils, leaders and ministers,
especially for...our Moderator,
...Moderator of the Church of South India,
...Metropolitan of the Mar Thoma Church;
for
any particular...of the Church...] (*pray for any particular work or need in the Church*)
particular persons...] (*pray for particular persons...*)
[After '...their oppressors...' add new line 'the unemployed...']
dying] the dying
commend all men] commend all

No. 18: [As in **EngA**, no. 29...] to keep God's commandments] by God's grace to keep his commandments
all men] all people

No. 20: their fellow men] one another
[After no. 20 the heading is changed to 'THE MINISTRY OF THE SACRAMENT']

No. 21: *Where it is the custom...be read*] *If the Scripture Warrant is to be used, it is read now, or after Section 27.*
[After no. 23 the heading is changed to 'THE PREPARATION OF THE BREAD AND WINE']

No. 29: have enlightened every man coming] enlighten every one who comes

No. 32: Again, after supper] In the same way, after supper
[After no. 34 the heading is changed to:

'THE COMMUNION

THE BREAKING OF THE BREAD AND
THE SHARING OF THE BREAD AND WINE']

No. 34: **because**] **for**
No. 37: [There is a new no. 37 (moving nos. 37, 38, 39 in **CNI** down one number):
'37 *The Prayer of Humble Access may be said.*
We do not presume...[CF 6 with addition]...**he in us. Amen**
drink his blood, that] drink his blood, that our sinful bodies and souls may be made clean by his most precious body and blood, and that
One or both of the following may be said or sung:
Blessed is he...[ICET 5(b)]...**in the highest.**
Jesus, Lamb of God...[ICET 8(a)]...**your peace.**]

No. 38 (now 39): *The ministers...the bread*] *The presbyters...the consecrated bread*
No. 39 (now 40): of Christ] of our Lord Jesus Christ TWICE
No. 40: OMIT
No. 42: *Seasonal*] OMIT
No. 43: by faith] with faith
No. 44: **benefits we thank you**] **benefits we thank you, and in union with your Son we offer you ourselves as a living sacrifice**
No. 45: *seasonal*] OMIT
No. 47: [Any changes are noted in Appendixes C and D]
No. 48: [Two separate texts are now printed out for the bread and the wine]

CHAPTER 14

THE ANGLICAN CHURCH IN KOREA

The 1973 liturgy (**Kor1**) printed in **FAL** was marginally revised through a decision of Synod on 20 November 1980, with authorization from 24 February 1982. The new text (known here as **Kor1A**) has the following changes from **Kor1** (the numbers refer to the paragraph numbering in **Kor1** in **FAL**).

THE KOREAN LITURGY REVISED 1982 (Kor1A)

General Instructions:

    Two more '*Instructions*' have been added on Ceremonial and five Miscellaneous ones have been added at the end (including one requiring the use of the 1979 version of the Korean Bible), making 24 Instructions in all.

  1: After this the Collect for Purity (CF1) is permitted as an option.

 11: The introduction 'Let us hear the Lord's Words' has been removed.

 14: The following forms of intercession are now provided:
    (i) The text in **Kor1** (but with the name of the bishop inserted into the first petition).
    (ii) The form in **EngA**, no. 21, on pages 6–7 above.
    (iii) 'Form III' from ECUSA Book of Common Prayer (page 387), similar to the forms on pp. 159–160 of **FAL** and shown as no. 88 on page 152 above.

 15: The Decalogue (in the **EngA**, no 78A, form) is permitted as an option, and the text is printed as an appendix to the rite.
    The absolution has been redrafted as follows:
    Almighty God, who forgives the sins of all who repent, by the merits of Jesus Christ have mercy on you, forgive you all your sins, give you power to do good, and grant you eternal life.

 17: Before the last sentence of the rubric, there is an addition:
    When the collection is brought up the priest says the offertory prayer.
    After the last sentence is the prayer itself:
    All things come from you, O Lord, and of your own do we give you.
    Lord, by this offering may your gospel be spread throughout the world. **Amen.**

 19: The embolism is omitted, and the Lord's Prayer runs straight through to the doxology.

 20: There is provision for adapting the Agnus Dei for Memorials of the dead.

 22: The first of the prayers from the schedule is now printed in the text:
    Almighty God, you have fed us with heavenly food, the body and blood of Christ, and made us one in the body of Christ. Help us by the Holy Spirit to sh   r lives in love and achieve all that you would have us do. Through...

 24: In the third line, the Blessing (CF10) replaces the previous text, and re   made to an appendix of seasonal blessings, virtually identical to those in **EngA** (see Appendix C in this book).

CHAPTER 15

THE REST OF ASIA

THE Episcopal Church in Jerusalem and the Middle East was formed from the old Jerusalem Archbishopric in 1976. It has little central provincial control over its scattered dioceses, and certainly no liturgical provision. The only diocese which had shown diocesan initiative previously was the diocese of Iran (there were eucharistic rites from Iran in **MAL** and **FAL**, **Iran** and **IranR**). This diocese has had enormous difficulties since the political changes of 1979, and has had little chance to handle liturgical revision further. The other dioceses tend to import English or American uses.

The Anglican Church of Sri Lanka remains the two independent dioceses mentioned in **FAL**. The diocese of Colombo has a duplicated English-language booklet, permitted for use by the bishop, which is traditional in its liturgical language, and follows **Cey** closely in the eucharistic prayer. However, it now includes acclamations during the prayer. It dates from 1982.

The Province óf Burma still uses the old C.I.P.B.C. Prayer Book (containing **Ind** and **IndR**), and has recently corrected its Burmese translation of this, as 'The Book of Common Prayer of Christ's Church in Burma'. Eucharistic revision is only a distant prospect.

The Council of the Church of South-East Asia did have in the late 1970s a Chinese language Prayer Book Revision Committee, and it produced texts known in English as 'Trial Use I' and 'Trial Use II' (1979), but actually composed in Chinese and rendered into English for a bilingual publication afterwards. However, there was some doubt about the status of the Committee, and little official acceptance of the rites can be traced. 'Trial Use II' states in an opening note that it is adapted from **Amer2–2** and **Eng3**. The former of these is dominant. The rite has had trial use in Hong Kong.

Nippon Sei Ko Kai has an alternative use to **Jap** of 1959, compiled in modern Japanese in 1978, and subject to various amending stages since then. The Liturgical Commission proposes to bring definitive texts in a modern-language Prayer Book to the General Synod in 1986.

In China itself there is now available in the West evidence of the rites in use in the 'post-denominational' church, in which ex-Anglicans are to be found. Space has excluded a translated eucharistic rite here.

The rites mentioned in the last three paragraphs above should take their place in any future volume succeeding this one.

CHAPTER 16

THE ANGLICAN CHURCH OF AUSTRALIA

THE eucharistic rites published in **FAL** (**Aus1A** of 1972 and **Aus4** of 1973) were not intended to be definitive. The General Synod in 1973 resolved that the Liturgical Commission should bring to the next General Synod in 1977 a complete book of modern services. The years between were to be used by the Commission to prepare for this.

Firstly, the texts themselves were to follow the established principle of having a modernized 1662 and also a further development of the 'experimental' liturgies (**Aus2**, **Aus3**, and **Aus4**). For the latter some testing was necessary, and in 1976 two editions of a booklet known as '*Australia '77*' were put out for experimental use. On the basis of the response the modernized 1662 ('**Aus1B**') and the 'Second Order' ('**Aus5**') were to be prepared by the Commission.

In April and October 1976 the Commission ran a series of 'Provincial Consultations', which covered the whole country and both enabled the responses to '*Australia '77*' to be collected, and also enabled confidence in the work of the Commission to grow.

The Commission itself did not take responsibility for the production and publication stages of the book, and these were handled by a 'Prayer Book Production Committee' appointed (at the request of the Commission) by the Standing Committee.

The Commission then finished its redrafting of the eucharistic rites (as of the whole draft book) early in 1977, and the book was published at the end of June as a draft '*An Australian Prayer Book*'. The Book came to the General Synod at the end of August. Some amendments were accepted when the Synod sat in committee (these are noted in the *apparatus* of the texts below), and then the Synod decided to proceed by 'ordinary bill' – a process of direct authorization, rather than of requiring the assent of all diocesan synods. On 31 August 1977 the Syond then authorized *An Australian Prayer Book* (as an alternative to the entrenched 1662 Book) overwhelmingly – there being but one opponent in the whole Synod. The Canon which undergirded the Book was also approved. The Book was then put into production, and printed copies became available on 5 April 1978. Different editions and offprints have followed. The Book as a whole, and particularly the 'Second Order' (**Aus5**), has passed uncontroversially into use throughout Australia.

THE LITURGIES FROM *AN AUSTRALIAN PRAYER BOOK* 1978 (AuslB, Aus5)

⟦The texts below are taken from *An Australian Prayer Book* (*AAPB*). *AAPB* has general 'Notes for the conduct of services' on page 15, and these include a conventional symbol for marking sections as optional. This symbol is omitted here. Rubics are in red in the original. The numbering is original. Variants are shown by *apparatus* where they come from '*Australia,* '77' ('1976(1)'), '*Australia,* '77 Revised' ('(1976(2))'), or the 1977 'Draft' of *AAPB* ('1977').⟧

THE HOLY COMMUNION

At communion time, the Table shall be covered with a clean white cloth.
The bread and wine for the communion shall be provided by the incumbent and churchwardens at the expense of the parish.
It is sufficient that the bread be such as is usually eaten.
For the significance of kneeling to receive the Lord's Supper, see the declaration which is printed at the conclusion of the Communion service in The Book of Common Prayer.

When the minister gives notice of the celebration of the communion, he may read this exhortation:
It is intended, on...next, to administer to all who shall be devoutly disposed, the most comforting sacrament of the body and blood of Christ, to be received by them in remembrance of his meritorious cross and passion, by which alone we obtain remission of our sins, and are made partakers of the kingdom of heaven.

We must thank our heavenly Father that he has given his Son our Saviour Jesus Christ, not only to die for us, but also to be our spiritual food and sustenance in that holy sacrament. This is so divine and strengthening a thing to those who receive it worthily, and so dangerous to those who presume to receive it unworthily, that it is my duty to exhort you, in the meantime, to consider the dignity of that holy mystery and the peril of the unworthy receiving of it, so that you may come holy and clean to such a heavenly feast.

The way to prepare yourselves is to examine your lives by the rule of God's commandments, and wherever you see you have offended in will, word, or action, there to repent and confess your sin to God, with full purpose of amendment of life. And if you think that you have injured not only God but also your neighbour, then you must ask his forgiveness as well, and make good, to the full extent of your ability, any injury or wrong that he has suffered at your hands. You must likewise forgive others who have injured you, if you desire God to forgive your offences. For if you receive the holy communion without God's forgiveness, you only increase the judgment under which you already stand. So then, should any of you be a blasphemer of God, a hinderer of his word, an adulterer, or be in malice, or envy, or in any other serious offence, repent of your sin, or else do not come to that holy table.

And since no one should come to the Lord's table without a full trust in God's mercy and a quiet conscience, if there is any one of you who cannot quieten his conscience by these means, but needs further help or counsel, let him come to me, or to some other discreet and learned minister of God's word, and open his grief, that by the ministry of God's holy word he may receive the benefit of absolution, together with spiritual counsel and advice, and so be quietened in his conscience, and resolve all scruples and doubts.

THE HOLY COMMUNION　FIRST ORDER (Aus1B)
THE WORD AND THE PRAYERS

1　*A psalm, hymn, or anthem may be sung when the ministers enter, or after
the sentence of scripture (§3).*

　*The priest may begin the service at the prayer desk, or at some other
convenient place.*

2　*The priest may greet the people*

　The Lord be with you.

　And also with you.

3　*A Sentence of Scripture appropriate to the day may be read.*

4　*The Litany (page...[i.e. elsewhere in AAPB]) may be said or sung.*
　If this is done, §§5, 6, and 17 of this Order may be omitted.

5　*The people kneeling, this Prayer of Preparation is said by the priest, or the
priest and people together*

　Let us pray.

　Almighty God,...[CF 1]...Lord. **Amen.**

　hid] hidden

6　*The priest reads aloud the Commandments, Exodus 20.1–17 (or the
alternative following, see Mark 12.30–31 and Matthew 22.37–40); and
the people ask God's forgiveness for their past transgressions, and grace to
keep God's laws in the future. The commandments may be read omitting
the words in brackets. They may also be read as a continuous whole without
the responses except that which follows the tenth commandment.*

　God spoke these words, and said:
　I am the Lord your God.
　You shall have...[CF 2 with response '**Lord, have mercy on us: and
incline our hearts to keep this law**' to first nine commandments, and with
variants as in **EngA**, no. 78B, except as shown below]...wife or his servant,
or his maid, or his ox, or his ass, or anything that is his.

　　**Lord, have mercy on us: and write your law in our hearts by your
　　Holy Spirit.**

　before me] but me
　that is in the earth] on the earth
　that is in the water] in the water
　serve] worship
　or your maidservant] your maidservant
　blessed the sabbath] blessed the seventh
　not kill] do no murder

　OPEN BRACKETS IN SECOND COMMANDMENT AT '(For I the Lord...)' AND IN
　FOURTH AT '(For in six days...)' AND OMIT BRACKETS IN FIFTH AND TENTH.

　*A shorter form of the Commandments is to be found on page...[i.e. **Aus5**, §5]*

Or this

Our Lord Jesus Christ said: You shall love...⟦CF 3⟧...as yourself. On these two commandments hang all the law and the prophets.

Lord, have mercy on us: and write your law in our hearts by your Holy Spirit.

heart...soul] heart, and...soul, and
first] great and first
The second is this: Love] And a second is like it: You shall love

Or on weekdays

Lord, have mercy on us.
Christ, have mercy on us.
Lord, have mercy on us.

7 *The priest says*
Let us pray.
He then says the Collect of the day.

8 *A Reading from the Old Testament (or as appointed) may be read. It is introduced.* The reading from..., chapter..., beginning at verse...; *and at the end*, Here ends the reading. *Or the reader concludes*, This is the word of the Lord, *and then the people may respond*, **Thanks to be God.**

9 *A psalm, hymn, or canticle may be said or sung between the readings.*

10 *The Epistle or Reading from the New Testament is read. It is introduced and concluded in the same manner as the Old Testament reading.*

11 *The people stand for the Gospel, which is introduced*

The holy Gospel is written in the...chapter of the Gospel according to Saint..., beginning at the...verse.

The people may respond
Glory to you, Lord Christ.

After the Gospel, the reader may say
This is the gospel of the Lord.
Praise to you, Lord Christ.

12 *The Sermon may be preached here, or after the creed.*

13 *The Nicene Creed is said or sung, all standing. It may be omitted on weekdays.*

We believe...⟦ICET 3⟧...come. Amen.

incarnate from] incarnate of
[and the Son]] OM BRACKETS
1977 HAS THE VERSION SHOWN IN **FAL** PAGE 325 AND CROSS-REFERS TO **Aus5**, §13

14 *The Sermon is preached here if it is has not been preached earlier.*

15 *The priest begins the Offertory, saying one or more of these verses*
⟦The Offertory Sentences which follow are to be found in Appendix B⟧

16 *While these sentences are being read, the alms and other offerings of the people are collected and brought to the priest who reverently presents and places them on the holy table.*

A hymn may also be sung during the collection.

And when there is a communion, the priest then places sufficient bread and wine on the table; or he may do so at §20.

17 *The priest may bid special prayers and thanksgivings.*

He then says the Intercession.

If there are no alms or oblations, the words in italics in the first paragraph of this prayer are omitted.

Let us pray for all people, and for the Church throughout the world.

Almighty and everliving God, we are taught by your holy word to make prayers and supplications and to give thanks for all people: we ask you in your mercy *to accept our alms and oblations and* to receive our prayers which we offer to your divine majesty.

We pray that you will lead the nations of the world in the ways of righteousness and peace, and guide their rulers in wisdom and justice for the tranquillity and good of all. Bless especially your servant Elizabeth our Queen, her representatives and ministers, her parliaments, and all who exercise authority in this land. Grant that they may impartially administer justice, restrain wickedness and vice, and uphold integrity and truth. And we ask you of your goodness, Lord, to comfort and sustain all who in this transitory life are in trouble, sorrow, need, sickness, or any other adversity.

We beseech you to inspire continually the universal Church with the spirit of truth, unity, and concord; and grant that all who confess your holy name may agree in the truth of your holy word, and live in unity and godly love.

Give grace, heavenly Father, to all bishops and other ministers [especially N our bishop and...], that, by their life and teaching, they may set forth your true, life-giving word, and rightly and duly administer your holy sacraments. And to all your people give your heavenly grace, and especially to this congregation here present, that they may receive your word with reverent and obedient hearts, and serve you in holiness and righteousness all the days of their life.

And we also bless your holy name for all your servants who have died in the faith of Christ. Give us grace to follow their good examples, that with them we may be partakers of your eternal kingdom.

Grant this, Father, for Jesus Christ's sake, our only mediator and advocate, who lives and reigns with you in the unity of the Holy Spirit, now and for ever.

Amen.

18 *If there is no communion, the service concludes here with the Lord's Prayer, other authorized prayers at the discretion of the minister, and the Grace or the Blessing.*

19 *A hymn may be sung here.*

THE LORD'S SUPPER

(An alternative order of §§20 to 27 is set out on pages... ⟦i.e. on page 217 below⟧*)*

20 *The priest places on the holy Table sufficient bread and wine for the communion (if he has not already done so) and reads this Exhortation, or at least the final paragraph (omitting 'then')*

Brothers and sisters in Christ, we who come to receive the holy communion of the body and blood of our Saviour Christ can come only because of his great love for us. For, although we are completely undeserving of his love, yet in order to raise us from the darkness of death to everlasting life as God's sons and daughters, our Saviour Christ humbled himself to share our life and to die for us on the cross. In remembrance of his death, and as a pledge of his love, he has instituted this holy sacrament which we are now to share.

But those who would eat the bread and drink the cup of the Lord must examine themselves, and amend their lives. They must come with a penitent heart and steadfast faith. Above all they must give thanks to God for his love towards us in Christ Jesus.

You, then, who truly and earnestly repent of your sins, and are in love and charity with your neighbours, and intend to lead a new life, following the commandments of God and walking in his holy ways, draw near with faith, and take this holy sacrament to strengthen and comfort you. But first, let us make a humble confession of our sins to Almighty God.

21 *A pause for self-examination may be observed.*
All then say this General Confession, kneeling

Almighty God, Father of our Lord Jesus Christ,
maker of all things, judge of all men,
we acknowledge with shame the sins we have committed,
by thought, word, and deed, against your divine majesty,
provoking most justly your wrath and indignation against us.
We earnestly repent, and are heartily sorry for all our mis-
doings.
Have mercy on us, most merciful Father.
For your Son our Lord Jesus Christ's sake
forgive us all that is past,
and grant that from this time forward
we may serve and please you in newness of life,
to the honour and glory of your name,
through Jesus Christ our Lord. Amen.

22 *The priest, or the bishop if he is present, stands and pronounces this Absolution*

Almighty God our heavenly Father, who of his great mercy has promised forgiveness of sins to all who with hearty repentance and true faith turn to him: have mercy on you; ...[[CF 5]]...our Lord. **Amen.**

life eternal] eternal life

23 *The Words of Assurance.*

The priest says one or more of these sentences

Hear the words of assurance for those who truly turn to Christ:
Jesus said: Come...[[CF 4]]...he is the perfect offering for our sins.
(1 *John* 2. 1, 2.)

Hear what...says] OM TWICE
true] sure
anyone does sin] any one sins

24 *The priest begins the Thanksgiving and Communion*

Lift up your hearts.
   We lift them to the Lord.
Let us give thanks to the Lord our God.
   It is right to give him thanks and praise.
It is indeed right, and our bounden duty, that we should at all times and in all places give thanks to you, Lord, holy Father, mighty Creator, and eternal God.

On certain days a special preface (see §25 below) is said here: otherwise the priest, or the priest and people together, continue

Therefore with angels and archangels, and with the whole company of heaven, we proclaim your great and glorious name, evermore praising you, and saying:
Holy, holy, holy, Lord God of hosts,
heaven and earth are full of your glory.
Glory to you, O Lord most high.

1977: **Lord God]** is the Lord
       your] his
       O Lord] Lord God

25 *Special prefaces*

[[The Proper Prefaces which follow here are to be found in Appendix C.]]

26 *After each of these prefaces the priest, or the priest and people together, continues*

Therefore with angels...[[as in §24]]...**most high.**

27 *Then the priest, kneeling down at the Lord's table, says this prayer in the name of all who are to receive the communion (or all may join with him in the prayer)*

We do not presume...[[CF 6]]...he in us. **Amen.**

this] OM

28 *When the priest has so arranged the bread and wine that he may more conveniently and appropriately take and break the bread before the people and take the cup into his hands, he says this Prayer of Consecration*

All glory to you, our heavenly Father, for in your tender mercy you gave your only Son Jesus Christ to suffer death on the cross for our redemption; who made there, by his one oblation of himself once offered, a full, perfect, and sufficient sacrifice for the sins of the whole world; and who instituted, and in his holy gospel commanded us to continue, a perpetual memory of his precious death until his coming again.

Hear us, merciful Father, and grant that we who receive these gifts of your creation, this bread and this wine, according to your Son our Saviour Jesus Christ's holy institution, in remembrance of his death and passion, may be partakers of his most blessed body and blood; who on the night he was betrayed *Here the priest takes the paten in his hands* took bread, and when he had given you thanks, *He breaks the bread* he broke it, and gave it to his disciples, saying, 'Take, eat; *He lays his hand on all the bread* this is my body which is given for you; do this in remembrance of me.' Likewise after supper *He takes the cup in his hands* he took the cup, and when he had given you thanks, he gave it to them saying, 'Drink from this, all of you; for *He lays his hand on the vessels in which is wine to be consecrated* this is my blood of the new covenant, which is shed for you and for many for the remission of sins; do this, as often as you drink it, in remembrance of me.'

All answer
Amen.

29 *The priest receives the communion in both kinds himself, and then distributes it similarly to the other communicants; first to any bishops, priests, and deacons, who are present, and then to the other communicants; into their hands, all kneeling.*

When the minister gives the bread he says
The body...[[CF 7(a)]]...with thanksgiving.
When the minister gives the cup he says
The blood...[[CF 7(b)]]...be thankful.

Instead of these words, the invitation together with the alternative words of distribution on page...[[i.e. at **Aus5**, §23, on page 227 below]] *may be used; and the communicant may answer* **Amen.**

During the Communion hymns or anthems (see page...[[i.e. in the 'Notes' following **Aus5**]]) *may be sung.*

30 *If the consecrated bread or wine prove insufficient for the communion, the priest is to consecrate more, beginning at* Our Saviour Christ on the night...*for the blessing of the bread; and at* Likewise after supper...*for the blessing of the cup.*

31 *When all have communicated, the minister reverently places on the table what remains of the consecrated elements.*
If he does not then consume them (see §36) he covers them with a clean white cloth.
A Sentence of Scripture may be said here or during the Communion.

32 *The priest says*

Let us pray. [As our Saviour Christ has taught us, we are confident to say,]

Our Father...⟦ICET 1⟧...**for ever. Amen.**

Save us...trial and] Lead us not into temptation, but
1977 HAS A TRADITIONAL ('THOU') FORM

33 *Then is said one or both of the prayers following*
Lord and heavenly Father...⟦as in **EngA**, no. 71⟧...for ever. **Amen.**
Almighty and everliving God...⟦as in **EngA**, no. 72⟧...for ever. **Amen.**

34 *This Hymn of Praise (Gloria in excelsis) is said or sung.*

Glory to God...⟦ICET 4⟧...**God the Father. Amen.**
1977 HAS THE TRADITIONAL FORM MODIFIED BY THE USE OF 'YOU'. A CROSS-REFERENCE TO **Aus5** POINTS TO THE ICET FORM

35 *The priest, or the bishop if he is present, lets the people depart with this Blessing*
The peace of God...⟦CF 10⟧...always. **Amen.**
among] amongst

36 *If any of the consecrated bread and wine remain it shall not be carried out of the church, but the priest and such other of the communicants as he shall request shall consume it after the Communion or immediately after the Blessing (see also §31).*

NOTES

1 *The reader may preface the announcement of the Gospel with the salutation,* 'The Lord be with you', *to which the people respond,* **'And also with you'.**

2 *The sermon may be omitted on weekdays.*

3 *Formal notices may be given before the service begins, before the sermon, after the Nicene Creed, or after the Intercession.*

4 *Another version of* 'Holy, holy, holy,...' *is to be found on page*...⟦i.e. in **Aus5**, §20⟧
1977: 4 *Another...on page...*] OM

ALTERNATIVE ORDER FOR §§20–27
1977: §§20–27] §§20–28
THE LORD'S SUPPER

20 *The priest places on the holy Table sufficient bread and wine for the communion (if he has not already done so), and says one or more of these sentences*
Hear the words...[as in §23 above]...our sins. (1 *John* 2. 1, 2)

21 *The priest continues*
You who truly...[as in §20 on page 213]...Almighty God.

22 *A pause for self-examination may be observed.*
All then say this General Confession, kneeling.
Almighty God...[as in §21 on page 213]...**our Lord. Amen.**

23 *The priest, or the bishop if he is present, stands and pronounces this Absolution*
Almighty God...[as in §22 on pages 213–14]...our Lord. **Amen.**

24 *Then this prayer may be said by the priest, kneeling down at the Lord's table, in the name of all who are to receive the communion (or all may join with him in the prayer)*
We do not presume...[as in §27 above]...**he in us. Amen.**

25 *All standing, the priest may give this Greeting of Peace*
The peace of the Lord be always with you.
  And also with you.

26 *When the priest has so arranged the bread and wine that he may more conveniently and appropriately take and break the bread before the people and take the cup into his hands, he begins the Thanksgiving and Communion*
[The Lord be with you.
  And also with you.]
Lift up your hearts. ...[as in §24 on page 214]... eternal God.
On certain days a special preface is said here: otherwise the priest, or the priest and people together, continue
Therefore with angels ...[as in §24 on page 214]...saying:

Holy, holy, holy is the Lord of hosts.
Heaven and earth are full of his glory.
Glory to you, Lord God most high.

27 *For the special prefaces see §§25 and 26 on page*...[i.e. in the main text]
[The Proper Prefaces which are printed there are to be found here in Appendix C]

28 *The priest continues with the Prayer of Consecration on page*...[i.e. at §28 on page 215 above]

THE HOLY COMMUNION SECOND ORDER (Aus5)

The parts of the service are set out for three different ministers : the presiding priest or bishop ; the deacon or assisting priest ; and other ministers or authorized assistants. The parts assigned to the deacon or assisting priest may be read by the priest, or all three parts may be read by the priest. When there is no communion, all three parts may be read by a deacon or authorized layman ; save that a deacon or authorized layman says 1 John 2. 1, 2 in place of the Absolution :

Hear these words of assurance from Saint John: If anyone sins, we have an advocate with the Father, Jesus Christ the righteous; and he is the perfect offering for our sins, and not for ours only but also for the sins of the whole world.

1976(1) AND 1976(2) PRESENT THIS SLIGHTLY DIFFERENTLY

THE WORD AND THE PRAYERS

1 *A Psalm, Hymn, or Anthem may be sung when the ministers enter or after the Greeting (§2).*

2 *The priest greets the congregation*
The Lord be with you.
And also with you.

[*During the Easter season he may add*
Christ is risen.
He is risen indeed.]

3 *A Sentence of Scripture appropriate to the day may be read.*
4 *This Prayer of Preparation is said*
[Let us pray.] **Almighty God**...⟦CF 1⟧...**our Lord. Amen.**
hid] hidden
1976(1): [Let us pray.]] OM

5 *The Ten Commandments or one of the forms below is used, and the people ask God's forgiveness and the grace to keep his word.*
a *The Ten Commandments (see Exodus 20. 1–17)*

The commandments may be read as a continuous passage, or after each commandment except the last the people may answer
Lord, have mercy on us: and incline our hearts to keep this law.
The full form of the commandments on page...⟦i.e. in **Aus1B**, §6 on page 210 above⟧ *may be used.*
1976(1), 1976(2): (*See Exodus 20. 1–17*)] OM
1976(1):   *The...passage, or*] OM
                REMAINING RUBRIC AND RESPONSE FOLLOW THE FIRST COMMANDMENT
                The full...may be used] OM
Hear the commandments which God gave his people Israel.
   1   I am the Lord your God who brought you out of the land of slavery; you shall have no other gods...⟦CF 2, omitting brackets ⟧...covet anything that is your neighbour's.

Lord, have mercy on us: and write your law in our hearts by your Holy Spirit.

any] a
nor the likeness] or any likeness
in the earth] that is on the earth ⟦1976(1), 1976(2): in⟧
in the water] that is in the water
nor worship] or serve
to keep holy the sabbath day] the sabbath day to keep it holy
you shall labour] shall you labour
not commit murder] do no murder ⟦1976(1): not kill⟧
1976(1), 1976(2): Six days...sabbath of the Lord your God] OM

b *The Two Great Commandments (see Matthew 22. 37–40 and Mark 12. 30–31)*

Our Lord Jesus Christ said:...⟦as **Aus1B**, §6⟧...**Holy Spirit.**
1976(1), 1976(2): (*see Matthew 22. 37–40 and Mark 12. 30–31*)] OM

c *Kyrie eleison*
These forms may be used together with either of the preceding forms, or they may be used by themselves.

Lord, have mercy on us.   *or*   **Lord, have mercy.**
Christ, have mercy on us.   **Christ, have mercy.**
Lord, have mercy on us.   **Lord, have mercy.**

and/or

Holy God, holy and mighty, holy and immortal, have mercy on us.

Kyrie eleison ('Lord, have mercy') *may be repeated according to local custom or the musical setting used for it.*
1976(1), 1976(2): *Kyrie eleison*] *Commandments* ⟦1976(2): *Words*⟧ *of the Lord Jesus*
        ADD SENTENCES FROM MARK 11. 25, MATTHEW 7. 12, MATTHEW 5. 44–45,
        JOHN 13. 34 BEFORE KYRIES WITH OTHER MINOR RUBRICAL VARIATION

6 *The Confession may be said here (instead of at §16). The deacon says*
In penitence and faith let us confess our sins to almighty God.
All kneel. A pause for self-examination may be observed.

Merciful God,
our maker and our judge,
we have sinned against you in thought, word, and deed:
we have not loved you with our whole heart,
we have not loved our neighbours as ourselves;
we repent, and are sorry for all our sins.
Father, forgive us.
Strengthen us to love and obey you in newness of life;
through Jesus Christ our Lord. Amen.
1976(1):   In penitence and faith] OM
1976(1), 1976(2): *All*] OM
1976(1):   **thought, word**] thought, and word
                  repent, and are sorry for] are truly sorry and repent of

The priest, or bishop if present, stands and pronounces this Absolution
Almighty God,
who has promised forgiveness to all who turn to him in faith,
pardon you and set you free from all your sins,
strengthen you to do his will,
and keep you in eternal life;
through Jesus Christ our Lord. **Amen.**

1976(1), 1976(2): *stands and*] OM

7 *This Hymn of Praise (Gloria in excelsis) may be sung or said, all standing*
Glory to God...[ICET 2]**...the Father. Amen.**

1976(1): *all standing*] stand

8 *The priest says*
Let us pray.
He then says the Collect of the Day.

1976(1), (1976(2): *He then says*] and

9 *All sit for the Reading from the Old Testament or as appointed.*
After each reading the reader may say
This is the word of the Lord.
Thanks be to God.

1976(1): *All sit for*] OM
1976(1), 1976(2): *After...***God**] IN §10
A Psalm may be sung or said.

10 *The Reading from the New Testament (other than from the Gospels).*

1976(1), 1976(2): *than from*] than

A Hymn or Anthem may be sung.

1976(1): *sung*] sung or said

11 *All stand for the Gospel Reading.*
The Gospel is announced
The gospel of our Lord Jesus Christ according to..., chapter...,
beginning at verse...

1976(1): *All...Reading*] Stand. The Gospel.
1976(1), 1976(2): *The Gospel is announced*] The deacon says

and there may be said
Glory to you, Lord Christ.

1976(1), (1976(2): *and*] When the Gospel is announced

After the Gospel, the reader may say
This is the gospel of the Lord.
Praise to you, Lord Christ.

1976(1), 1976(2): *reader*] deacon

12 *The Sermon is preached here, or after the Creed.*

13 *All stand for the Nicene Creed which is said or sung.*
   It may be omitted on weekdays.

   1976(1): *All...which*] Stand. *The Nicene Creed*
   1977: ADD *Another version of the Nicene Creed is to be found on page* ... ⟦i.e. **Aus1B**, §13⟧

   We believe... ⟦ICET 4⟧ ...**to come. Amen.**
   incarnate from] **incarnate of**
   [and the Son]] OM BRACKETS

   1976(1), 1976(2): VERSION SHOWN IN **FAL** PAGE 325
   1977:   ICET 1971 VERSION

14 *The Prayers are offered by one or more persons.*
   They may follow the form printed below or one of the forms given on pages ... ⟦i.e. on pages 230–231 below⟧.

   Pauses may be allowed for silent prayer and thanksgiving.

   The response
        Lord, in your mercy
        hear our prayer
   may be used after the detailed additions instead of the response printed after each section.

   For the use of the following form see also Note 9 on page ... ⟦i.e. page 230⟧

   The priest says

   Let us pray for all people and for the Church throughout the world.
   The minister says
   Almighty God, your Son Jesus Christ has promised that you will hear us when we ask in faith: receive the prayers we offer.

   For the church
   We give thanks for... We pray for... *the church in other countries; the church in Australia; this diocese; N our Bishop; this parish;* ...

   Strengthen your people for their witness and work in the world, and empower your ministers faithfully to proclaim the gospel and to administer your holy sacraments. Unite in the truth all who confess your name, that we may live together in love and proclaim your glory in all the world.

        Father, hear our prayer,
        through Jesus Christ our Lord.

   ⟦And similarly after each of the following three paragraphs⟧

For all peoples
We give thanks for... We pray for... *the peoples of the world; their leaders; Elizabeth our Queen; Australia, and those who make and administer our laws; all who have responsibility; all men and women in their daily work...*

Give wisdom to those in authority in every land, and guide all peoples in the ways of righteousness and peace, so that they may share with justice the resources of the earth, work together in trust, and seek the common good.

For our community
We give thanks for... We pray for... *one another; our local community; people known to us (especially...);...*

We commend to your keeping, Father, ourselves and each other, our families, our neighbours, and our friends. Enable us by your Spirit to live in love for you and for one another.

For those in need
We pray for...*those who suffer; the sick; the poor; the distressed; the lonely; the outcast; the persecuted; those who mourn; those who care for them;...*
We give thanks for...

Comfort and heal, merciful Lord, all who are in sorrow, need, sickness, or any other trouble. Give them a firm trust in your goodness; help those who minister to them; and bring us all into the joy of your salvation.

Thanksgiving for the faithful departed
We give thanks for *the life and work of...*

We praise you, Lord God, for your faithful servants in every age, and we pray that we, with all who have died in the faith of Christ, may be brought to a joyful resurrection and the fulfilment of your eternal kingdom.

1976(1), 1976(2) INCLUDE IN RUBRICS THE PROVISIONS OF NOTE 9 ON PAGE 230 BELOW, AND INCLUDE THE VERSICLE AND RESPONSE ('Father, hear...') IN THE OPENING RUBRICS

1976(1):	throughout the world] ADD *Kneel*	
1976(1), 1976(2):	*Australia and those who make and administer our laws*] *our country*	
1976(1), 1976(2):	they may share] we may share	
1976(1):	*one another*] OM	
1976(1), 1976(2):	and each other] OM	
1976(1), 1976(2), 1977:	*the poor : the distressed*] OM ⟦1976(1) also omits '*the sick*'⟧	
1976(1), 1976(2):	those who minister] us to minister	
1976(1), 1976(2):	all into the joy] the joy ⟦1976(1): all the joy⟧	

The priest says either
Hear us, Father, through Jesus Christ our Lord,
Who lives and reigns with you
in the unity of the Holy Spirit,
one God now and for ever. Amen.
1976(1) **in the unity of**] **and**

or

Accept our prayers through Jesus Christ our Lord, who taught us to pray,

Our Father in heaven... [ICET 1] **...for ever. Amen.**
Save us from the time of trial and] Lead us not into temptation, but
1976(1), 1976(2): *The priest says*] OM
1976(1)   *either...or...*] REVERSE THE TWO SECTIONS
[The 1976(1) and 1976(2) text is a traditional form of the Lord's Prayer (except the first line) with 'thy' etc. replaced by '**your**']
When there is no Communion, the Lord's Prayer should be used here and the Confession at §6, and the service ends with [a hymn, during which the gifts of the people may be received and presented] the General Thanksgiving (page... [i.e. elsewhere in *AAPB*])*, and the Grace.*

PREPARATION FOR THE LORD'S SUPPER

15 *One or more of these (or other suitable verses of Scripture) may be read*
Jesus said: Come to me all who labour and are heavy laden, and I will give you rest. Take my yoke upon you, and learn from me; for I am gentle and lowly of heart, and you will find rest for your souls. For my yoke is easy and my burden is light.   (*Matthew* 11. 28–30)

Jesus said: I am the bread of life; he who comes to me shall not hunger, and he who believes in me shall never thirst.   (*John* 6. 35)

Jesus said: A new commandment I give to you, that you love one another, even as I have loved you.   (*John* 13. 34)

Whenever you stand praying, forgive, if you have anything against any one; so that your Father also who is in heaven may forgive you your trespasses.
                                          (*Mark* 11. 25)

God so loved the world that he gave his only Son, that whoever believes in him should not perish but have eternal life.   (*John* 3. 16)

Saint Paul said: As often as you eat the bread and drink the cup of the Lord, you proclaim the Lord's death until he comes. Whoever, therefore, eats the bread or drinks the cup in an unworthy manner will be guilty of profaning the body and blood of the Lord. Let a man examine himself, and so eat of the bread and drink of the cup.   (*I Corinthians* 11. 26–28)

1976(1), 1976(2): *of Scripture*] ADD *e.g. Heb. 4. 12–13; Heb. 4. 14–16; 1 Cor. 12. 31b–13. 7: Matt. 5. 3–12* [Omit John 13. 34 and Mark 11. 25]

The Exhortation on page... [i.e. on page 213 above] *may be read here. If the Confession is not to follow immediately, this Exhortation should end with the words...*to strengthen and comfort you.

1976(1), 1976(2): *The Exhortation...*comfort you] OM

16 *This Prayer may be said, all kneeling*
[Let us pray.] **We do not presume...** [CF 6] **...he in us. Amen.**
this] OM
1976(1):   REVERSES §§16 AND 17. HAS SEPARATE RUBRIC *Kneel*
1976(1), 1976(2): *Prayer*] *Prayer of Approach*

17 *The Confession is said here, if it has not been said at §6. The deacon says:*
In penitence...[as in §6 including the Absolution]...our Lord. **Amen.**

18 *All stand, and the Greeting of Peace is given by the priest (see also Note 10 on page...[i.e. on page 230 below])*

We are the body of Christ.
His Spirit is with us.
The peace of the Lord be always with you.
And also with you.

1976(1): *All stand, and the] Stand. The*   1976(2): *Note 10] Note 9*
    (see...page...)] OM

A hymn may be sung.

19 *The gifts of the people are brought to the Lord's Table. They may be presented in silence, or the following prayer may be used*

Blessed are you, Lord God our Father;
through your goodness we have these gifts to share.
Accept and use our offerings for your glory
and for the service of your kingdom.
Blessed be God for ever.

1976(1), 1976(2): *the following prayer] one of the following prayers*
                    ADD BEFORE THE PRAYER *All things come from you, O Lord*
                            and of your own do we give you.
                                    or

THE THANKSGIVING

20 *The priest takes the bread and wine for the communion, places them upon the Lord's Table, and says this Prayer of Thanksgiving and Consecration (or one of the forms on pages...[i.e. on pages 231–6 below]. On certain days special additions may be made to this Prayer, and these are to be found on pages...[i.e. §20d, page 236 below].*

[The Lord be with you.
And also with you.]
Lift up your hearts.
We lift them to the Lord.
Let us give thanks to the Lord our God.
It is right to give him thanks and praise.
All glory and honour, thanks and praise
be given to you at all times and in all places,
Lord, holy Father, true and living God,
through Jesus Christ our Lord.
For he is your eternal Word
through whom you have created all things from the beginning
and formed us in your own image.

In your great love you gave him
to be made man for us and to share our common life.

In obedience to your will
your Son our Saviour offered himself as a perfect sacrifice,
and died upon the cross for our redemption.
Through him you have freed us from the slavery of sin
and reconciled us to yourself,
our God and Father.

He is our great high priest
whom you raised from death
and exalted to your right hand on high
where he ever lives to intercede for us.

Through him you have sent upon us
your holy and life-giving Spirit
and made us a royal priesthood
called to serve you for ever.

Therefore with angels and archangels
and with all the company of heaven
we proclaim your great and glorious name,
for ever praising you and saying:

**Holy, holy, holy Lord, God of power and might,
heaven and earth are full of your glory.
Hosanna in the highest.**

Merciful Father, we thank you
for these gifts of your creation, this bread and this wine,
and we pray that we who eat and drink them
in the fellowship of the Holy Spirit
in obedience to our Saviour Christ
in remembrance of his death and passion
may be partakers of his body and his blood,

> *He takes the bread into his hands and says*

who on the night he was betrayed took bread;
and when he had given you thanks
he broke it, and gave it to his disciples, saying,
'Take, eat. This is my body which is given for you.
Do this in remembrance of me.'

> *He takes the cup into his hands and says*

After supper, he took the cup,
and again giving you thanks

he gave it to his disciples, saying,
'Drink from this, all of you.
This is my blood of the new covenant
which is shed for you and for many
for the forgiveness of sins.
Do this, as often as you drink it, in remembrance of me.'

Christ has died;
Christ is risen;
Christ will come again.

Father, with this bread and this cup,
we do as our Saviour has commanded;
we celebrate the redemption he has won for us;
we proclaim his perfect sacrifice
made once for all upon the cross,
his mighty resurrection and glorious ascension;
and we look for his coming
to fulfil all things according to your will.
Renew us by your Holy Spirit,
unite us in the body of your Son,
and bring us with all your people
into the joy of your eternal kingdom;
through Jesus Christ our Lord,
with whom and in whom,
by the power of the Holy Spirit,
we worship you, Father almighty,
in songs of never-ending praise:

Blessing and honour and glory and power
are yours for ever and ever. Amen.

1976(1): *On certain days…pages…*]　REPLACE BY PROPER PREFACES IN MAIN TEXT
1976(1), 1976(2): your Son our Saviour offered himself] he offered himself to you
1976(1): slavery] bondage
1976(1): all the company of heaven]　ADD with the patriarchs and apostles and with
　　the whole church in heaven and earth
1976(2): all the company of heaven]　REPLACE BY ABOVE FROM 1976(1) WITHOUT 'with'
1976(1): and we pray…fellowship of the Holy Spirit] and we pray that by your Holy
　　Spirit we who eat and drink them
1976(2): and we pray…fellowship of the Holy Spirit] and in the power of your Holy
　　Spirit we pray that we who eat and drink them
1976(1): we do…commanded]　OM
　　he has won] our Saviour has won
　　mighty]　OM
　　glorious]　OM
　　we look…your will] the outpouring of your Spirit upon your people.

21 *If the Lord's Prayer has not already been said, it is said here or after the*
   Communion
   As our Saviour Christ has taught us, we are confident to say,

   1976(1), 1976(2): As...say] Let us pray with confidence to the Father as our Saviour
      Christ has taught us:
   1977:   say] pray

   Our Father in heaven...⟦ICET 1 as at §14⟧...**for ever. Amen.**

THE COMMUNION

22 *The priest breaks the bread before the people.*
   He may do so in silence, or he may say
   [We who are many are one body in Christ,
   for we all share in the one bread.]

   1976(1): *before*] *in the sight of*
      ADDS *Kneel* AND THEN THE FIRST FOUR LINES OF §23 WITH 'Let us remember'

23 [*The priest may say*
   Come let us take this holy sacrament of the body and blood of Christ
   in remembrance that he died for us, and feed on him in our hearts by
   faith with thanksgiving.]

   The priest and the other communicants receive the holy communion.

   When the minister gives the bread he says

   The body...⟦CF 7(a)⟧...with thanksgiving.
   or
   The body of Christ keep you in eternal life.
   or
   Take and eat this in remembrance that Christ died for you, and be
   thankful.

   1976(1): *or* Take...thankful] OM
   1976(2): and...remembrance] eat: remember

   The communicant may answer **Amen.**

   When the minister gives the cup he says
   The blood...⟦CF 7(b)⟧...be thankful.
   or
   The blood of Christ keep you in eternal life.
   or
   Drink this in remembrance that Christ's blood was shed for you, and
   be thankful.

   1976(1): *or* Drink...thankful] OM
   1976(2): this in remembrance] from this: remember

   The communicant may answer **Amen.**

During the Communion, hymns or anthems (see Note 1 on page... ⟦*i.e.
page 229 below*⟧*) may be sung.*

AFTER COMMUNION

24 *A Sentence of Scripture may be said.*

25 *If the Lord's Prayer has not been said earlier, it is used here.*
The priest says
Let us pray. As our Saviour...⟦as at §21⟧...**for ever. Amen.**
1976(1): *used] to be used*

26 *The priest may say this or another suitable prayer (see page...* ⟦*i.e.
page 237 below*⟧*).*

[Let us pray]
Father, we thank you
that you feed us who have received these holy mysteries
with the spiritual food of the body and blood of our Saviour, Jesus
    Christ.
We thank you for this assurance of your goodness and love,
and that we are living members of his body
and heirs of his eternal kingdom.
Accept this our sacrifice of praise and thanksgiving,
and help us to grow in love and obedience,
that with all your saints we may worship you for ever.

1976(1):   [Let us pray.]] OM
1976(1), 1976(2): Father] Almighty and everliving God
               that you feed] for feeding
               who...mysteries] OM
               We thank...goodness and love, and,] and for assuring us who have
                  received these pledges of his love ⟦1976(1): who...love] in these
                  holy mysteries⟧
1977:   love, and that] love; that
1976(1):   grow in love and obedience] live as true members of the body of your
               Son
1976(1), 1976(2): for ever] for ever. We ask this through Christ our Lord. **Amen.**
               ⟦1976(2) omits 'we ask this'⟧

27 *All say together*
Father, we offer ourselves to you
as a living sacrifice
through Jesus Christ our Lord.
Send us out in the power of your Spirit
to live and work to your praise and glory. Amen.

1976(1), 1976(2): **as a living sacrifice]** OM
                through] in

28 *A hymn may be sung, which may be Gloria in excelsis (see page...* [*i.e.
§7 above*]*) if it has not already been used at §7.*

29 *The priest, or bishop if present, says this or the appropriate seasonal Blessing (see below)*

The peace... ⟦CF 10⟧ ...always. **Amen.**

among] amongst BUT NOT IN 1976(1) AND 1976(2)

30 *The deacon may say*

Go in peace to love and serve the Lord:
In the name of Christ. Amen.

1976(1), 1976(2): *may say] says*

Seasonal Blessings which may be used at §29

⟦The Seasonal Blessings which are printed here are to be found in Appendix D⟧

Other suitable sentences, such as those at the end of the services in Morning and Evening Prayer Second Form (pages... ⟦*i.e. elsewhere in AAPB*⟧*) may also be used when appropriate before the words* and the blessing...

NOTES

⟦In all the items in section 1 below the page numbers, referring to pages in *An Australian Prayer Book*, have been omitted without further explanation⟧

1 *The following canticles and anthems are suitable :*

When the ministers enter or after the Greeting
Psalm 95 (page...)
Judith 16. 13–15 (page...)
Tobit 13. 1–4, 6 (page...)
Hebrews 10. 19–22 (page...)
Psalms 23; 43; 93; 96. 1–6; 96. 7–13; 100; and 150.

Before the Gospel Reading
The Song of Zechariah (page...)
The Song of Mary (page...)
The Song of Creation (page...)
Ephesians 2. 4–7 (page...)
Great and wonderful (page...)
Psalm 23

During the Communion
Psalm 67
A Song of Christ's Glory (page...)
Saviour of the World (page...)
The Easter Anthems (page...)
Gloria in excelsis (page...)
Blessed... ⟦ICET 5(b)⟧ ...highest
Jesus... ⟦ICET 8(a)⟧ ...peace
Lamb of God... ⟦ICET 8(b)⟧ ...peace

Before the Blessing
Te Deum (page...)
The Song of Simeon (page...)
The Hymn to the Word (page...)
Ephesians 1. 3–6 (page...)
A Song to the Lamb (page...)
A Song of Christ's Glory (page...)

2 *When Baptism or Confirmation is to be administered, or Holy Matrimony is to be solemnized, during this service, or when there is no communion, it is appropriate that the Confession be at §6.*

3 *The optional Sentence of Scripture permitted at §3 may be sung as an anthem by the choir at §3, or before the opening Greeting ; or it may be used immediately before the Collect at §8.*

4 *Gloria in excelsis may be used wherever a hymn is permitted instead of at §7 ; it may be omitted during Advent and Lent and on weekdays.*

5 *A pause for reflection may be observed at any of the following : before the Collect ; after any of the Readings ; before the Confession ; and after all have received the holy communion.*

6 *The reader may preface the announcement of the Gospel reading with the salutation. '*The Lord be with you*', to which the people respond* **'And also with you.'**

7 *Although the recommended position for the Sermon is after the Gospel Reading it may be after the creed, or before or after any of the readings. A sermon should normally be preached at this service.*

8 *The plural* **'we believe'** *is original to the Nicene Creed, which was a corporate declaration of faith ; while the singular is appropriate to the Apostles' Creed which is an act of personal commitment at baptism. Nevertheless, in this service, the Nicene Creed may be used in the singular.*

9   *The form of Intercession on page...* [i.e. at §14], *may be offered as a single prayer without the detailed additions suggested or responses.*
    The minister need not use all the detailed suggestions on each occasion, nor need he use the precise form. 'We give thanks for... We pray for...'. Any forms should be clearly addressed to God, and not biddings to the congregation. The congregation may join in saying the invariable paragraphs of the prayer.

10 *The priest exchanges the Greeting of Peace, §18, with the congregation by using the versicle and response. When circumstances permit, all may then exchange the greeting, saying, for example, 'Peace be with you', which they may accompany with a handclasp or other similar action.*

11 *It is appropriate for all to remain standing during the Thanksgiving and Consecration (§20) and the Breaking of the Bread (§22). However, it may be considered desirable, at the discretion of the local congregation, for the people to kneel.*

12 *The consecrated elements may be distributed immediately after the words of institution. In this case, the bread is to be broken at the words 'he broke it', and* **'Amen'** *or one of the acclamations (e.g.* **'Christ has died,...'**) *is said after '...in remembrance of me.'*
    After the Communion, the service resumes at §25 or §26.

13 *If the consecrated bread and/or wine are insufficient for the communion, the priest is to take more bread and/or wine saying the appropriate portions of §20, beginning, 'Merciful Father' and ending 'in remembrance of me'.*

14 *If any of the consecrated bread and wine remain it shall not be carried out of the church, but the priest and such other of the communicants as he shall request shall reverently consume it after the Communion or immediately after the Blessing.*

15 *Notices may be given before the Prayers (§14) or before the final Blessing (§29).*

16 *The Readings from the Old and New Testaments (§§8 and 10) are introduced, 'A reading from..., chapter..., beginning at verse...'*

1976(1): NOTES] ADDITIONAL NOTES AND DIRECTIONS
          OMITS NOTES 3, 4, 5, 6, 9, 10 AND 16, AND RENUMBERS ADDING '10' RE HYMNS
1976(2): OMITS NOTES 9 AND 16 AND RENUMBERS
1977:   OMITS NOTE 16

ALTERNATIVE FORMS FOR §14
THE PRAYERS

14a *The Intercession (§17) from The Holy Communion First Order (page...* [i.e. in **Aus1B**]) *or the Prayer for all people (page...* [i.e. elsewhere in *AAPB*]) *may be used.*
    When it is desired to say the Lord's Prayer after the Prayer of Intercession, the priest introduces it with the words
    Accept our prayers through Jesus Christ our Lord, who taught us to pray...

14b *The Litany (page...* [i.e. elsewhere in *AAPB*]) *may be used; it may begin with §4 Receive now our prayers and end with the Lord's Prayer; on weekdays selected petitions from the Litany may be used.*
    1976(1): PRINTS OUT 14a AND ADDS 'ALL SORTS AND CONDITIONS' AS 14b AND RELETTERS

14c *The priest says*
    Let us pray for all people and for the Church throughout the world.
    When the following form is used, the minister may add names of particular persons or needs to the several petitions; he may add other similar petitions.

    Almighty God, whose Son Jesus Christ has promised that you will hear us when we ask in faith: receive the prayers we offer.

    We pray for the peace of the world and the welfare of your holy Church.
    Lord, in your mercy,
    hear our prayer.
    [The versicle and response recur after each paragraph]

    We pray for our Bishop *N*, and for all the clergy and people.

    We pray for Elizabeth our Queen, for the leaders of the nations, and for all in authority.

[We pray for seasonable weather, and for an abundance of the fruits of the earth.]

[We pray that we may share with justice the resources of the earth, and live in trust and goodwill with one another.]

We pray for the aged and the infirm, for widows and orphans, and for the sick and suffering.

We pray for the poor and oppressed, for prisoners and captives, and for all who care for them.

We pray for ourselves and for each other.

We praise you, Lord God, for the communion of saints, and for the glorious hope of the resurrection to eternal life.

1976(1), 1976(2): and the welfare...Church] the welfare...Church and for the unity of all
                mankind
                the infirm] infirm
                care] remember and care

⟦Two endings follow as in § 14, with variants as shown there.⟧

14d   *The priest says*
Let us pray for all people and for the Church throughout the world.

The minister says
Father, we pray for your holy catholic Church;
    that we all may be one in Christ.

Grant that every member of the Church may truly and humbly serve you;
    that your Name may be glorified by everyone.

We pray for all bishops, priests, and deacons;
    that they may be faithful ministers of your word and sacraments.

We pray for all who govern and exercise authority in the nations of the world;
    that there may be peace and justice among all.

Give us strength to do your will in all that we undertake;
    that we may be blessed in all our works.

Have compassion on those who suffer or are in grief or trouble;
    that they may be delivered from their distress.

We praise you for all your saints who have entered into joy;
    may we also share in your heavenly kingdom.

1976(1):   We pray for all bishops...**sacraments**] OM
1976(1), 1976(2): strength] courage

⟦Two endings follow as in § 14, with variants as shown there.⟧

ALTERNATIVE FORMS FOR §20–30

⟦1976(1) includes here as §20a, called 'A Second Form', the Thanksgiving with Seasonal Additions. §20b, entitled 'A Third Form', corresponds to 'A Second Form' below, and is shown as an *apparatus* to it. §20c, entitled 'A Fourth Form', is printed out in Appendix E. 1976(2) begins with the same pattern, but does not call the form at §20a 'A Second Form'. At §20b it has a distinct 'A Second Form' printed below in Appendix E. At §20c it has 'A Third Form' related to 'A Second Form' below and shown as an *apparatus* to it. At §20d it has a distinct 'A Fourth Form' printed below in Appendix E. There is considerable relationship between the distinct forms printed in the Appendix and 'A Third Form' below, but it is too complicated to be shown by an *apparatus*. In 1976(2) each Form is followed by provision for §§21–22. New texts are provided at §22 as follows:

§22a   Let us keep a joyful and holy feast with the Lord.
    All that the Lord has spoken we will do and be obedient.

§22b The cup of blessing which we bless
is it not a sharing in the blood of Christ?
The bread which we break,
is it not a sharing in the body of Christ?
Risen Lord, be known to us in the breaking of the bread.]

A SECOND FORM OF THE THANKSGIVING

20a *The priest takes the bread and wine for the Communion, places them upon the Lord's table,
and says this Prayer of Thanksgiving and Consecration.*
[The Lord be with you.
And also with you.]
Lift up your hearts.
We lift them to the Lord.
Let us give thanks to the Lord our God.
It is right to give him thanks and praise.

All thanks and praise, glory and honour,
be yours at all times, in every place,
creator Lord, holy Father, true and living God.

We praise you that through your eternal Word
you brought the universe into being
and made man in your own image.
You have given us this earth to care for and delight in,
and with its bounty you preserve our life.

We thank you that you bound yourself to mankind
with the promises of a gracious covenant
and called us to serve you in love and peace.

Above all, we give you thanks for your Son,
our Saviour Jesus Christ;
by the power of the Holy Spirit
he was born a man and lived our common life;
to you he offered his life in perfect obedience and trust;
he has delivered us from our sins, brought us new life,
and reconciled us to you, Father, and to one another.

Therefore we join with angels and all created things,
with patriarchs, prophets, and apostles,
and the whole church in heaven and earth,
in their unending song:

**Holy, holy, holy Lord, God of power and might,
heaven and earth are full of your glory.
Hosanna in the highest.**

And now, Father, we thank you
for these gifts of your creation, this bread and this wine,
and we pray that we who eat and drink them
in the fellowship of the Holy Spirit
in obedience to our Saviour Christ
may be partakers of his body and blood,
and be made one with him and with each other
in peace and love.

The priest takes the bread into his hands and says
For on the night he was betrayed he took bread;
and when he had given you thanks
he broke it, and gave it to his disciples, saying,

'Take, eat. This is my body which is given for you.
Do this in remembrance of me.'
He takes the cup into his hands and says
After supper, he took the cup
and again giving you thanks
he gave it to his disciples, saying,
'Drink from this, all of you.
This is my blood of the new covenant
which is shed for you and for many
for the remission of sins.
Do this, as often as you drink it, in remembrance of me.'

**With this bread and this cup
we show forth Christ's death
until he comes in glory.**

With thanksgiving, Father, for the gift of your Son,
we proclaim his passion and death,
his resurrection and ascension,
the outpouring of his Spirit,
and his presence with his people.

Renew us by your Holy Spirit
that we may be united in the body of your Son
and serve you as a royal priesthood
in the joy of your eternal kingdom.

Receive our praises, Father almighty,
through Jesus Christ our Lord,
with whom and in whom,
by the power of the Holy Spirit,
we worship you in songs of never-ending praise:

**Blessing and honour and glory and power
are yours for ever and ever. Amen.**

1976(1):	bound] bond
1976(1):	common] human
1976(1), 1976(2):	created things] the heavenly host
1976(1), 1976(2):	these gifts of your creation] OM
1976(1), 1976(2):	and we pray...in obedience]
	they are gifts from your creation and pledges of your saving love. We pray that, by your Holy Spirit, we [1976(2): In the power of your Spirit we pray that we] who eat and drink them in obedience.
1976(1), 1976(2):	given you thanks] given thanks
1976(1):	**show forth] proclaim**
1976(1), 1976(2):	that we may be united...and serve] as we offer ourselves in Christ our Saviour to serve
1976(1):	**power] might**

21 *Please turn to page...* [i.e. §21 on page 236 below]

A THIRD FORM OF THE THANKSGIVING

20b *The priest takes the bread and wine for the Communion, places them on the Lord's table,
and says this Prayer of Thanksgiving and Consecration.*
[The Lord be with you.
  And also with you.]

Lift up your hearts.
We lift them to the Lord.
Let us give thanks to the Lord our God.
It is right to give him thanks and praise.

All thanks and praise, glory and honour,
be yours at all times and in all places,
creator Lord, holy Father, true and living God.

We praise you for your only-begotten Son
through whom you brought the universe into being
and made man in your own image.
You have given us this earth
that we might care for it and delight in it,
and through its bounty you preserve our life.

Above all we thank you
that you sent your Son, our Saviour Jesus Christ:
he is your eternal Word and the clear image of your glory.
By the power of the Holy Spirit
he was made man of the flesh of Mary, his virgin mother;
he took the form of a servant
and, with perfect trust in you,
he lived our common life.
He obeyed you in all things,
even to death on the cross.

He is the true passover Lamb
who was offered for us.
By his death he has destroyed death,
has taken away our sin and the sin of all the world,
and has reconciled us to you, Father,
and to one another.
By his rising to life again
he has brought us into new and everlasting life.

We thank you because you have bound yourself to us
and all mankind
by the promises of the new testament in his blood,
calling us into the fellowship of your saints
to serve you in love and peace,
to witness to the gospel,
and to show forth the fruit of the Spirit in our lives.

Therefore with angels and archangels,
and with all the company of heaven,
we proclaim your great and glorious name,
for ever praising you and saying:
Holy, holy, holy Lord, God of power and might,
heaven and earth are full of your glory.
Hosanna in the highest.

Hear us, merciful Father,
and grant that we who receive these gifts of your creation,
this bread and this wine,
in obedience to our Saviour Christ,
may be partakers of his body and blood,
and be made one with him and with each other
in peace and love.

The priest takes the bread into his hands and says
For on the night he was betrayed he took bread;
and when he had given thanks
he broke it, and gave it to his disciples, saying,
'Take, eat. This is my body which is given for you.
Do this in remembrance of me.'

He takes the cup into his hands and says
After supper, he took the cup
and again giving you thanks
he gave it to his disciples, saying,
'Drink from this, all of you.
This is my blood of the new covenant
which is shed for you and for many
for the remission of sins.
Do this, as often as you drink of it, in remembrance of me.'

With this bread and this cup *or* **Christ has died;**
we show forth Christ's death **Christ is risen;**
until he comes in glory. **Christ will come again.**

We give thanks to you, Father,
for your gift to us of Christ your Son,
our great high priest;
we celebrate and proclaim his perfect sacrifice
made once for all upon the cross,
his resurrection from the dead,
and his ascension into heaven to reign with you in glory.

We thank you for the outpouring of the Spirit upon your saints;
renew us, we pray, by the same Holy Spirit,
as we offer ourselves to you through Christ our Saviour
to serve you as a royal priesthood;
and grant that, when he returns to the earth
in power and majesty to judge the living and the dead,
we with all your pilgrim people
may be ready to meet him,
and may worship you for ever.

Receive our prayer and praise, Father,
through Jesus Christ our Lord,
with whom and in whom,
by the power of the Holy Spirit,
we worship you, Father almighty,
in songs of never-ending praise:
Blessing and honour and glory and power
are yours for ever and ever. Amen

21 *Please turn to page...* [i.e. §21 on page 236 below].

A FOURTH FORM OF THE THANKSGIVING

20c *The priest takes the bread and wine for the Communion, places them upon the Lord's table,*
and says this Prayer of Thanksgiving and Consecration

[The Lord be with you.
  And also with you.]
Lift up your hearts.
  We lift them to the Lord.

Let us give thanks to the Lord our God.
It is right to give him thanks and praise.

All glory and honour, thanks and praise,
be yours now and always,
Lord, holy Father, mighty Creator, everliving God.
We give thanks and praise for your Son, our Saviour Jesus Christ,
who by his death on the cross
and rising to new life
offered the one true sacrifice for sin
and obtained an eternal deliverance for his people.

Therefore with the whole company of heaven
we proclaim your great and glorious name,
for ever praising you and saying:

Holy, holy, holy Lord, God of power and might,
heaven and earth are full of your glory.
Hosanna in the highest.

And now, Father, we pray
that we who receive these your gifts of bread and wine
according to our Saviour's word
may be partakers of his body and blood.

The priest takes the bread into his hands and says:
For on the night he was betrayed he took bread;
and when he had given thanks to you, his almighty Father,
he broke it, and gave it to his disciples, saying,
'Take, eat. This is my body which is given for you.
Do this in remembrance of me.'

He takes the cup into his hands and says:
After supper, he took the cup
and again giving you thanks
he gave it to his disciples, saying,
'Drink from this, all of you.
This is my blood of the new covenant
which is shed for you and for many
for the remission of sins.
Do this, as often as you drink it, in remembrance of me.'

With this bread and this cup   *or*   **Christ has died;**
we show forth Christ's death   **Christ is risen;**
until he comes in glory.   **Christ will come again.**

We offer our prayer and praise, Father,
in the fellowship of the Holy Spirit,
through Jesus Christ our Lord:
Blessing and honour and glory and power
are yours for ever and ever. Amen.

21 *Please turn to page...* ⟦i.e. §21 below⟧.

THE PRAYER OF THANKSGIVING AND CONSECRATION WITH SEASONAL ADDITIONS

20d ⟦There follows here the main Thanksgiving from §20 above, set out to include the Proper Prefaces, which are to be found in Appendix C.⟧

21–22 ⟦These are set out again as in the main text above. 1976(1) omits them.⟧

THE COMMUNION

23 ⟦The text of the invitation and of rubrics cross-referring to the main text are set out here. 1976(1) does not print them.⟧

AFTER COMMUNION

4–25 ⟦These correspond to §§24 and 25 in the main text. 1976(1) omits them.⟧

26 *The priest may say one of the following prayers, and the congregation responds with the prayer at §27* ⟦1976(1) omits the rubric and adds four prayers not intended for the eucharist in *AAPB*. 1976(2) omits '*and...at §27*'⟧.

[Let us pray.]
Father, we thank you...⟦as in §26 on page 228, with 1977 variant⟧...for ever.

or this
Father of all...⟦CF 8⟧...praise your Name.

or this
Father, you graciously feed us
who have received these holy mysteries
with the bread of life and the cup of eternal salvation.
May we who have reached out our hands to receive this sacrament
be strengthened in your service;
we who have sung your praises
tell of your glory and your truth in our lives;
we who have seen the greatness of your love
see you face to face in your kingdom.
For you have made us your own people
by the death and resurrection of your Son our Lord
and by the life-giving power of the Spirit.

1976(1), 1976(2):   graciously feed] have graciously fed
1976(1):   who have received] in
1976(1), 1976(2), 1977: this sacrament] your gifts
1976(1), 1976(2):   ADD A DOXOLOGY

or this
Father,
we who believe in your Son Jesus Christ
and have received these pledges of his love,
thank you because you graciously feed us
with the spiritual food of his body and his blood.
By this you assure us of your love and forgiveness,
and that we and all your faithful people
are true members of his body and of each other in him.
Remember your church which you have purchased by his blood,
and gather it in holiness into the kingdom you have prepared for it.
Make us faithful witnesses of the Lord Jesus and his resurrection,
that at his coming we may go out with great joy to meet him,
and be found worthy to worship you
with all your saints for ever.

1976(1): OMIT

or either of the prayers at §33 of The Holy Communion, First Order (page... ⟦i.e. in **Aus1B** on page 216⟧*) may be used, and one of the prayers from §§8–11 of the Prayers for Various Occasions (page....* ⟦i.e. elsewhere in the *AAPB*⟧*) may be added.*

7–30 ⟦These sections are exactly as on pages 228–9 above. 1976(1) omits them.⟧

CHAPTER 17

THE ANGLICAN PROVINCE OF PAPUA NEW GUINEA

THE 'Niugini' rite (**NG**) was published in 1970, and printed in **FAL**. The rite was revised in 1974, when the 1971 ICET texts replaced the previous more local ones. The Province of Papua New Guinea was formed in 1978, and the rite was revised in 1983 and approved by the Provincial Council. The revision (entitled '**PNG**') is shown below by description only, using **NG** as the point of reference.

THE REVISED PAPUA NEW GUINEA LITURGY 1983 (PNG)

〚This is published in a booklet with black and white illustrations. The numbering below is the editorial numbering of **NG** as presented in **FAL**, now related to **PNG**. Pronouns for God do not now have capital letters.〛

THE EUCHARIST

Before the rite: there are now printed 'A Prayer of Thanksgiving', which is a very simplified form of The General Thanksgiving, and 'A Prayer before Holy Communion' ('*This prayer may be said sometime before the Eucharist, or before receiving the Blessed Sacrament*'), which is the Prayer of Humble Access, worded as in no. 22.

Nos. 1–8: These come in the order 4, 5 (with salutation before), 6[1], 1, 2, (with addition after '**we have sinned against you**' of '**and each other**'), 3, 7 (1971 ICET text), 8.

Nos. 9–10: *A lesson from the Bible shall be read. On Sundays two lessons shall be read with a canticle or psalm (said or sung) between them. After each reading may be said:*

Reader This is the Word of the Lord.
People **Thanks be to God.**

Then a psalm, canticle, or hymn may be said or sung.

Stand

Priest The Lord be with you.
People **And with you.**

No. 11: *Then a lesson from the Gospels shall be read.*
All Before: +**Glory be to you, Lord Christ.**[2]
At the end the reader may say: This is the Gospel of Christ.
After which, or at the end all say: **Praise be to you, Lord Christ.**

---

[1] An error in **FAL** means that no. '6' appears in the margin there, and at first sight the Kyries are contained with the Prayer of Humble Access under '5'. They are meant to be '6'. In **FAL** they are presented for fully congregational recitation, here they are printed for responsive recitation.

[2] The '+' here represents a dagger symbol in the original found in nos. 3, 7 (final line), here, twice in no. 17 (see on page 240 below), accompanying both the words of administration in no. 23, and in no. 26.

No. 12: *Sit On Sundays and special days the Sermon follows.*

No. 13: Add '*Nicene*' in rubric omit '*then*' and add '*Stand*' before text (ICET 1971, without brackets).

No. 14: This is so changed as to be set out in full:

THE PRAYERS OF THE CHURCH . . . THE INTERCESSION

The Priest or one or more of the people shall offer the Prayers of the Church.

Reader Let us pray:
Almighty God, you have taught us to give thanks for all people; we thank you for.... Father we thank you

People **Through Jesus Christ our Lord.**

Reader You have promised to hear the prayers of those who ask in faith, we pray for all our brothers and sisters in Christ throughout the world...and that your whole Church may grow in unity and love. Lord, in your mercy

People **Hear our prayer.**

Reader For this Province of Papua New Guinea, especially for the work of the Church in...: Lord, in your mercy

People **Hear our prayer.**

Reader For...our bishop/s; for all our priests and deacons; For Evangelists, Church Councillors and other lay workers; For the Brothers and Sisters of Religious Communities; For the members of this congregation; Lord, in your mercy

People **Hear our prayer.**

Reader For those who have lost you, that they may find you again; For those who have rejected you, that they may repent; For unbelievers, that they may come to know the truth in Christ; Lord, in your mercy

People **Hear our prayer.**

Reader For peace and justice throughout the world; For the leaders of all nations, especially for our Queen, Elizabeth; and her deputy here...our Governor General. For our nation, Papua New Guinea; For those in authority.... For this place.... and for all who live here; Lord, in your mercy

People **Hear our prayer.**

Reader For our homes, and for all parents and children; For teachers, and all who lead others by their words, writings and actions; For students that they may know wisdom and truth; Lord, in your mercy

People **Hear our prayer.**

Reader For all men and women in their daily work; For our food and crops, that they may grow well; For the businesses and industries of our nation; For all who travel by land, sea and air; Lord, in your mercy

People **Hear our prayer.**

Reader That you may give healing and comfort to those who are sick or suffering... sorrowful or needy... worried or frightened... and that you may bless all who serve them...; Lord, in your mercy

People **Hear our prayer.**

Reader For our ancestors, for our fathers in the faith, and for all Christian people who have died...that they may have your light and peace; Lord, in your mercy

People **Hear our prayer.**

Reader For ourselves, that we may follow the holy saints and martyrs...in being good soldiers and servants of Christ, and that we may have a holy and happy death, rest in paradise, and a share in your glory.

People **Grant these prayers of ours, merciful Father, for the sake of your Son, our Saviour, Jesus Christ. Amen.**

No. 15: The four lines in **NG** come as follows: 3, 4, 1 (first half by priest), 1 (second half by people), 2 (omitting 'Try to' and 'to')

No. 16: After the rubric there is optional provision for the Roman Catholic 'Offertory Prayers' (see **Scotl**, no. 16 on page 50 above, but here reading 'may it become...'), and (between the two) for the Roman prayer 'By the mystery...' at the preparation of the chalice. Then comes the rubric ' *Then shall always be said* ', followed by the versicle and response in **NG**. Optional provision follows for two more prayers of preparation, and ' *A Hymn may be sung at this time.* '

No. 17: The differences from **NG** can be generally shown by *apparatus*:
THE PROPER PREFACES ALL FOLLOW 'life-giving Spirit' AND ARE SHOWN IN APPENDIX C HERE
So through Him, with angels] So, with angels

SANCTUS AND BENEDICTUS QUI VENIT USE 1971 ICET TEXTS (' + ' BEFORE BENEDICTUS)
(*Bell, Drum or Rattle*)] OMIT (TWICE)
O Father...O Lord] OMIT 'O'
and make these gifts] and by the power of the Holy Spirit make these gifts
as often as] whenever
O Lord] Father
the coming of his kingdom] his coming again in glory
that we may be filled] so that we may be filled
Christ our Lord] Jesus Christ our Lord
AFTER 'Amen': *All* **Christ has died.+**
Christ is risen.
Christ will come again.

No. 18: Opening rubrics are omitted. It begins: ' *Priest* As our Saviour Christ has commanded and taught us, we pray.' The text is ICET 1974 with '**Lead us not into temptation**'.

No. 19: The rubric omits '*which has been blessed*' and has '*consecrated bread*'. The people's responses change the question format to 'is a sharing...'

No. 20: the text is unchanged (apart from the omission of 'O'), but includes provision for a Requiem ('give them rest...rest eternal').

No. 21: and thanksgiving] with thanksgiving

No. 22: has been moved to the beginning of the rite (and the '*Bell or Drum or Rattle*' rubric has disappeared).

No. 23: There is a + before the words of distribution.

No. 25: There are now three paragraphs, the second beginning 'We thank you for keeping...' and the third 'We pray that we may...'. 'Body of your Son' is 'Mystical Body...' and 'faithful' is 'believing'.

No. 27: This is omitted.

After the Rite: There are alternative intercessions, the first based on **Eng2**, and the second on American Form III in **FAL** p. 159. There is also a form of 'THE SACRAMENT OF PENANCE', and 'AN ACT OF PENITENCE: THE COMMANDMENTS'.

CHAPTER 18

THE CHURCH OF THE PROVINCE OF NEW ZEALAND

THE 1970 Liturgy (**NZR**, in **FAL**) remained the sole modern language of the Province until 1984. In 1982 the second line of the Lord's Prayer was altered to 'Hallowed be. . . .' In addition a draft eucharistic rite produced by the Prayer Book Commission was distributed to selected parishes in 1982. This enabled the Commission to take soundings and bring new texts to the 1984 General Synod. The Synod received the proposed alternatives warmly in May 1984, and authorized them for use, and the requisite confirmation by diocesan synods followed.

The rites comprise a principal alternative (**NZ1**), a two-in-one more experimental rite (**NZ2**), and an outline structure (**NZ3**). The language is 'inclusive', and at points original and highly imaginative. The 1986 General Synod will be invited to make the rites definitive, and there is a possibility of inclusion in a more permanent and larger book of services after that. The rites were published as a booklet in early 1985.

THE NEW ZEALAND LITURGIES 1984 (NZ1, NZ2, NZ3)

[The notes 'Concerning the Liturgy' relate to each of the rites. At points in the rites a Maori equivalent of English versicles and responses has been printed in the English version, and these are included here, indented slightly as in the original as alternatives to the English at those points. A full 'diglot' version is planned by the Liturgical Commission for **NZ1**. The numbering in this edition is editorial. The lining out of the original has been followed very closely. The 'Seasonal Variants' at §§48, 75, 85, whilst in the duplicated text authorized, are not in the printed booklet, though it makes reference to them.]

CONCERNING THE LITURGY

1. *The Eucharist is a celebration of the whole Community of Faith, whose worship is led by the presiding priest and lay ministers.*
2. *No change in Eucharistic doctrine from that implied by the Book of Common Prayer is intended by the changes in structure or language of this rite.*
3. *It is fitting that the presiding priest, whether bishop or priest, be assisted by other priests, deacons or lay ministers.*
4. *Lay members of the community may be appointed to read the lessons, lead the prayers of the people and where licensed by the bishop, assist in the administration of Communion.*
5. *All who are to receive communion should prepare themselves with prayer, penitence and forgiveness.*

THE LITURGY OF THE EUCHARIST (NZ1)

THE MINISTRY OF WORD AND PRAYER

THE PREPARATION

1 *All standing, the presiding priest or minister greets the congregation.*

2 *The theme may be introduced and subjects of special concern or thanksgiving suggested.*

3 *Any of the following greetings may be used.*
Grace and peace to you from God.
    Kia tau ki a koutou, te atawhai me te rangimarie a te Atua.
God fill you with truth and joy.
    Ma te Atua koe e whaka kii, ki te pono me te hari.
The Lord be with you.
    Kia noho a Ihowa ki a koutou.
The Lord bless you.
    Ma Ihowa koe e manaaki.
This is the day which the Lord has made.
    Ko te ra tenei i hanga a Ihowa.
Let us rejoice and be glad in it.
    Kia hari, kia koa tatou.

4 *The sentence of the day may be read.*

5 *The following may be said.*
Almighty God...[CF 1]...through our Saviour, Jesus Christ. **Amen.**
hid] hidden   perfectly] truly
that] so that   magnify] praise

6 *The following may be said or sung here, or after the Absolution.*
Glory to God...[ICET 4]...**God the Father. Amen.**

7 *The congregation kneels.*
The Ten Commandments (page...[i.e. §91]), or one of the following may be used.
The Summary of the Law
Hear these words of Jesus Christ: You shall love...[CF 3]...your neighbour as yourself.
Spirit of God search our hearts.
heart...soul] heart and...soul and
first] first and greatest
The second] And a second
A New Commandment
Jesus said: A new commandment I give to you, that you love one another as I have loved you.
Spirit of God, search our hearts.

*The Kyries may be used as an alternative response, repeating each three
times if desired.*

Lord, have mercy.

E te Ariki, kia aroha rapea.

Christ, have mercy.

E te Karaiti, kia aroha rapea.

Lord, have mercy.

E te Ariki, kia aroha rapea.

Kyrie eleison.

Christe eleison.

Kyrie eleison.

8 *One or more of these sentences may be read.*

Hear God's word to all who turn to Christ.

God so loved the world that he gave his only Son,
that whoever believes in him should not perish
but have eternal life.

If we confess our sins, God is faithful and just,
and will forgive our sins and cleanse us from all
unrighteousness.

Jesus said
There is joy among the angels of God
over one sinner who repents.

Come to me all who labour and are heavy laden
and I will give you rest.

9 *The presiding priest or minister says*

God has promised forgiveness
to all who truly repent
turn to Christ in faith
and are themselves forgiving.

In silence we call to mind our sins.

Silence

10 Let us confess our sins.

Merciful God,
we have sinned
in what we have thought and said,
in the wrong we have done
and in the good we have not done.
We have sinned in ignorance:
we have sinned in weakness:
we have sinned through our own deliberate fault.
We repent and turn to you.
Forgive us, for our Saviour Christ's sake,
and renew our lives to the glory of your name. Amen.

11 *The Absolution is declared by the presiding priest.*
By the authority of Jesus Christ
I declare that God has mercy on you
pardons you and sets you free.
Know that your sins are forgiven
through Jesus Christ our Saviour.
God strengthen you in all goodness
and keep you in life eternal. **Amen.**

If a priest is not present the following shall be said
Hear the word of God to all.
God shows his love for us in that,
while we were yet sinners Christ died for us. **Amen.**

12 *The Gloria in excelsis – Glory to God in the Highest – may be said or
sung here, all standing.*

THE READINGS

13 *The following may be used.*
The peace of Christ rule in our hearts.
   Kia mau te rongo o te Karaiti ki o tatou ngakau.
The word of Christ dwell in us richly.
   Kia hira ake te noho o tana kupu ki a tatou.

14 *The sentence of the day may be read.*

15 *The collect of the day shall be said here, or before or after the Sermon.*

16 *The congregation sits.*
One or two lessons, as appointed, are read, the reader first saying
A reading from . . . . (chapter . . . . beginning at . . . .)
Silence may follow each reading.
The reader may say
Hear what the Spirit is saying to the church.
Thanks be to God.

17 *A psalm, hymn or anthem may follow each reading.*

18 *Then, all standing, the reader of the Gospel says*
The Holy Gospel according to . . . . (chapter . . . . beginning at . . . .)
Praise and glory to God.
After the Gospel silence may be kept.
The reader says
This is the Gospel of Christ.
Praise to Christ, the Word.

THE PROCLAMATION

19 The SERMON *may be preached here.*

20 The NICENE CREED *may be said or sung, all standing.*

We believe...⟦ICET 3⟧...**world to come. Amen.**
us men] us
[and the Son]] OM BRACKETS

THE PRAYERS OF THE PEOPLE

21 *The presiding priest says*

Let us pray for the Church and the world,
thanking God for his goodness.

Three other forms of intercession and thanksgiving are provided on pages...⟦i.e. at §§45–47 below⟧

Or, intercessions and thanksgivings may be offered by a minister or members of the congregation in their own words.

The following subjects are offered as a guide

the church throughout the world	families and friends
the parish, the diocese	children
bishops, clergy and all who minister	people in their daily lives
those who have died, the saints of God	
	the sick and suffering
the nations of the world	and those who care for them
this country and its leaders	those in need
the local community	those who mourn

Periods of silence may be kept.

During the prayers any of the following may be used

After thanksgiving : For your love and goodness
We give you thanks, O God.

Let us bless the Lord
Thanks be to God.

Give thanks to our God who is gracious
Whose mercy endures for ever.

After intercession : God of love
Grant our prayer.

Hear us, Lord
Lord, hear our prayer.

Lord, in your mercy
Hear our prayer.

Lord, hear our prayer
And let our cry come to you.

The prayers of the people may conclude with an appropriate collect or one of the following

God of mercy,
you have given us grace to pray
with one heart and one voice;
and have promised to hear the prayers
of two or three who agree in your Name;
Fulfil now, we pray,
the prayers and longings of your people
as may be best for us and for your kingdom.
Grant us in this world to know your truth,
and in the world to come to see your glory. **Amen.**

Almighty and eternal God,
ruler of all things in heaven and earth;
mercifully accept the prayers of your people,
and strengthen us to do your will;
through Jesus Christ our Lord. **Amen.**

Those things, good Lord,
that your servants have prayed for,
give us grace to work for;
and in the purpose of your love
answer our prayers and fulfil our hopes
for Jesus' sake. **Amen.**

Now to God who is able to do immeasurably more
than all we can ask or conceive,
by the power which is at work among us,
be glory in the church and in Christ Jesus
throughout all ages. **Amen.**

The Lord's Prayer (which is to be used at least once in the service) may be said here.

As Jesus taught us, we pray

Our Father in heaven...
[ICET 1]...**for ever. Amen.**

[In the booklet the Maori text is set out beneath the English.]

E to matou Matua i te rangi,
  Kia tapu tou Ingoa,
  Kia tae mai tou rangatiratanga.
  Kia meatia tau e pai ai
    ki runga ki te whenua,
    kia rite ano ki to te rangi.
Homai ki a matou aianei
  he taro ma matou mo tenei ra.
Murua o matou hara,
  Me matou hoki e muru nei
    i o te hunga e hara ana ki a matou.
Aua hoki matou e kawea kia whakawaia;
  Engari whakaorangia matou i te kino:
Nou hoki te rangatiratanga, te kaha,
  me te kororia,
    Ake ake ake. Amine.

THE MINISTRY OF THE SACRAMENT
THE PEACE

22 *All stand. The presiding priest says to the people*

The peace of Christ be always with you.
Kia tau tonu te rangimarie o te Ariki ki a koutou.
And also with you.
A ki a koe ano hoki.

23 *The priest may invite the people to exchange a sign of peace according to local custom.*

24 *The priest says*

Brothers and sisters, we are the body of Christ.
E te whanau, ko tatou te Tinana o te Karaiti.
By one Spirit we were baptised into one Body.
Na te Wairua kotahi tatou i iriiri hei Tinana kotahi.

Keep the unity of the Spirit in the bond of peace.
Kia mau te kotahitanga o te Wairua he mea paihere na te rangimarie.
Amen. We are bound by the love of Christ.
Amine. Kua paiheretia tatou ki te aroha o te Karaiti.

THE PREPARATION OF THE GIFTS

25 *A hymn or anthem may be sung.*

26 *During or after the hymn representatives of the congregation may bring the bread and wine to the Holy Table or Altar. The offerings of the people are presented.*

27 *The presiding priest may say*

To you, Lord, belongs the greatness,
and the power, and the glory,
and the victory and the majesty.
All that is in the heavens and the earth is yours,
and of your own we give you.

28 *Or the priest may offer praise for God's gifts in the following, or other appropriate words*

Blessed are you, God of all creation;
through your goodness we have these gifts to share.
Accept and use our offerings for your glory
and for the service of your kingdom.
Blessed be God for ever.

THE GREAT THANKSGIVING

29 *An alternative Great Thanksgiving is provided on page... [[i.e. §49]]*
Seasonal variants in the Great Thanksgiving may be used.

30 *It is recommended that the people stand or kneel throughout the following prayer.*

31 *The presiding priest says or sings*
The Lord is here.
God's Spirit is with us.
Lift up your hearts.
We lift them to the Lord.
Let us give thanks to the Lord our God.
It is right to give him thanks and praise.

It is right indeed, it is the joy of our salvation, holy Lord,
almighty Father, everlasting God, at all times and in all places
to give you thanks and praise through Christ your only Son.

You are the source of all life and goodness;
through your eternal Word you have created all things
from the beginning and formed us in your own image;
male and female you created us.

Any Seasonal Variant either replaces or follows this section.

When we turned away from you
you called us back to yourself
and gave your only Son to share our human nature.
He made the one perfect sacrifice for the sin of the world
and by his death on the cross,
he freed us from the bondage of sin.

You raised him to life triumphant over death;
you exalted him in glory.

In him you have called us to be a holy people
by sending upon us your holy and lifegiving Spirit.

Therefore with the faithful who rest in him,
with angels and archangels and all the company of heaven,
we proclaim your great and glorious name,
for ever praising you and saying:
Holy, holy, holy Lord, God of power and might,
heaven and earth are full of your glory.
Hosanna in the highest.
Tapu, tapu, he tapu te Ariki
Te Atua o te mana me te kaha,

ki tonu te rangi me te whenua i tou kororia.
Ohana i runga rawa.

The following may also be used
Blessed is he who comes in the name of the Lord.
Hosanna in the highest.
Whakapaingia a ia e haere mai nei i runga i te Ingoa o te
Ariki.
Ohana i runga rawa.

All glory and thanksgiving to you, Holy Father;
on the night before he died
your Son, Jesus Christ, took bread;
when he had given you thanks,
he broke it, gave it to his disciples, and said:
Take, eat, this is my body
which is given for you;
do this to remember me.

After supper he took the cup;
when he had given you thanks,
he gave it to them and said:
Drink this, all of you,
for this is my blood of the new covenant
which is shed for you and for many
for the forgiveness of sins;
do this as often as you drink it,
to remember me.

Glory to you, Lord Christ:
your death we show forth:
your resurrection we proclaim:
your coming we await:
Amen: Come Lord Jesus.

Therefore loving God,
recalling your great goodness to us in Christ,
his suffering and death,
his resurrection and ascension,
and looking for his coming in glory,
we celebrate our redemption with this bread of life
and this cup of salvation.
Accept our sacrifice of praise and thanksgiving
which we offer through Christ our great High Priest.

Grant that through your Holy Spirit
these gifts of bread and wine which we receive
may be to us the body and blood of Christ.
Fill us with your Spirit
by whose grace and power
you make us one in the body of Christ.

With all who share these holy things
we worship you in songs of everlasting praise.

**Blessing, honour and glory be yours,
here and everywhere,
now and forever. Amen.**

Silence may be kept.

THE COMMUNION

32 *The priest may say*

As Jesus taught us, we pray

Our Father in heaven...⟦ICET 1⟧...for ever. Amen.

33 *The priest breaks the bread.*

Silence may be kept.

We break this bread
to share in the body of Christ.

**We who are many are one body,
for we all share the one bread.**

34 *The following may be used before or during Communion or as private devotions.*

We do not presume...⟦CF 6⟧...he in us. **Amen.**
this your] your holy
manifold and great mercies] great mercy
so much as to gather up] ever to gather
flesh] body

Lamb of God...⟦ICET (b)⟧...grant us your peace.
sins] sin

Jesus, Lamb of God...⟦ICET 8(a)⟧...give us your peace.

35 *The priest says*

Draw near and receive the Body and Blood of our Saviour Jesus Christ in remembrance that he died for us.

Let us feed on him in our hearts by faith with thanksgiving.

36 *The Bread and the Cup are given to each person with one of the following*

The body of Christ given for you.

Ko te Tinana o to tatou Ariki, i tukua nei mou.

The blood of Christ shed for you.

    Ko nga Toto o to tatou Ariki, i whakahekea nei mou.

The body of our Lord Jesus Christ given for you.

    Ko te Tinana o to tatou Ariki, i tukua nei mou.

The blood of our Lord Jesus Christ shed for you.

    Ko nga Toto o to tatou Atiki, i whakahekea nei mou.

The body of Christ keep you in eternal life.

    Ma te Tinana o te Karaiti, koe whakau ki te ora tonu.

The blood of Christ keep you in eternal life.

    Ma nga Toto o te Karaiti koe whakau ki te ora tonu.

The communicant may respond. **Amen. Amine.**

37 *If there is insufficient Bread and Wine for the number of communicants, the presiding priest is to return to the Holy Table and say*

Almighty God, obeying the command of your Son, Jesus Christ, who took break and said: 'This is my body', we also take this bread, and pray that through your Word and Spirit it may be for us the Sacrament of the body of Christ. **Amen.**

Almighty God, obeying the command of your Son, Jesus Christ, who took the cup and said: 'This is my blood', we also take this wine, and pray that through your Word and Spirit it may be for us the Sacrament of the blood of Christ. **Amen.**

AFTER COMMUNION

38 *An appropriate sentence of scripture may be said.*

Silence may be kept.

39 *The Lord's Prayer (if it has not been used before) shall be said or sung here.*

40 *A seasonal prayer of thanksgiving may be used, with or without one of the following.*

41 Father of all...⟦CF 8⟧...praise your name;
Send us out...⟦CF 9⟧...praise and glory. Amen.
in this hope that we have grasped] firm in the hope you have set before us
Or

42 Almighty God, giver of all good things,
we thank you for feeding us with the spiritual food
of the precious Body and Blood of our Saviour, Jesus Christ.
We thank you for your love and care
in assuring us of your gift of eternal life
and uniting us with the blessed company
of all faithful people.

**Therefore, everliving God,
keep us steadfast in your holy fellowship.
And now we offer ourselves, soul and body,
to serve you faithfully in the world,
through Jesus Christ our redeemer,
to whom with you and the Holy Spirit
be all honour and glory, now and for ever. Amen.**

43 *The presiding priest, or the bishop when present, may bless the congregation.*

44 *The congregation is sent out with these words*
Go in peace to love and serve the Lord.
>Haere i runga i te rangimarie i runga i te aroha me te ngakau hihiko ki te mahi ki te Ariki.

**Amen. We go in the name of Christ.
Amine. Ka haere matou i runga i te ingoa o te Karaiti.**

FORMS OF INTERCESSION AND THANKSGIVING
45 *FIRST FORM*

This form may be used as a continuous prayer, or each section may conclude with particular intercessions, and a versicle and response.
God of heaven and earth, through Jesus Christ you promise to hear us when we pray to you in faith with thanksgiving.

We pray for one another, for our families and friends, through whom we learn to love and to be loved. Thank you for all who care for us. Give us grace to serve Christ by serving our neighbours and our community, loving others as he loves us.
Silence [and so after each paragraph]
We thank you for the unfailing love you hold out to everyone in Jesus Christ. Comfort and heal those in sorrow, need, sickness or any other trouble. Give them courage and hope in their distress, and bless those who minister to them.

We remember with gratitude your many gifts to us in creation and the rich heritage of these islands. Help us and people everywhere to share with justice and peace the resources of the earth. Give wisdom to those in authority among us and to all leaders of the nations.

We pray for your church throughout the world, thanking you for all who serve Christ and his kingdom. By your Spirit strengthen your people for their work and witness in the world. Unite us in your truth and love, that we who confess your name may also reflect your glory.

We remember with thanksgiving all who have died in Christ, and we rejoice at the faithful witness of your saints in every age, praying that we may enter with them into the unending joy of your heavenly kingdom.

Merciful God, you look with compassion on all who turn to you. Hear the prayers of your people.

**Grant that what we have asked in faith
we may by your grace receive;
through Jesus Christ our Lord. Amen.**

46 SECOND FORM

The leader and people pray responsively.
The minister may insert biddings for thanksgiving and intercession before any section.

Blessed are you eternal God
To be praised and glorified for ever.

Heavenly Father, hear us as we pray for the unity of your church.
May we all be one that the world may believe.

Grant that every member of the church may truly and humbly serve you.
That the life of Christ may be revealed in us.

We remember those who have died.
Father, into your hands we commend them.

(Remembering......)
We praise you for all your saints who have entered your eternal glory.
May we also come to share your heavenly kingdom.

Have compassion on those who suffer from sickness, grief or trouble.
In your presence may they find strength.

Look with your kindness on our homes and families.
Grant that your love may grow in our hearts.

Make us alive to the needs of our community.
Help us to share one another's joys and burdens.

Inspire and lead those who hold authority in the nations of the world.
Guide us and all people in the way of justice and peace.

Strengthen all who minister in Christ's name.
Give us courage to proclaim your Gospel.

47 THIRD FORM

Heavenly Father, you have promised to hear when we pray in the name of your Son.
Therefore in confidence and trust:

We pray for the church: (*Particular intercessions/thanksgivings may be offered*)
Father, enliven the church for its mission in the world.
That we may be salt of the earth and light to the world.

Breathe fresh life into your people.
Give us power to reveal Christ in word and action.

We pray for the world: (*Particular intercessions/thanksgivings may be offered*)
Creator of all, lead us and every people into ways of justice and peace.
That we may respect one another in freedom and truth.

Awaken in us a sense of wonder for the earth and all that is in it.
Teach us to care creatively for its resources.

We pray for the community: (*Particular intercessions/thanksgivings may be offered*)
God of truth, inspire with your wisdom those whose decisions affect the lives of others.
That all may act with integrity and courage.

Give grace to all whose lives are linked with ours.
May we serve Christ in one another, and love as he loves us.

We pray for those in need: (*Particular intercessions/thanksgivings may be offered*)
God of hope, comfort and restore all who suffer in body, mind or spirit.
May they know the power of your healing love.

Make us willing agents of your compassion.
Strengthen us as we share in making people whole.

We remember those who have died and those who mourn: (*Particular intercessions/thanksgivings may be offered*)

We remember with thanksgiving, those who have died in the faith of Christ and those whose faith is known to you alone.
Father, into your hands we commend them.

We praise you for (.......and) all your saints who have entered your eternal glory.
May their example inspire and encourage us.

We pray for ourselves and our ministries: (*Particular intercessions/thanksgivings may be offered*)

Either:

Lord, you have called us to serve you
Grant that we may walk in your presence:
your love in our hearts,
your truth in our minds,
your strength in our wills:
until, at the end of our journey,
we know the joy of our homecoming
and the welcome of your embrace,
through Jesus Christ our Lord. Amen.

Or:

Your word is a lamp for my feet
In darkness and in light,
in trouble and in joy,
help us, Heavenly Father,
to trust your love,
to serve your purpose,
and to praise your name,
through Jesus Christ our Lord. Amen.

48 〚SEASONAL VARIANTS IN THE GREAT THANKSGIVING: Proper Prefaces provided here in the duplicated text (see page 241) are to be found in Appendix C.〛

AN ALTERNATIVE GREAT THANKSGIVING
49 '*CELEBRATING THE GRACE OF GOD*'

The Lord is here.
God's Spirit is with us.

Lift up your hearts.
We lift them to the Lord.

Let us give thanks to the Lord our God.
It is right to give him thanks and praise.

Honour and worship are indeed your due,
our Lord and our God, through Jesus Christ,
for you created all things;
by your will they were created
and for your glory they have their being.

In your loving purpose you chose us before
the foundation of the world to be your people;
you called Abraham, Isaac and Jacob,
and bestowed your favour on the Virgin Mary.
Above all we give you thanks and praise
for your grace in sending Jesus Christ,
not for any merit of our own
but when we had turned away from you.
We were bound in sin,
but in your compassion you redeemed us
reconciling us to yourself with the precious blood of Christ.

In your Son you suffered with us and for us,
offering us the healing riches of salvation
and calling us to freedom and holiness.

Therefore with people of every nation, tribe and language,
with the whole church on earth and in heaven,
joyfully we give you thanks and say:

Holy, holy, holy Lord, God of power and might,
heaven and earth are full of your glory.
Hosanna in the highest.

All glory and honour to you, God of grace,
for you gave your only Son Jesus Christ
once for all on the cross
to be the one perfect sacrifice for the sin of the world
that all who believe in him might have eternal life.
The night before he died, he took bread,
and when he had given you thanks
he broke it, gave it to his disciples, and said:
Take, eat, this is my body which is given for you,
do this to remember me.

After supper he took the cup,
and when he had given you thanks
he gave it to them and said:
Drink this, all of you,
for this is my blood of the new covenant
which is shed for you and for many
for the forgiveness of sins;
do this as often as you drink it,
to remember me.

Therefore heavenly Father,
in this sacrament of the suffering and death of your Son,
we now celebrate the wonder of your grace
and proclaim the mystery of our faith.

Christ has died,
Christ is risen,
Christ will come in glory.

Redeemer God, rich in mercy, infinite in goodness,
we were far off until you brought us near
and our hands are empty until you fill them.
As we eat this bread and drink this wine,
through the power of your Holy Spirit
feed us with your heavenly food,
unite us in Christ,
and bring us to your everlasting kingdom.
O the depths and riches of your wisdom, O God.
How unsearchable are your judgments
and untraceable your ways.

From you, and through you, and to you are all things.
To you be the glory for ever.
through Christ our Saviour. Amen.

ALTERNATIVE EUCHARISTIC LITURGY (NZ2)
'THANKSGIVING AND PRAISE'
'CREATION AND REDEMPTION'

50 *These Alternative Liturgies have a common Ministry of the Word.*

The section to the end of the Absolution may be used as decided by the presiding priest. Parts may be omitted but a greeting should establish the community, and Absolution should be given to the penitent.

THE MINISTRY OF THE WORD

51 *A minister may greet the people informally.*

In the name of God: creator, redeemer and giver of life. **Amen.**

52 *The sentence of the day may be said.*

53 Grace to you and peace
from God our Creator,
the love at our beginning
and without end,
in our midst and with us.

God is with us,
here we find new life.
Let us give thanks
for the coming of God's reign of justice and love.

Jesus Christ is good news for the poor,
release for the captives,
recovery of sight for the blind
and liberty for those who are oppressed.

54 *An appropriate psalm, canticle or hymn may be used, or the following*

Glory to God...[ICET 4]...**God the Father. Amen.**

55 *One of the following may be used.*

Hear these words...[as at §7 above]...as yourself.
Spirit of God, search our hearts.

or

Lord, have mercy.
Christ, have mercy.
Lord, have mercy.

or

Our Lord Jesus Christ says:
A new commandment I give to you
that you love one another as I have loved you.
Spirit of God, search our hearts.

56 *One of the following three alternative forms is used.*
Either

In silence we remember our need for God's forgiveness
Silence

God is merciful.
Holy and merciful God,
we confess that we have sinned against you
in thought, word and deed.
We have not loved you
with all our heart, mind and soul.
We have not loved others
as our Saviour Christ loves us.
We have not done what Christ has called us to do.

The presiding priest says

God is love.
Through Christ your sins are forgiven.
Take hold of this forgiveness
and live your life
in the Spirit of Jesus. Amen.

57 *Or*

Happy are those whose sins are forgiven,
whose wrongs are pardoned.
I will confess my sins to the Lord,
I will not conceal my wrongdoings.

Silence

God forgives and heals us.

We need your healing, merciful God:
give us true repentance.
Some sins are plain to us;
some escape us,
some we cannot face.
Forgive us;
set us free to hear your word to us;
set us free to serve you.

The presiding priest says

God forgives you;
forgive others;
forgive yourself.

Pause

Through Christ, God has put away your sin:
approach your God in peace.

58 *Or*

In silence before God,
let us confess our sins.

Silence

The presiding priest says
God forgives you; be at peace.

THE READINGS

59　*The collect of the day shall be said here, or before or after the sermon.*

60　*The congregation sits.*
One or two lessons, as appointed, are read, the reader first saying
A reading from . . . .(chapter. . beginning at. . . .)
Silence may follow each reading.

61　*The reader may say*
Hear what the Spirit is saying to the church.
Thanks be to God.

62　*A psalm, hymn or anthem may follow each reading.*

63　*Then, all standing, the reader of the Gospel says*
The Holy Gospel according to. . .(chapter. . .beginning at. . .)
Praise and glory to God.
After the Gospel silence may be kept. The reader says
This is the Gospel of Christ.
Praise to Christ the Word.

THE PROCLAMATION

64　*SERMON.*

65　*The NICENE or APOSTLES' CREED may be said here.*

THE PRAYERS OF THE PEOPLE

66　*The presiding priest says*
Let us pray for the Church and for the world,
thanking God for his goodness.

Three forms of intercession and thanksgiving are provided on pages. . . ⟦*i.e. at §§45–47 above*⟧

Or, intercessions and thanksgivings may be offered. . .⟦*as at §21 to The Lord's Prayer in English*⟧. . .**ever. Amen.**

'THANKSGIVING AND PRAISE'

The Ministry of the Sacrament for the other Alternative Eucharistic Liturgy 'Thanksgiving for Creation and Redemption' is found on page. . . ⟦*i.e. at §76*⟧

THE MINISTRY OF THE SACRAMENT
THE PREPARATION OF THE GIFTS

67　*The offerings of the people are presented and the table prepared.*

The presiding priest says
Blessed be Christ the Prince of Peace.
He breaks down the walls that divide.
The peace of God be always with you.
Praise to Christ who is our peace.

THE PEACE

68 *The people may greet each other and exchange a sign of peace.*

THE GREAT THANKSGIVING

69 *The presiding priest says or sings*
Christ is risen!
He is risen indeed.
Lift up your hearts.
We lift them up to God.
Let us give thanks to God.
It is right to offer thanks and praise.
It is the joy of our salvation
God of the universe,
to give you thanks
through Jesus Christ.

You said, 'Let there be light'.
There was light.
Your light shines on in our darkness.
For you the earth has brought forth life
in all its forms.
You have created us
to hear your Word,
to do your will
and to be fulfilled in your love.

It is right to thank you.
You sent your Son to be for us
the way we need to follow
and the truth we need to know.
The seasonal variants for Advent, Christmas and Epiphany may be inserted here. [See §75]

You sent your Son to give his life
to release us from our sin.
His cross has taken our guilt away.
The seasonal variants for Lent, Palm Sunday, Passiontide, Good Friday, Easter, Ascensiontide and Pentecost may be inserted here. [See §75]

You send your Holy Spirit
to strengthen and to guide,
to warn and to revive your Church.

Therefore, with all your witnesses
who surround us on every side,
countless as heaven's stars,
we praise you for our creation
and our calling,
with loving and with joyful hearts.

Holy God, holy and merciful, holy and just,
glory and goodness come from you.
Glory to you most high and gracious God.

Blessed are you, most Holy, in your Son,
who washed his disciples' feet.
'I am among you,' he said, 'as one who serves.'

On the night before he died,
he took bread, gave you thanks.
He broke it, gave it to his disciples,
and said,
'Take, eat, this is my body,
which is given for you.
Do this to remember me.'

After supper, he took the cup,
he gave you thanks.
He gave it to them and said,
'Drink this. It is my blood of the new covenant
shed for you, shed for all,
to forgive sin.
Do this to remember me.'

Therefore God of the past and present,
with this bread and wine,
we your people remember your Son.
We thank you for his cross and resurrection
and we take courage from his ascension.
We look for his coming in glory
and in him we give ourselves to you.

Through your Holy Spirit,
may we who receive Christ's body,
be indeed the body of Christ.

May we who share his cup,
draw strength from the one true vine.
Called to follow Christ,
help us to reconcile and unite.
Called to suffer,
give us hope in our calling.

THE COMMUNION

70 Christ's body was broken for us on the cross.
Christ is the bread of life.
His blood was shed for our forgiveness.
Christ is risen from the dead.
Come God's people,
come to receive Christ's heavenly food.

71 *At the distribution the minister says*
The body of Christ... ⟦the first four lines of § 36⟧...nei mou.
The communicant may respond. **Amen. Amine.**

AFTER COMMUNION

72 Blessed be God who called us together.
Praise to God who makes us his people.

Blessed be God who has forgiven our sin.
Praise to God who gives us hope and freedom.

Blessed be God whose Word is proclaimed.
Praise to God who is revealed as love.

Blessed be God who has called us to serve.
Amen. Blessed are you, our God,
for you alone have called us,
you alone make us your ministers.

Therefore, we offer you all that we are
and all that we shall become.

Accept our sacrifice of praise,
accept our thanks for all you have done;
our hands were empty and you filled them.

73 *A general blessing or one appropriate to the theme may be given.*
The priest may use one of the Gospel sayings of Jesus.

74 *The congregation is sent out with these words*
Go in peace.
Amen. We go in the name of Christ.

75 ⟦SEASONAL VARIANTS IN THE GREAT THANKSGIVING: Proper Prefaces provided in the duplicated text (see page 241) are to be found in Appendix C.⟧

'THANKSGIVING FOR CREATION AND REDEMPTION'

76 *The Ministry of the Word which precedes this Ministry of the Sacrament is found on page...* ⟦i.e. at §51 above⟧

THE MINISTRY OF THE SACRAMENT

THE PEACE

77 *All stand. The presiding priest says to the people*
The peace of God be with you all.

In God's justice is our peace.

(Brothers and sisters) Christ calls us to be God's people.
Baptised into Christ we seek to live in the Spirit of Christ.

Christ is the end of all false barriers,
even of race, class or sex.
May we share Christ's sufferings,
may we know the power of his resurrection.

The priest may say
Let us give one another a sign of peace.
All may exchange a sign of peace.

THE PREPARATION OF THE GIFTS

78 *The offerings of the people are presented and the table prepared.*
The presiding priest says

God of all creation, you bring forth
bread from the earth
and fruit from the vine.

By your Holy Spirit this bread and wine
will be for us
the body and blood of Christ.
All you have made is good.
Your love endures for ever.

THE GREAT THANKSGIVING

79 *The presiding priest says or sings*
The Spirit of God be with you.
And also with you.

Lift up your hearts.
We lift them up to God.

Let us give thanks to God.
It is right to offer thanks and praise.

It is right indeed to give you thanks
most loving God
through Jesus Christ, our redeemer,
the first born from the dead,
the pioneer of our salvation,
who is with us always,
one of us,
yet from the heart of God.

For with your whole created universe,
we praise you for your unfailing gift of life.
We thank you that you make us human
and stay with us
when we turn from you to sin.

God's love is shown to us,
in that while we were yet sinners,
Christ died for us.

In that love, dear God,
righteous and strong to save,
you came among us in Jesus Christ
our crucified and living Lord.
You make all things new:
in Christ's suffering and cross
you reveal your glory
and reconcile all peoples to yourself,
their true and living God.

A Seasonal Variant may be inserted here.

In your mercy you are now our God.
Through Christ you gather us,
new-born in your Spirit,
a people after your own heart.
We entrust ourselves to you,
for you alone do justice
to all people, living and departed.

Now is the acceptable time,
now is the day of salvation.

Therefore with saints and martyrs,
apostles and prophets,
with all the redeemed,
joyfully we praise you and say:
Holy, holy, holy:
God of mercy, giver of life;
earth and sea and sky
and all that lives,
declare your presence and your glory.
All glory to you, giver of life
sufficient and full for all creation.
Accept our praises,
living God,
for Jesus Christ,
the one perfect offering
for the world,
who in the night that he was betrayed,
took bread,
and when he had given thanks,
broke it,
gave it to his disciples and said:
'Take, eat, this is my body
which is given for you.
Do this to remember me.'
After supper he took the cup;
and when he had given thanks,
he gave it to them and said:
'Drink this, all of you.
This is my blood of the new covenant
which is shed for you, and for many,
to forgive your sin.
Do this as often as you drink it
to remember me.'
Therefore, God of all creation,
in the suffering and death
of Jesus our redeemer,
we meet you in your glory.
We lift up the cup of salvation
and call upon your name.
Here and now,
we celebrate your great acts of liberation.

ever-present and living in Jesus Christ,
crucified and risen,
who was and is and is to come.
Amen. Come Lord Jesus.
May Christ ascended in majesty
be our new and living way,
our access to you, Father,
and source of all new life.
In Christ we offer ourselves
to do your will.
Empower our celebration with your Holy Spirit,
fire us with your love,
confront us with your justice,
and make us one in the body of Christ
with all who share your gifts of love.
Through Christ,
in the power of the Holy Spirit,
with all who stand before you
in earth and heaven,
we worship you, all loving God. Amen.
Silence
THE COMMUNION
80 *The Lord's Prayer may be said here or at the Preparation of the Gifts.*
As Jesus taught us, we pray:
Our Father in heaven...⟦ICET 1⟧...**for ever. Amen.**
81 *The priest breaks the bread.*
The bread we break
is a sharing in the body of Christ.
We who are many are one body
for we all share the one bread.
The cup of blessing
for which we give thanks
is a sharing in the blood of Christ.
Bread and wine; the gifts of God
for the people of God.
May we who share these gifts
be found in Christ
and Christ in us.
82 *The Communion is distributed with the following words*
The body...⟦as in §71⟧...**Amen. Amine.**

AFTER COMMUNION

83 *The priest says*
Most loving God, creator and redeemer,
we give you thanks
for this foretaste of your glory.
Through Christ, and with all your saints,
we offer ourselves
and our lives to your service.
Send us out in the power of your Spirit,
to stand with you in your world.
We ask this through Jesus Christ
our friend and brother. Amen.
Silence may be kept.
84 *The congregation is sent out with these words*
Grace be with you.
Thanks be to God.
Go in peace.
Amen. We go in the name of Christ.

85 ⟦SEASONAL VARIANTS IN THE GREAT THANKSGIVING: Proper Prefaces provided in the duplicated text (see page 241) are to be found in Appendix C.⟧

AN ORDER FOR CELEBRATING THE EUCHARIST (NZ3)

86 *This rite requires careful preparation by the priest and participants. It is intended for special occasions and not for the regular celebration of the Eucharist.*

THE PEOPLE AND PRIEST
87   *Gather in the Lord's Name*
        Proclaim and respond to the Word of God
The proclamation and response may include readings, music, dance and other art forms, comment, discussion and silence. A reading from the Gospel is always included.

88   *Pray for the world and the church*
        Exchange the Peace
        Prepare the table and set bread and wine on it
        Make Eucharist
The President gives thanks in the name of the assembly. The President uses one of the Eucharistic Prayers provided (pages... ⟦i.e. §§31, 49, 69, 79⟧), or the framework provided on page... ⟦i.e. §90⟧

89   *Break the Bread*
        Share the gifts of God
The bread and wine are shared reverently. When all have received, any of the sacrament remaining is then consumed.

90 ## *A GREAT THANKSGIVING FOR SPECIAL OCCASIONS*

The following Eucharistic Prayer may be used either as a framework within which insertions may be made or as a continuous whole. It contains within a short compass all the essential elements of a Eucharistic Prayer.

The Lord is here.
God's Spirit is with us.

Lift up your hearts.
We lift them to the Lord.

Let us give thanks to the Lord our God.
It is right to give thanks and praise.

The celebrant gives thanks to God for the work of creation and God's self revelation. The following or any other suitable words are used. The particular occasion being celebrated may also be recalled.

It is indeed right, always and everywhere,
to give thanks to you, the true and living God,
through Jesus Christ.
You are the source of life for all creation
and you made us in your own image.

The celebrant now gives thanks for the salvation of the world through Christ. The following or any other suitable words are used.

In your love for us
you sent your Son to be our Saviour.
In the fulness of time he became incarnate,
and suffered death on the cross.
You raised him in triumph
and exalted him in glory.
Through him you send your Holy Spirit
upon your church
and make us your people.

If the Sanctus is to be included, it is introduced with these or similar words.

And so, we proclaim your glory, as we say:
Holy, holy, holy Lord, God of power and might:
heaven and earth are full of your glory.
Hosanna in the highest.

Then follows

To you indeed be glory, almighty God,
because on the night before he died,
your Son Jesus Christ took bread;
when he had given you thanks,
he broke it, gave it to his disciples, and said:
'Take, eat; this is my body,
which is given for you.
Do this to remember me.'

After supper, he took the cup;
when he had given you thanks,
he gave it to them, and said:
'Drink this, all of you.
This is my blood of the new covenant,
which is shed for you and for many
for the forgiveness of sins.
Do this as often as you drink it,
to remember me.'

The people may say this or some other acclamation

Christ has died,
Christ has risen,
Christ will come in glory.

Then follows

Therefore, loving God,
recalling now Christ's death and resurrection,
we ask you to accept
this our sacrifice of praise.
Send your Holy Spirit upon us
and our celebration
that we may be fed with the body and blood of your Son
and be filled with your life and goodness.
Unite us in Christ
and give us your peace.

The celebrant may add further prayer that all may receive the benefits of Christ's work and renewal in the Spirit.

The prayer ends with these or similar words

All this we ask through your Son
Jesus Christ our Lord,
to whom with you and the Holy Spirit
be all honour and glory
now and for ever. **Amen.**

APPENDIX

91 ### THE TEN COMMANDMENTS

Hear the commandments which God gave to the people of Israel by his servant Moses.

After each commandment, or after the fourth and the tenth, the people shall reply
Spirit of God, search our hearts.

1. You shall have no other... [CF 2, omitting bracketed parts] ...covet anything which belongs to your neighbour.

   for yourself any graven image] yourself idols
   bow down to nor worship] worship or serve
   to keep holy the Sabbath day] the sabbath day and keep it holy
   commit murder] murder

92 ### ADDITIONAL DIRECTIONS

The holy table should be covered with a clean white cloth during the celebration.

The presiding priest at the Eucharist should wear a cassock and surplice with stole or scarf or an alb with the customary vestments.

Readings : [There are then lectionary provisions.]

When appropriate the Scriptures may be read in other languages in addition to or instead of English.

The bread for the Eucharist shall be as good a quality wheaten bread (either loaf or wafer) as may be obtained and the wine for the Eucharist shall be a good quality wine.

If there is insufficient bread and wine for the number of communicants, the celebrant is to return to the holy table and say :

[Text as at §37]

Unless any remaining consecrated bread and wine is required for the communion of the sick, or for the administration of communion when a priest is not available, the celebrant or assistants and other communicants reverently eat and drink it, either after the communion of the people or after the dismissal.

There shall be no celebration of the Eucharist unless at least one other person is present to receive communion with the presiding priest.

CHAPTER 19

THE CHURCH OF THE PROVINCE OF MELANESIA

THE text published as **Mel** in **FAL** was contained in the *Melanesian Prayer Book* (1973). The Provincial Commission on Liturgy and Worship has been preparing forms for inclusion in a new Provincial Prayer Book to be submitted to the Provincial Synod in 1986. In the course of this a new eucharistic rite has been drafted, 'Second Form' (**Mel** being 'First Form', and due for republication in the new Book).

This text ('**MelR**', 1984) is in use in a duplicated format, and includes the use of 1974 ICET texts (but the Lord's Prayer follows 1971), a revised intercession, Roman Catholic offertory prayers, and a revised eucharistic prayer, which is published below, with the proper prefaces in Appendix C.

THE EUCHARISTIC PRAYER FROM MelR 1984

The Lord be with you.
And also with you.
Lift up your hearts.
We lift them up to the Lord.
Let us give thanks to the Lord our God.
It is right to give him thanks and praise.
Father, all powerful and ever-living God, it is right that we give you all glory and honour, thanksgiving and praise, at all times and in all places, THROUGH Jesus Christ our Lord. He is your eternal word. Through him you created the whole world, making us in your own likeness, and giving us this earth, to care for it, to enjoy it, and to use its fruits for our food.

[*Proper preface* – see Appendix C]

Therefore we praise you, joining our voices with Angels and Archangels and with all the company of heaven, who forever sing this hymn to proclaim the glory of your name:

Holy, holy...[ICET 5(a) (b)]]...**in the highest.**
The people kneel or remain standing. Celebrant continues:
Holy and gracious Father, we thank you for these gifts you have made, this bread and this wine. We ask you to pour your Holy Spirit on us and on them, so that as we eat and drink them, in obedience to our Saviour Christ in remembrance of his suffering and death we may be partakers of his body and blood.

He takes the bread into his hands and says:
For on the night he was betrayed he took bread, and when he had given you thanks he broke it, and gave it to his disciples and said; 'TAKE THIS AND EAT IT. THIS IS MY BODY WHICH IS GIVEN FOR YOU. DO THIS IN REMEMBRANCE OF ME.'

He takes the cup into his hands and says:
After supper he took the cup, and again giving you thanks he gave it to his disciples, saying, 'DRINK FROM THIS, ALL OF YOU. THIS IS MY BLOOD OF THE NEW COVENANT, WHICH IS SHED FOR YOU AND FOR MANY FOR THE FORGIVENESS OF SINS. DO THIS AS OFTEN AS YOU DRINK IT, IN REMEMBRANCE OF ME.'

The Celebrant continues
Let us proclaim the mystery of faith:
Christ has died.
Christ is risen.
Christ will come again.
Father, we offer you this bread of life and this cup of salvation, as our Saviour commanded. We celebrate and show forth his perfect sacrifice, made once for all upon the cross, his rising again from the dead and his going into heaven to reign with you in glory, and we look for his coming to fulfil all things according to your will.

Renew us with your Holy Spirit, unite us in the body of your Son, Jesus Christ and bring us with all your people into the joy of your eternal kingdom.

Through him,
with him,
in him.
In the unity of the Holy Spirit, all glory and honour is yours
Almighty Father,
for ever and ever.
Amen.

COMMON FORMS

As in **FAL**, the 'Common Forms' used here are all texts which address God as 'you', divided into two sets, the most recent 'ICET'[1] ones, and other common ones, largely drawn from **Eng3**.

The ICET texts follow the '1974' forms, published as *Prayers we have in Common* by SPCK and Seabury in 1975. Most of the modern-language rites in this volume employ the 1974 versions, but the 1970 and 1971 variants are here published as an *apparatus* (reversing the pattern of **FAL**), for reference purposes.[2]

The other 'CF' forms follow the **FAL** selection exactly, but with one addition. Of the **FAL** texts, only two – that is, the Decalogue and the Words of Administration – were not from **Eng3**, and that is still the case. The addition is the 'First Post-Communion Prayer' from **Eng3** (numbered 'CF 8' below), which has been widely adopted in texts subsequent to **Eng3**.

Rites which address God as 'thou' have reference to '**MAL** CF', and the forms of these are in most cases the well-known 1662 forms.

The citations use the convention '⟦ICET 4⟧', '⟦CF 7⟧', etc. Variants from the forms below are shown by an *apparatus* in the rite. If the cue words at the beginning or end include a variant, then it is not shown by *apparatus*, and sometimes the cue words are extended to a long sentence to convey such changes. Omissions also may be similarly inferred. Differences of punctuation, capitalization, and 'lining out', have been ignored here. Congregational recitation is shown by bold type in the text, and not here. Where one marginal number is shown in the Decalogue, or one biblical reference in the Comfortable Words, then the whole set of such numbering from the CF is indicated.

Some tiny errors in **FAL** have been corrected.[3]

A. ICET Forms

ICET 1 (1974). THE LORD'S PRAYER

Our Father in heaven,
    hallowed be your Name,

---

[1] 'International Consultation on English Texts' – this met between 1969 and 1974, and is described in **FAL** pages 10–12.

[2] That is, the complete set from the successive *Prayers we have in Common*, except Benedictus, Nunc Dimittis, and Magnificat. Te Deum was in **FAL**, but is not here.

[3] These mostly relate to the 1974 texts, shown by variant in **FAL**, as only duplicated sheets were available at the time of **FAL** going to press. See **FAL** corrigenda sheet re pages 393, 396, and 397. Printed copies of 1974 texts still have a capital for 'Our' in 'Let us give thanks to the Lord Our God'.

your kingdom come,
your will be done,
    on earth as in heaven.
Give us today our daily bread.
Forgive us our sins
    as we forgive those who sin against us.
Save us from the time of trial
    and deliver us from evil.
For the kingdom, the power, and the glory are yours
    now and for ever.

1970, 1971: hallowed] holy
      Save us from the time of trial and] Do not bring us to the test but

ICET 2 (1974). THE APOSTLES' CREED

I believe in God, the Father almighty,
    creator of heaven and earth.

I believe in Jesus Christ, his only Son, our Lord.
    He was conceived by the power of the Holy Spirit
        and born of the Virgin Mary.
    He suffered under Pontius Pilate,
        was crucified, died, and was buried.
    He descended to the dead.
    On the third day he rose again.
    He ascended into heaven,
        and is seated at the right hand of the Father.
    He will come again to judge the living and the dead.

I believe in the Holy Spirit,
    the holy catholic Church,
    the communion of saints,
    the forgiveness of sins,
    the resurrection of the body,
    and the everlasting. Amen.

ICET 3 (1974). THE NICENE CREED

We believe in one God,
    the Father, the Almighty,
    maker of heaven and earth,
    of all that is, seen and unseen.

We believe in one Lord, Jesus Christ,
    the only Son of God,
    eternally begotten of the Father,

God from God, Light from Light,
true God from true God,
begotten, not made,
of one Being with the Father.
Through him all things were made.
For us men and for our salvation
  he came down from heaven:
by the power of the Holy Spirit
  he became incarnate from the Virgin Mary, and was made man.

For our sake he was crucified under Pontius Pilate;
  he suffered death and was buried.
  On the third day he rose again
    in accordance with the Scriptures;
  he ascended into heaven
    and is seated at the right hand of the Father.
He will come again in glory to judge the living and the dead,
  and his kingdom will have no end.

We believe in the Holy Spirit, the Lord, the giver of life,
  who proceeds from the Father [and the Son].
With the Father and the Son he is worshiped and glorified.
He has spoken through the Prophets.
We believe in one holy catholic and apostolic Church.
We acknowledge one batism for the forgiveness of sins.
We look for the resurrection of the dead,
  and the life of the world to come. Amen.

1970, 1971: is, seen] is seen
       of one Being] one in Being
       became incarnate from] was born of
       was made] became
       suffered death] suffered, died
       in accordance with] in fulfilment of

ICET 4 (1974). GLORIA IN EXCELSIS

Glory to God in the highest,
  and peace to his people on earth.

Lord God, heavenly King,
almighty God and Father,
  we worship you, we give you thanks,
  we praise you for your glory.

Lord Jesus Christ, only Son of the Father,
Lord God, Lamb of God,

you take away the sin of the world:
  have mercy on us;
you are seated at the right hand of the Father:
  receive our prayer.

For you alone are the Holy One,
you alone are the Lord,
you alone are the Most High,
  Jesus Christ,
  with the Holy Spirit,
  in the glory of God the Father. Amen.

ICET 5(a) (1974). SANCTUS

Holy, holy, holy Lord, God of power and might,
heaven and earth are full of your glory.
  Hosanna in the highest.

ICET 5(b) (1974). BENEDICTUS QUI VENIT

Blessed is he who comes in the name of the Lord.
  Hosanna in the highest.

ICET 6 (1974). GLORIA PATRI

Glory to the Father, and to the Son, and to the Holy Spirit:
  as it was in the beginning, is now, and will be for ever. Amen.

1970, 1971: it was]OM   is] so   will be]OM

ICET 7 (1974). SURSUM CORDA

The Lord be with you.
And also with you.

Lift up your hearts.
We lift them to the Lord.

Let us give thanks to the Lord Our God.
It is right to give him thanks and praise.

1970: The Lord be] The Spirit of the Lord be

ICET 8(a) (1974). AGNUS DEI – 1970 TEXT

Jesus, Lamb of God:
  have mercy on us.
Jesus, bearer of our sins:
  have mercy on us.
Jesus, redeemer of the world:
  give us your peace.

ICET 8(b) (1974). AGNUS DEI – ALTERNATIVE

Lamb of God, you take away the sins of the world:
  have mercy on us.
Lamb of God, you take away the sins of the world:
  have mercy on us.
Lamb of God, you take away the sins of the world:
  grant us peace.

B. Other Common Forms

CF 1. THE COLLECT FOR PURITY (**Eng3**)

Almighty God,
to whom all hearts are open,
all desires known,
and from whom no secrets are hid:
cleanse the thoughts of our hearts
by the inspiration of your Holy Spirit,
that we may perfectly love you,
and worthily magnify your holy Name;
through Christ our Lord. Amen.

CF 2. THE DECALOGUE (A 'consensus' text).

God spoke these words and said:

1. I am the Lord your God; you shall have no other gods but me.

2. You shall not make for yourself any graven image, [nor the likeness of anything that is in heaven above, or in the earth beneath or in the water under the earth]. You shall not bow down to them, nor worship them.

3. You shall not take the Name of the Lord your God in vain.

4. Remember to keep holy the sabbath day. [Six days you shall labour, and do all that you have to do; but the seventh day is the Sabbath of the Lord your God.]

5. Honour your father and your mother.

6. You shall not commit murder.

7. You shall not commit adultery.

8. You shall not steal.

9. You shall not bear false witness [against your neighbour].

10. You shall not covet.

CF 3. THE SUMMARY OF THE LAW (**Eng3**)

Our Lord Jesus Christ said: The Lord our God is the only Lord. You shall love the Lord your God with all your heart, with all your soul, with all your mind, and with all your strength. This is the first commandment. The second is this: Love your neighbour as yourself. There is no other commandment greater than these.

CF 4. THE COMFORTABLE WORDS (**Eng3**)

Hear the words of comfort our Saviour Christ says to all who truly turn to him.

Come to me, all who labour and are heavy-laden, and I will give you rest.   (*Matthew* 11.28)

God so loved the world that he gave his only Son, that whoever believes in him should not perish but have eternal life.   (*John* 3.16)

Hear what St Paul says.

This saying is true and worthy of full acceptance, that Christ Jesus came into the world to save sinners.   (1 *Timothy* 1.15)

Hear what St John says.

If anyone does sin, we have an advocate with the Father, Jesus Christ the righteous; and he is the expiation of our sins.   (1 *John* 2.1)

CF 5. THE ABSOLUTION (**Eng3**)

Almighty God, who forgives all who truly repent, have mercy upon you, pardon and deliver you from all your sins, confirm and strengthen you in all goodness, and keep you in life eternal; through Jesus Christ our Lord. Amen.

CF 6. THE PRAYER OF HUMBLE ACCESS (**Eng3**)

We do not presume
to come to this your table, merciful Lord,
trusting in our own righteousness,
but in your manifold and great mercies.
We are not worthy
so much as to gather up the crumbs under your table.
But you are the same Lord
whose nature is always to have mercy.
Grant us therefore, gracious Lord,
so to eat the flesh of your dear Son Jesus Christ,
and to drink his blood,
that we may evermore dwell in him,
and he in us. Amen.

CF 7(a). THE WORDS OF ADMINISTRATION FOR THE BREAD (**Eng2**)

The Body of our Lord Jesus Christ, which was given for you, preserve your body and soul to everlasting life. Take and eat this in remembrance that Christ died for you, and feed on him in your heart by faith with thanksgiving.

CF 7(b). THE WORDS OF ADMINISTRATION FOR THE CUP (**Eng2**)

The Blood of our Lord Jesus Christ, which was shed for you, preserve your body and soul to everlasting life. Drink this in remembrance that Christ's Blood was shed for you, and be thankful.

CF 8 (not in CF in **FAL**) THE FIRST POST-COMMUNION PRAYER (**Eng3**)

Father of all, we give you thanks and praise that when we were still far off you met us in your Son and brought us home. Dying and living, he declared your love, gave us grace, and opened the gate of glory. May we who share Christ's body live his risen life; we who drink his cup bring life to others; we whom the Spirit lights give light to the world. Keep us in this hope that we have grasped; so we and all your children shall be free, and the whole earth live to praise your Name; through Christ our Lord. Amen.

CF 9. POST-COMMUNION PRAYER OF THANKSGIVING AND SELF-OFFERING (**Eng3**)

Almighty God,
we thank you for feeding us
with the body and blood of your Son Jesus Christ.
Through him we offer you our souls and bodies
to be a living sacrifice.
Send us out
in the power of your Spirit
to live and work
to your praise and glory. Amen.

CF 10. THE BLESSING (**Eng3**)

The peace of God, which passes all understanding, keep your hearts and minds in the knowledge and love of God, and of his Son Jesus Christ our Lord;
And the blessing of God Almighty, the Father, the Son, and the Holy Spirit, be among you, and remain with you always. Amen.

B. OFFERTORY SENTENCES

THIS separate appendix of a fading usage is kept for the sake of continuity with the previous volumes.[1] There are now no seasonal sentences. The notes on **FAL** page 401 apply. The first number in brackets is the **FAL** one, the second the **LiE/MAL** one).

Dt. 16. 6–17 (**LiE** 27)	Ire2	Acts 20. 35 (9, 21)	Ire2
1 Chron. 29. 11 (11, 32)	Amer1–1, 2–2	Rom 12. 1 (13,34)	Amer1–1, 2–2,
Ps. 27. 6 (**LiE** 25)	Wall		Wall
Ps. 50. 14 (10, 24)	Amer1–1, 2–2,	2 Cor. 9. 6, 7 (4, 9)	Aus1B
	Aus1B, Ire2	Gal. 6. 6 (5, 10)	Aus1B
Ps. 50. 15 (16, 38)	Aus1B	Gal. 6. 10 (6, 11)	Aus1B
Ps. 50. 23 (17, 39)	Aus1B	Eph. 5. 2 (12, 33)	Amer1–1, 2–2
Ps. 96. 8 (14, 36)	Amer1–1, 2–2,	Heb. 4. 14, 16 (**LiE** 47)	Wall
	Ire2, Wall	Heb. 13. 15 (18, 40)	Aus1B
Ps. 116. 15, 16 (**LiE** 34)	Wall	Heb. 13. 15, 16 (new)	Amer1–1, 2–2
Matt. 5. 16 (1, 1)	Aus1B, Wall	Heb. 13. 16 (7, 15)	Aus1B, Ire2
Matt. 5. 23, 24 (15, 37)	Amer1–1, 2–2	1 John 3. 17 (8, 16)	Aus1B
Matt. 7. 21 (3, 4)	Aus1B, Ire2	Rev. 4. 11 (**FAL** 20)	Amer1–1, 2–2
		Bidding (**FAL** p. 402)	Amer1–1, 2–2

C. PROPER PREFACES

As in **FAL**, Proper Prefaces are shown on a folding table, here placed in a pocket in the inside back cover. The seasons and occasions follow a similar order to that in **FAL**. Some are on the reverse side. Note also:

1. **Scot2** has an invariable preface. **NZ1** and **NZ2** refer to 'seasonal additions', but do not provide them in the booklet; they are taken here from the duplicated texts passed by Synod.
2. **Amer1–1**, **EngB** (and **Eng1–2B**), **Can1A**, and **Wall** have 'thou' form texts. **Amer1–1** is very close to **Amer2–2**, and can be inferred by substituting 'thou' (and its cognates) for 'you': other variants are shown by *apparatus*. **EngB** has for the first thanksgiving the **Eng1** provision from **MAL** (i.e. nos. 5, 12, 29, 30, 32, 37, 40, 63, 71, 91) along with two for 'Funerals' which can be inferred from the last two Easter prefaces of **EngA**, with 'thou' substitution:[2] for the second thanksgiving the provision is

---

[1] The origin of these was in the giving of *money* – the meaning of 'Offertory' in 1549 and 1662. As the meaning has become indistinct, so has the provision become rare.

[2] The variations from **Eng1** are listed in **FAL**, page 405, footnote 3. The two adapted from **EngA** begin 'because through thy Son Jesus Christ our Lord'. **Eng1–2B** uses 'Whitsunday' for 'Pentecost'.

almost exactly that of **Eng3** in **FAL**, with substitution.[1] **Can1A** follows **CanR** (**LiE** nos. 3, 5, 13, 18, 19, 52), but has altered those for Pentecost (21) and Trinity (as **Amer1–1**), and added three for Sundays, and one each for weekdays, Lent, Last Sunday after Pentecost, Marriage, and the Commemoration of the Departed.[2] **Wal1** has **MAL** nos. 1, 5, 12, 17, 22, 30, 32, 36 (or 37), 40, 79.[3]

3.   **CNIR**, **Nig**, and **PNG** are shown as variants on **EngA**

4.   **Can3** differs from **Can4** in its opening lines, and these are shown here once – further variants being shown as variants:

Can3	Can4
It is right, and a good and joyful thing,	Blessed are you, gracious God,
always and everywhere to give thanks to you,	creator of heaven and earth,
Father Almighty, creator of heaven and earth	we give you thanks and praise

5.   Proper Prefaces are included for **TanR** and **MelR**, though there are not full rites set out in the respective chapters.

D. OTHER PROPERS

THESE texts are on the reverse of the folding table of Proper Prefaces. The footnote in **FAL**, page 408, applies, in that the only material included here is that which in principle could have been set out within the rite, or its appendices. Similar matter not allocated to a season is usually printed in the main text here. Rubrical directions must also be discerned from the main text.

E. SOME EUCHARISTIC PRAYERS

THE second folding table is used to set out in parallel columns the following selections of eucharistic prayers:

Table E1:   The development of the first eucharistic prayer in **EngA**.
Table E2:   The development of 'A Third Form' in **Aus5**.
Table E3:   Some texts of Hippolytus and of prayers derived from Hippolytus, not necessarily inter-dependent.

---

[1] There are additions for Thursday before Easter and Transfiguration (both adapted from the **Eng1** provision (**MAL** nos. 29 and 63), and two for 'Funerals' (adapted from those for the first thanksgiving (see note 2 on p. 277)). The 'Christmas, Presentation, Annunciation' Preface is taken from the **Eng2** provision (**MAL** no. 6). In the 'Easter' Preface the last clause is changed to 'by his rising to life again has restored to us everlasting life'. **Eng1–2B** uses 'Whitsunday' for 'Pentecost'.

[2] These, exceptionally, are shown on the folding table, as variants from **Can4**.

[3] Variants are those for **Wal** plus 'Spirit' for 'Ghost' and 'has' for 'hath' throughout, and also:

No. 1   unto] to   well-beloved]OM   in great humility] our Saviour Jesus Christ   wilt] thou wilt   shall come again] returns   his glorious majesty] glory   in righteousness]OM.
No. 5   that without spot of sin, to] being himself without sin he might
No. 17   all ways] every way   that by his] and by whose   may overcome all] are able to overcome
No. 37   did pour] poured